TOM AND HUCK
DON'T LIVE HERE ANYMORE

Other Books by Ron Powers

The Newscasters:
The News Business as Show Business

Face Value (a novel)

Toot-Toot-Tootsie, Good-Bye (a novel)

Super Tube: The Rise of Television Sports

White Town Drowsing: Journeys to Hannibal

Far from Home: Life and Loss in Two American Towns

The Beast, the Eunuch and the Glass-Eyed Child:
Television in the 80s

The Cruel Radiance:
Notes of a Prosewriter in a Visual Age

Dangerous Water:
A Biography of the Boy Who Became Mark Twain

Flags of Our Fathers (with James Bradley)

The Man Who Flew the Memphis Belle:
Memoir of a World War II Bomber Pilot
(with Col. Robert Morgan, USAFR, Ret.)

TOM ⚌ HUCK DON'T LIVE HERE ANYMORE

CHILDHOOD AND MURDER IN THE HEART OF AMERICA

RON POWERS

ST. MARTIN'S PRESS   NEW YORK

www.stmartins.com

Library of Congress Cataloging-in-Publication Data

Powers, Ron
   Tom and Huck don't live here anymore : childhood and murder in the heart of America.
Ron Powers.—1st ed.
   p. cm.
Includes index.
ISBN 0-312-26240-X
   1. Children—United States—social conditions. I. Title.
HQ792.U5 P67 2001
305.23'0973—dc21

2001041612

First Edition: October 2001

1   3   5   7   9   10   8   6   4   2

Once again, to Dean and Kevin

Once again, to Honoree

CONTENTS

ACKNOWLEDGMENTS

I am grateful to the people of Hannibal who agreed to talk to me about matters of unimaginable personal sorrow even though they had no incentive to do so beyond simple decency and hospitality. I hope that their stories, as rendered in this book, justify their trust. To the many others who offered professional insights and matters of record, most of whom are quoted herein, I am also grateful.

John Fougere, public information officer for the Missouri Department of Corrections, was helpful in arranging certain interviews. Mary Lou Montgomery, editor of the *Hannibal Courier-Post*, provided essential guidance, wisdom, and encouragement. I thank my sister, Joyce Myers, for sharing her rich and acute memories of our Hannibal childhoods and for the use of her photographic scrapbook.

I owe an enormous debt to my editor at St. Martin's Press, Tim Bent, for his superb skills in helping me organize and clarify many interlinking thematic ideas and for his unparalleled insistence on the proper care of a sentence. (Any uncared-for sentences in here are my responsibility alone.) And to Jim Hornfischer, a friend and source of strong social ideas as well as a champion literary agent.

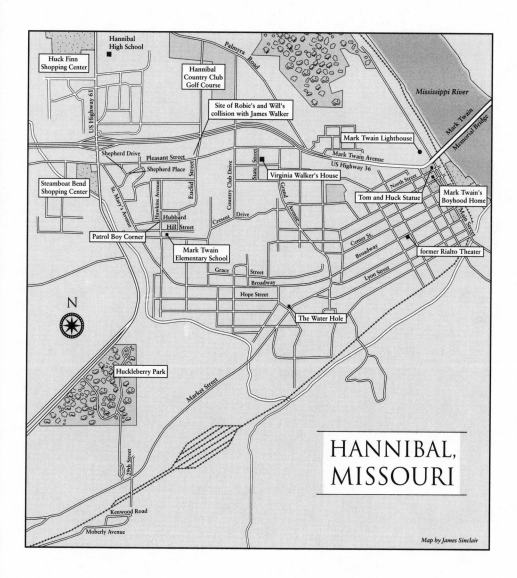

Huck Finn
Shopping Center

Hannibal
High School

Palmyra Road

Mississippi River

Mark Twain Memorial Bridge

Hannibal
Country Club
Golf Course

US Highway 61

Site of Robie's and Will's
collision with James Walker

Mark Twain Lighthouse

Mark Twain Avenue

US Highway 36

Shepherd Drive

Pleasant Street

State Street

Shepherd Place

Virginia Walker's House

North Street

Steamboat Bend
Shopping Center

St. Mary's Avenue

Euclid Street

Country Club Drive

Grand Avenue

Tom and Huck Statue

Mark Twain's
Boyhood Home

Main Street

Hawkins Avenue

Hubbard
Hill Street

Cresent Drive

Patrol Boy Corner

Mark Twain
Elementary School

Grace Street

Center St.

Broadway

former Rialto Theater

Broadway

Lyon Street

Hope Street

The Water Hole

N

Huckleberry Park

Market Street

29th Street

HANNIBAL,
MISSOURI

Kenwood Road

Moberly Avenue

Map by James Sinclair

You see, I'm kind of a hard lot—
least everybody says so,
and I don't see nothing against it.
—Huckleberry Finn

TOM AND HUCK
DON'T LIVE HERE ANYMORE

PROLOGUE

In the waning days of 1997, I learned of a killing in my hometown of Hannibal, Missouri. Six weeks later I received word of a second. The killings were carried out by adolescent boys. My first reaction to each bit of news, even though I had left the town thirty-eight years earlier and presently lived some nine hundred miles away, was: *That sort of thing is not supposed to happen here.*

News of a killing in a small town is news of an especially dark kind. It fuels a dread that seeps in deeper than the revulsion and pity evoked by any willful taking of life. In addition to their human victims, small-town killings assault one of the most cherished surviving myths in a myth-starved society: the myth of the hearth, the safe inner circle that protects a loving enclave against the cruelties of a barbarous world. Small towns—abandoned so promiscuously in the early decades of the last century—have come to symbolize the hearth for Americans taking stock of their own rootlessness. Small towns are where Americans now return, or aspire to return, to recapture, in a densely interconnected community, a state of tranquility and security, especially for their children.

Thus when the killers in a small town turn out to be adolescents—the very "children" that towns are presumed to nurture—the news carries an even deeper payload of dread.

I grew up knowing that I shared my native ground with a god of American literature. Hannibal is nationally celebrated as the boyhood home of Samuel Clemens, who as Mark Twain drew on his memories of the Mississippi River village to create stories that virtually enshrined boyhood as a sacred phase of life. On the strength of that connection, Hannibal advertises itself as "America's Home Town."

Thus the dread, in this instance, takes on the awful weight of ironic prophecy.

I was born in Hannibal a hundred two years after the boy Sammy Clemens moved there at age four with his family, from the nearby hamlet of Florida in November of 1839. I left the town at age seventeen, the same age as Sammy when he departed, when my Fuller Brush Man father lit out for a new territory in a larger city halfway across the state. Until then, I lived a life that—while it may not have approached "the greatest boyhood ever lived," in Justin Kaplan's assessment of Sammy's—was enriched by many of the same forces of nature and humanity. Surprisingly many, in fact, given the transforming onslaught of that particular hundred-year interval.

These forces included the great river that flowed along the town's eastern rim, of course, and the intimate wooded fields along the high bluffs to the north and south, and the deliciously terrifying cave that snaked deep into the limestone darkness three miles south of town. They included the rituals of town life—seasonal festivals, traveling circuses and ballgames and parades and school pageants and extravagant, sometimes downright scary, displays of Christian worship. And they included friendships: friendships with other boys, and sometimes with girls. From these friendships sprang adventures. The adventures led in turn to narratives, a constantly accumulating local history.

That history, and its kinship with myth, depended for its power on a crucial ingredient: isolation.

Our town was out there by itself on the great Midland prairie, its vastness interrupted only by that longitudinal slash of Mississippi. We were contiguous to no larger place. Distance separated us from bigger towns and great cities, but not from the surrounding farms and farm villages that supported Hannibal's merchant economy. Thus distance did not shrink us or trivialize us; it did the opposite. We felt a grandeur in the distances between Hannibal and everyplace else. Our existence, even as kids—maybe especially as kids—had meaning and function that could be heightened as it resonated against the invisible membrane enclosing our finite universe.

I believe that Samuel Clemens felt the same thing, at least for a long while. He returned to Hannibal some seven times after his leave-taking, in a century when Hannibal was even harder to get to than it is today. His last visit was in 1902, eight years before his death. As Mark Twain, he saturated his canonical works with depictions of the town and the people in it, nearly all of them idealized, fantastical, suggesting a hallowed place of eternal, safe-kept childhood. Only in the helpless candor of his embittered old age did Twain acknowledge the dark ghosts that haunted his memories of the town.

· · ·

THE MEMBRANE WAS never quite as resilient as we had imagined. It could not hold its shape against the tremendous encroaching forces of postwar America, the forces of agribusiness, centralized commerce, urban migration. Inevitably, the membrane gave way. The sanctifying distances collapsed. Like many other once-distinctive places that had nourished their own narratives and myths—Faulkner's Oxford, Steinbeck's Salinas, Thomas Wolfe's Asheville come to mind—Hannibal gradually saw its local culture absorbed into the template of an un-differentiated America.

I had revisited my hometown in the summer of 1985, the one-hundred-fiftieth anniversary of Samuel Clemens's birth, to witness the first great upheaval caused by that absorption. Hannibal was struggling against hard times then. Local businesses had folded, the surrounding farms were drying up, the population was aging as the young fled elsewhere. At a time when local places all over the country were suffering the same fate—and when theme parks and faux-"heritage" development were transforming those places into desperate cartoon versions of themselves—my hometown had made an awkward grasp toward cashing in. Spurred by the urgings of an Eastern-based "commemorations specialist," the mayor, the chamber of commerce, and several leading businesspeople had launched an overwrought (and underplanned) eight-month festival, long on garishly produced "attractions" and short on coherence, ballyhooed as the Mark Twain Sesquicentennial.

My resulting book, *White Town Drowsing: Journeys to Hannibal*,* examined the process of the town's self-defilement as the price of a mass-marketed economic fix (which never materialized, in any case). I thought that perhaps I had witnessed and described the fullest measure of loss that a community could experience in an age of accelerating materialism and extractive wealth.

I was wrong. I had not looked deeply enough into the town I'd thought I knew by heart. What interested me then was the changing civic face of Hannibal, the backings and fillings of its political and mercantile leaders as they pillaged and trivialized the town's cultural legacy in their quest for a marketing niche.

But this was only the surface of the town, its public veneer. I had not gone deeper. I had not walked into the peeling older neighborhoods, the edgy public schools, the drying-up shops, or the empty playing fields of the town. I had not spoken with families about their prospects, or about their children. I don't recall having paid much attention whatsoever to the children of Hannibal in that summer. There weren't many visible children in any case, a fact that should have triggered some warning system in the mind of a former child of the town.

But I had not looked deeply enough.

Twelve years later, at a time of skyrocketing anxiety about violent children and their alienation from their native places—places often denatured and demythified by the harsh architecture of colonizing commerce—the news reached me that the unthinkable had happened in America's Home Town. And then, six weeks later, had happened again.

And so I went back there to look more deeply: to take an accounting of the killings and find some narrative that made sense of them, if I could.

I found more than I had bargained for. I found that the atrophy of civic and familial cohesion—of "social capital," as it is lately being called by sociologists—had reached more deeply into much of the town than I could possibly have imagined, and that children, from earliest infancy through the end of adolescence, endured the greatest suffering from its effects.

---

*Published in 1986 by Atlantic Monthly Press, New York.

I also discovered, or rediscovered, that this present-day atrophy did not explain everything. Like its forward-looking host nation, and like the machine-dreaming author who once lived there, Hannibal remained profoundly in the often-violent jurisdiction of its past. Many of its discontents had moved through the generations in an almost biological progression, passed quite literally from father to son.

It was only when I sat in an idling car one day, looking out through a rainy mist at the general scene of one of the crimes, that I finally rediscovered how inseparable were the agonies of Hannibal's lost children from my personal past, and how unmodified by passing time. It was only then, at that moment, that my own memories of an idyllic childhood place shifted to accommodate the inclusion of my late brother Jimmy.

What I found forms the contents of this book. I owe many of these new discoveries to the honest, courageous conversations of deeply wounded people who had no particular reason to trust the stranger I had become. The rest I owe to the old ghosts I encountered as I physically explored the remnants of a Hannibal-that-was, including the ghosts of my father, my brother, and my childhood self.

—Ron Powers
Middlebury, Vermont
February 21, 2001

ROBIE AND WILL

Late on a Tuesday afternoon in November 1997, around supper-time, two sixteen-year-old Missouri boys got into a 1988 Ford Bronco II and went out looking for some way to pass the time before heading over to the local Baptist college to watch a basketball game. They slipped into the continental cortege, the perpetual flow of kids in cars looking for something to do, some way to break through the blankness.

Their town was Hannibal, Missouri—"America's Home Town," as it billed itself in tourist brochures, a salute to its legacy as the boyhood home of Mark Twain. The teenagers were named William D. Hill and Robie Wilson. Wilson (he pronounced his name "Robbie"), a serious-faced boy with short-cut blond hair and a sturdy build, was the son of a Hannibal city councilman and letter carrier named Kyle Wilson. He did not live with his father, who was twice divorced, but with his mother and her new husband. Hill, also blond, was an athlete, tall and muscular. He had recently moved to town from Iowa with his mother and stepfather.

With Hill at the wheel, the two kids cruised around town for a while, looking for girls, for friends, for anything besides what they knew was and wasn't there.

Not much to do.

They stopped for a snack at a fast-food franchise, then headed out onto the streets again.

It was around six P.M. when they spotted the jogger.

They had found themselves rolling aimlessly along Pleasant Street—Pleasant Street of America's Home Town. The figure trotting toward them, up the grade, was a sixty-one-year-old machinist with Car Quest Auto Parts and an amateur railroad enthusiast named James Walker. Like Robie, he was a lifelong Hannibal resident. An army veteran, he had been married to Virginia Elliott Walker since 1957. Virginia, a pale and soft-spoken woman, had for a time served as the president of the Helen Cornelius Fan Club. Ms. Cornelius, a Hannibal native and country-western singer, had enjoyed some success as a three-time winner on the *Ted Mack Amateur Hour* and later as an RCA recording artist in the 1970s. Her best-known hits were "We Still Sing Love Songs in Missouri" and "Tweedle-de-dee." The couple had one son, Michael Ray Walker, who lived in St. Louis.

Just now, James Walker was about midway through his five-mile run, which he made several times a week, always along the same route. He was at work on his goal of completing fifty-seven miles of running by the end of the month. Another fifty-seven, to be chalked up in December, would give him a thousand miles of running for the year.

Pleasant Street is an east-west road, both arterial and residential, near the western edge of town, two lanes of asphalt, no sidewalks. It had originated as a wooden plank road in about 1835, some sixteen years after first settlement, by a man named Fry, who cut it through three miles of hardwood forest in return for half of the fledgling town's remaining unsold lots. 1835 was the year of the birth, near Hannibal, of Samuel Langhorne Clemens—Mark Twain, the great mythifier of American boyhood.

Winter dusk had settled in on this November afternoon. The street-lights had been turned on, and Walker was wearing his customary bright yellow shorts, reflective vest, and orange fluorescent hat.

Walker chugged eastward on Pleasant, on the left side of the road, facing traffic. Hill and Wilson cruised westward on the downgrade. As they drew near the approaching figure, one of the boys—it was never conclusively established which—asked the other, "Do you want to door him?"

It was William Hill, the owner of the Bronco and a promising high school baseball player, who had clued Robie Wilson in on "dooring" or "awarding the door prize." The two had talked about it the previous summer, while idly tooling around a small lake. "Dooring" was a car stunt pulled occasionally in Iowa high school parking lots. It entailed a driver drawing alongside a student on foot while the front-seat passenger opened the door, giving the student an unexpected whack.

On this Tuesday, though, the recipient was to be not a high school student but an elderly man. And the "door prize" was to be administered not at a parking-lot crawl but at thoroughfare speed.

The Bronco closed on Walker in the 2500 block of Pleasant, a longish stretch in which the edge of the asphalt gave directly onto steep grassy lawn. The unsuspecting Walker had no route of escape.

What happened next differs slightly in the retelling by each boy. In either version, they made two runs at Walker before they struck the man.

William Hill later testified that it was Robie's idea to "door" the running man. Hill went along with it more or less offhandedly.

On the first pass, Hill swerved in Walker's direction, but perhaps because of the wind, Robie Wilson had trouble pushing the door open. "I missed him," he told Hill. Hill would testify that Robie urged him to go back.

Hill was reluctant, he said, but drove to the bottom of Pleasant and turned around. The Bronco retraced its route up the grade, overtook Walker, and continued up Pleasant a little way. Then Will Hill U-turned and made his second run.

Robie insisted that the first time they passed Walker, nothing happened; there was no discussion about "dooring." At the bottom of Pleasant, Hill made a right turn onto U.S. Highway 61 and headed north toward Hannibal–La Grange College, the site of the game. But after a block, Hill turned right again and looped back along a road parallel to Walker's route.

Whichever version of the story was correct, the Bronco was soon bearing down on James Walker for a second time.

Reemerging on Pleasant, with the trotting figure in his sights, Hill angled the car toward the man and, according to Robie, ordered Robie to open the door. Scared and confused, Robie complied.

Whatever the truth, James Walker paid the consequences. He never grasped what was about to happen. As the car approached, he made no effort to dodge out of the way. Robie Wilson pushed his door open. The onrushing steel caught Walker full in the face with explosive impact. The window glass burst, sending an eruption of shards back into the Bronco and outward along the pavement. The force was such that the window behind the passenger's seat shattered as well.

Robie Wilson glanced back at the collapsed figure and yelled, "Go! Go! Go!" Hill gunned his damaged car down Pleasant Street. He veered left into a more secluded, curving street called Shepherd Place, hurried along its tree-lined downhill contours until its terminus at St. Mary's Avenue. There he turned left again and took off along the central spine of Hannibal. At some point, Hill turned right off that spine—now Broadway—and plunged the Bronco down into one of the town's older, shabbier enclaves: a latticework of short, sharply angled streets fronted by century-old bungalows with peeling white paint; by sheds, freestanding garages, truck gardens. He drove a couple of blocks through this area to Market Street, a long and narrow winding hive of taverns and storefront businesses, early-century brick and wood frame, that once had teemed with raucous honky-tonk nightlife but now lay mostly dust-caked, abandoned, and Gothic. He pulled up near a cramped little bar and pool hall called the Water Hole, where he knew he could find his stepfather.

The Water Hole and the sagging storefronts alongside it formed a line of decay that was interrupted, less than a block to the east, by a jarringly spotless structure, all right angles and chrome and assertive colors. It spread, still under construction, like a nesting starship that had touched down on a dead planet. This was a half-completed service station.

New service stations and old bars formed a conspicuous proportion of commercial Hannibal, a glum dialectic. Corporate prosperity shouldering in on local subsistence. A vacuum of organic, self-sustaining community, scaled and designed for harmonious habitat by human beings. In their economic and architectural extremes, and in what was missing in between, the bar and the service station represented a significant vision of the America that in the 1990s presented itself to its young.

Before entering the tavern, Will Hill took his billfold out of his back pocket and put it on the seat of the Bronco. Then he found a rock and placed it inside the truck's cab. These items were meant to buttress the story that was already forming in Hill's mind, the story he would tell the Hannibal police.

Inside the Water Hole, Will Hill located his stepfather and told him the story he had rapidly formulated. Then he telephoned the Hannibal police and gave them the same version: his Bronco had just been vandalized, he said; someone had thrown a rock through the window, probably to get at the billfold that he had accidentally left on the driver's seat. (Why the billfold should still be on the seat after the vandal struck, Hill was perhaps not prepared to say.) When a squad car arrived at the bar a few minutes later, Will got in and sat beside Officer Darren Smith while he elaborated on the lie. He'd gone inside the bar to play pool at about five-thirty, he said, and when he came out an hour later he saw that someone had broken two windows in his car.

After Hill told his story, the officer let him go and he drove the damaged Bronco home, exchanged it for another car in the family, and the two boys went on to the basketball game.

A neighborhood man driving home from work came upon James Walker as he lay unconscious with massive face and brain injuries amid the glass shards. He called an ambulance. Emergency medical technicians tried to give Walker first aid at the scene; then they took him to Hannibal Regional Hospital, recently relocated from the town center to a field a few miles west of town. The next day Walker was transferred to a trauma unit at Blessing Hospital in neighboring Quincy, Illinois. He lasted another day, and then, on November 14, he died.

•   •   •

THE NET BEGAN to close on Will and Robie almost at once. While they were still at the game, the Hannibal police, who had never really bought Hill's "vandalizing" story, had begun collecting evidence linking the Bronco to the bloody hit-and-run on Pleasant Street. Sometime during the evening, Officer John Dean drove out to the Hill house on Moberly Avenue and examined the vehicle. Moberly is a short east-west street on the extreme southwestern edge of Hannibal, about two miles from the Mississippi riverfront and perhaps a mile west of the Water Hole. It dead-ends near an abandoned Moose lodge and the grounds of the Northeast Missouri Humane Shelter. The little street forms a southern border of a small community called Oakwood: once a settlement, later joined to Hannibal by the spine of another nineteenth-century plank road, and finally incorporated when that road became Market Street. Moberly lies below Market in an old cluster of floodplain bungalows wedged between the Norfolk Southern railroad tracks and Bear Creek. The tracks and the creek parallel Market in a meandering line toward the town center.

Checking out the Bronco's badly dented right door, Officer Dean found some orange fibers, the same color as the material in James Walker's fluorescent hat. He also collected some glass from the mostly hollowed-out passenger window; it would prove to match samples of the glass taken from the point of impact on Pleasant Street—glass that was demonstrably from a Ford product. Officer Dean spoke with Hill's mother, informing her of the pedestrian collision.

Mrs. Hill confronted Will with this information when he got back home. Panicky now, Will called Robie's house. Robie lived several hundred yards east of Will, on Kenwood Street. Robie's stepfather, Jim Beilsmith, answered the phone. A service garage owner, Jim had just returned home from an evening attending EMT classes; he was training to be an EMT to bolster his skills as a reserve deputy sheriff for Marion County. At the training site he had heard some radio transmissions detailing the collision; later, he had met some of the EMTs who'd been at the scene and listened as they described the injuries to Walker.

"It's after ten," Jim pointed out to Will. "No calls." "It's an emergency," Will replied. "Right," said Jim. "Everything's an emergency. You're a teenager." "No," Will said. "This is really an emergency." Jim handed the phone to Robie—who had started to undress for bed and was without a shirt—and gave him a two-minute time limit.

Nita Beilsmith, Jim's wife and Robie's mother, pondered this exchange as the two withdrew from Robie. A former EMT herself, Nita had a job with the Marion County Ambulance District and kept a police scanner at home. Nita had heard the transmission too, and just now, as she and Jim headed for their bedroom, she was thinking about something Robie had said in passing as he darted into the house and toward his bedroom, twenty minutes past his curfew: The window in Will's Bronco had been broken.

Robie listened to his friend for a few seconds before he tore into his parents' bedroom and shouted, "I gotta go to Will's. It's an emergency!" Then he fled the house into the late-autumn night, still half clad. A few minutes later he called from the Hill house: "Come over. We've got to talk. Something's happened. Someone's been hurt."

At the Hill house, anxiety and wariness reigned. Two reconstituted families, unfamiliar with one another, groping in the night to comprehend the horror their children might have wrought and what to do about it. There was some discussion about how to deal with the police and disparities in the two boys' stories. In later court proceedings, it was suggested that someone in the group—a tangential adult who may have been drinking—loudly warned the boys, "You better get your stories straight! You better get them together!"

It was Jim Beilsmith who reached a point of resolve that ended the confusion. The reserve deputy sheriff abruptly stood up and said, "We're leaving. That's it." He returned to his house, phoned the police department, and told the clerk that his stepson Robie Wilson had information relevant to the collision with the jogger.

· · ·

WHEN ROBIE ENTERED the police station after school the next day, he told the same story that Will Hill had told to Officer Smith. At the high school, he and Hill had behaved as though nothing of particular importance had happened to them. But they could not keep completely silent. A girlfriend of Hill's would later testify that before Walker died and before any charges were filed, Will admitted to her that his Bronco did indeed strike the running man. They'd only planned to scare him, Will told her; he guessed he'd gotten too close. In the months of rumor, gossip, and embellishment that inevitably ensued, some Hannibal High students would recall that one or the other of them had actually bragged about the dooring. At least one young woman thought she'd heard them boast that they had practiced on dogs.

On November 20, a week after James Walker died, Hannibal police arrested William Hill and Robie Wilson. Hill was picked up at Hannibal High School, Wilson at the Hannibal Alternative School, a separate facility for "problem" students.

This time, the two boys presented a new version of their essential innocence. Yes, they had been driving on Pleasant Street on that Tuesday afternoon, they acknowledged. Yes, they may have struck something. But the evening was dark, the pavement on that stretch extremely bumpy, and besides, the passenger door of Hill's Bronco did not shut properly; he had to keep a towel wrapped around it so it would stay shut. If anything resembling the charges against them actually happened, it was purely an accident.

The two were charged with involuntary manslaughter, leaving the scene of an accident, hindering prosecution, tampering with evidence, and concealing an offense. Their names were withheld from the local newspapers, radio, and TV for several weeks, even though nearly all of Hannibal soon learned their identities. They were only sixteen. Juveniles.

Children.

. . .

BY 1997, AMERICA may have been a country in the throes of a "great escape" back to its small-town roots, but it was also a country in the early throes of a dreadful reckoning: it had somehow lost connection with its children. These two truths were in some ways interlinked. The dimensions of this breach, as they grew ever more insistently visible, were vaster than any of the partial symptoms that mainstream America had been fitfully acknowledging since the end of World War II: "juvenile delinquents," "beatniks," "hippies," "dropouts," "slackers," "rebellious" children of "dysfunctional" families.

The disconnection—or whatever it was—could no longer be tidily expressed in terms of fringes or aberrations of extremes (though many Americans, especially those in public life, continued to try). In the pit of its stomach, at the base of its nighttime fears, America was starting to perceive that something horrible had metastasized. America's children, *as a category*, had unaccountably turned alien.

Many of the country's thirty-four million adolescents had withdrawn from, or had never engaged, America as it was understood by older adults: a grand social fabric of laws, economics, family cohesion, responsibilities, education, opportunities, meaningful work, a history expressed in mythic idealism.

Hundreds of thousands had drifted from households (most often broken and abusive households) into the burgeoning gangland netherworld. A million and a quarter had run away from home, whether toward some demimonde or simply toward the horizon. Another 273,000 were homeless.

Violence, particularly gun violence and its ceaseless depictions in media, saturated the consciousness of children. American kids killed and were killed by guns. Drugs and alcohol absorbed countless millions.

Gun homicide committed by teenagers tripled from 1986 to 1993, even as murders by people over twenty-five showed a significant decline. Early adolescents were the prime victims of assault. A million kids a year between the ages of twelve and nineteen were victims of violent crime.

In 1995, some 2,227 kids were suicides (an increase of about 120 percent over 1980). A Harvard Medical School study found that 23 percent of its 8,098-member study group had serious depressions before turning twenty.

Marijuana use more than doubled between 1991 and 1994. In addition, the National Institute on Drug Abuse found that two-thirds of eighth graders reported having tried alcohol; a quarter said they were current drinkers; 28 percent admitted they had been drunk at least once. Eleven thousand died each year in car crashes, half of them as a result of drunk driving.

The evidence of extreme youthful alienation had not exactly been obscure before the dreadful reckonings at the end of the decade and century. It had been accumulating in America for some time. In late June of 1990—at about the same time the $1.5 billion Hubble Space Telescope was found to contain a debilitating flaw; about the same time that the tab for the savings and loan bailout was being estimated at $500 billion; about the same time the ex-mistress of the ex-mayor of the nation's capital city was testifying about crack cocaine, opium, and marijuana escapades with His Honor—the *New York Times* announced on its front page that "today's youth" could not care less about any of it.

Citing the results of two recent national studies, the *Times* quoted one of them as declaring that the generation of young adults then aged eighteen to twenty-nine "knows less, cares less, votes less and is less critical of is leaders and institutions than young people of the past." This generation—a "backwash of the baby boom" composed of the "baby bust"—seemed almost to be rebelling, as the *Times* phrased it, against rebellion. It went on: "The indifference of this generation—to politics, to government, even to news about the outside world—is beginning to affect American politics and society . . . helping to explain such seemingly disparate trends as the decline in voting, the rise of tabloid television and the effectiveness of negative advertising."

A report prepared by People for the American Way framed these trends as a "citizenship crisis," noting that for the first time in fifty years, younger members of the public were not as well informed about issues in the world as older people. As recently as 1972, half the population between the ages of eighteen and twenty-four had voted. By 1988, the percentage had dropped to thirty-six. When asked about what did matter to them, most young respondents mentioned getting jobs, relief from "stress," and the fear of AIDS and drug addiction. Some mentioned their concern that the minimum drinking age had gone up. A few others cited "rights"—mostly, as it turned out, the "right" not to be hassled by the police. One young woman cited as an example of "rights" infringement a security guard's insistence at a rock concert that she and her boyfriend stop turning on their cigarette lighters.

By the end of the decade—the years of Robie Wilson's and Will Hill's midadolescence—that generation of "young adults" had matured toward early middle age. Now they were watching (or not watching) as new generations of the young edged even further from the core. The so-called gen X materialized, flared brightly, and then receded from pop consciousness. Its replacement was something darker, more amorphous: a formless mélange of statistics, images, styles, news reports, warnings, and behaviors that as yet had no organizing logo or name.

Whatever it was, this new manifestation of "youth" drew adults into responses far more intense than mere perplexity, exasperation, or puzzlement. It ignited a potent mixture of anger, hatred, and terror. It fueled a growing rejection of social institutions that had been designed and refined for more than a century to safeguard the interests of the young. Welfare, public-school funding, and the criminal-justice system became principal targets of this rejection.

But mainstream America's response to the youth crisis took other, more paradoxical forms as well, forms that seemed to spring from some deep schizophrenic wound in the national psyche.

Even as grass-roots America fretted, fulminated, and recoiled at the multiplying pathologies of youthful behavior, corporate America found ways to encourage and exploit that very same behavior for commercial profit.

Beginning in the mid-1980s and continuing throughout the nineties, the interlocked legions of advertising, entertainment, marketing, and technology unleashed a fusillade of imagery designed to exalt the most morbid symbols of teenage fear and alienation. Historic restraints and self-restraints melted away: restraints built over generations to shield the young from violence and its mimetic attraction, from the burdens of premature sexuality, from irrational material greed and envy, from a loss of empathy, from a collapse of faith in loving intimacy and communal purpose. From gangsta-rap music to shock-jock radio to slasher movies to interactive computer/video games saturated in images of extreme violence, to TV programs and commercials glorifying sexual obsession and predatory, "outlaw" aggression, the corporations drove home the ethos of nihilism and despair: soul-blights to be soothed, however temporarily, only by extreme stimulation and consumption.

This orgy of dark imagery, this extended national episode of wound worrying, begged comparisons to the sadomasochistic compulsions of a severely disturbed individual. It made a rough kind of rational sense only when one considered that many of the young corporate designers and brokers of these images were themselves recent émigrés of the same youth culture that had absorbed milder versions of this onslaught since birth.

•   •   •

BY THE AUTUMN of 1997, a new mimetic response would form, one that in time would finally focus the full attention of the host society: shooting assaults by adolescent boys in public schools.

Six weeks before Will and Robie got into the Bronco, a sixteen-year-old boy in Pearl, Mississippi, brooding over a breakup with his girlfriend, shot his mother to death, then made his way to the town high school and shot nine students, two of them fatally. It was the third school shooting in America in less than two years. There would be more. West Paducah, Kentucky, would erupt within two weeks; Jonesboro, Arkansas, four months after that; then Edinboro, Pennsylvania, in April 1998; then Pomona, California, four days after that; then in May, Fayetteville, Tennessee, and Houston, and Onalaska, Washington, and Springfield, Oregon. Littleton awaited.

By the mid- and late 1990s, fully one-half of America's teens had experimented with some form of high-risk or moderately high-risk behavior, some action that made them dangerous to themselves or others. A few extreme eruptions of such behavior (the school shootings, some inexplicable suicides, the odd gang rape) made national headlines and fueled a growing but inchoate national debate. Most episodes, however, were simply absorbed, endured, and folded back into the fabric of American community life.

· · ·

AS WILL AND Robie awaited their fates, life in the town, the state, and America went on.

The Christmas season drew near, and the state of Missouri focused its public energies on several pressing issues: the impending collapse of the public-school system in St. Louis, the rising popularity of casino gambling, and an epidemic of methamphetamine production and use, which the governor of the state called "an epidemic of evil."

In mid-December, St. Louis mayor Clarence Harmon announced that he was prepared to take over a school system beset by violence, racial tensions, and abysmal performance scores by largely impoverished students. He likened the system to "a giant snowball rolling down the hill toward St. Louis" and flattening everything in its path. He said he was considering removing the St. Louis school board and replacing it with a chief executive to be appointed by himself.

A good education, the mayor said, was the only hope for many of the children in the system. "We've got some neighborhoods that are sort of like third-world countries," he remarked. "And I'm not the first person to say that."

At about the same time, a Missouri state senator named Ronnie DePasco, a Democrat, was putting the finishing touches on a constitutional amendment that would grant license protection for existing riverboat gambling casinos that float in artificial basins. The so-called boats in moats had begun to sprout up on landlocked sites around Missouri after the state approved "riverboat gambling" in 1994; the state supreme court later ruled that "riverboat gambling" meant gambling on actual surface streams of the Missouri and Mississippi rivers.

While the senate anticipated DePasco's amendment, it debated for several hours a bill that would expand the state's Medicaid system to provide health insurance to more than ninety thousand uninsured young people. The measure never made it to a vote.

On December 18, a campaign was launched in St. Louis aimed at helping compulsive gamblers overcome their addictions. The campaign was sponsored by the Missouri Riverboat Gaming Association (a pro-gambling trade group), the state Gaming Commission, the Missouri Lottery, and the Department of Mental Health.

The methamphetamine crisis had seized hold of the entire rural Midwest by the late 1990s. Since 1996, some sixty-two meth manufacturing labs had been shut down in the Hannibal area alone. The epidemic had hit the heartland just a few years earlier—the result, experts believed, of shrewd market-expansion forays by Mexican traffickers based in California. Its ingredients were easily accessible: ephedrine, an over-the-counter component of cold and asthma tablets; fertilizer; battery acid. Intensely addictive, easy to make, savage in its paranoiac aftereffects, meth was a cottage-industry product in a thousand midwestern barns, sheds, shanties, and basements. Its leading consumers were teenagers.

On December 22, William Hill, who had by then turned seventeen, was certified to be tried as an adult. His parents hired a lawyer. Hill immediately agreed to testify against Robie Wilson. The Marion County prosecuting attorney, Tom Redington, dropped all charges against Hill except leaving the scene of an accident. He posted bail on a bond set at $25,000 and returned to school.

Robie Wilson remained in custody in a St. Louis–area detention center.

A few weeks after classes resumed at the start of the new year, a teacher at Hannibal High School overheard some boys talking about Will Hill in the school library.

The boys were hoping that Hill's case would get settled pretty soon. The baseball season was coming up in a few weeks. We really need Will on the team, one of the boys was saying. We're countin' on him.

· 2 ·

ZACH AND DIANE

It was only a few weeks after the killing of James Walker that America's Home Town absorbed its second shock involving youthful mayhem.

On Wednesday night, January 28, a young Ohio state trooper named Richard Noll was sitting in his parked cruiser monitoring eastbound traffic at a crossover on Interstate 70 in Preble County, near the Ohio-Indiana border. At about ten forty-five P.M. Noll, on assignment with the force's Drug Interdiction Unit, spotted a red Chevy 4×4 pickup truck with no rear license plate. He could make out two figures inside. Noll accelerated onto the interstate and flipped on his flashing lights. The Chevy's driver immediately slowed and pulled over onto the right berm. As the patrolman began his amble toward the pickup, a match flared inside the cabin; the driver had lit a cigarette. The driver turned out to be a teenage boy, fair-haired and good-looking, with eyebrows slanted upward toward the middle of his brow in a way that gave him a look of slightly perplexed good humor. His companion was a younger teenage girl, small and compact, with chopped and dyed black hair. The girl was pale and pretty in the manner of a very young Jacqueline Kennedy, but she radiated tension.

Trooper Noll poked his head inside the passenger window, where he met the girl's riveting gaze, and asked the driver for his license and registration. No license, the boy responded. No ID. He'd lost his wallet. The glove box proved empty of identifying papers.

Trooper Noll escorted the boy back to his cruiser. En route, he learned—or so he thought—that the two teens had left Missouri on a "road trip," in the truck lent to them by the girl's uncle. Their destination was the Mall of America in Detroit. This struck the patrolman as peculiar, given that the Mall of America was above and behind them in Minneapolis.

By now, Noll had been joined at the scene by another trooper, Joe Beghart. While Beghart inspected the red truck, Noll sat in the cruiser and prepared to move ahead with his routine questioning. He was abruptly interrupted in a manner that made his throat go dry.

"You want to hear a confession?" the boy suddenly asked. "You want to know about the owner of the truck? I'll tell you. You'd better listen up, 'cause I'm only going to tell you once, and one time only.

"The owner of the truck, I shot him. I blew his motherfuckin' head off."

· · ·

THREE HOURS LATER, at the Eaton Highway Patrol post on State Route 127, the details of the boy's confession were spooled up on Ohio State Patrol videotape. "We didn't ask very many questions at all," Trooper Noll remembered some months later. "Everything he gave us was just voluntary statements that he just kept talking about."

The driver's name was Zachary Wilson. He was seventeen. His companion was a fifteen-year-old girl named Diane Myers. The truck they were driving belonged to Diane's step-grandfather, a sixty-seven-year-old retired farmer and part-time auto salesman named J. D. Poage of Hunnewell, a decrepit farming hamlet of 219 residents living mostly in mobile homes some twenty miles southwest of Hannibal.

Zachary was the stepson of Kirk Wilson, the older brother of Kyle Wilson, Robie's father.

J. D. Poage was dead, Zachary told the Ohio troopers, a fact they soon verified by inquiries to the Missouri Highway Patrol. Zachary had killed him late on Monday night. He had blasted Poage twice with a shotgun the two had stolen from Diane's stepfather. Then he took the dead man's wallet and the $120 in cash that it contained. The two jumped into Poage's 4×4, with Diane's dogs in the truck bed, and sped into the night. Zachary drove to Hannibal, through the streets of the sleeping town. Somewhere, they remembered to free the dogs. Then they impulsively headed across the Mississippi River into Illinois on the old Mark Twain Bridge.

At the far end of the bridge—on a woebegone little patch of riverbank known portentously as the John Hay Recreation Area—Diane asked him to stop the truck. Zachary would testify later that he'd thought she wanted to have sex, but what she in fact wanted was to get rid of the shotgun. In one later version of Zachary's confession, Diane had sobbed and said she was going to hell for this, that her stepfather would find her and kill her. The two teenagers walked out to the river's edge, facing Hannibal across the river, their breath making puffs in the cold night air. Zachary heaved the weapon as far as he could. It spun and skidded on the Mississippi ice and disappeared into the darkness. It was recovered days later by divers. Diane placed her step-grandfather's billfold under a rock. Then the two drove to a nearby RV park, where Zachary fell asleep. Diane tried to drive the truck but managed to enmire it in a field. Zachary awoke, took over the driving, and the two resumed their flight, improvising all the way.

They drove first to neighboring Quincy, Illinois, for fast-food hamburgers, but Diane was so upset she could not swallow the ground meat. Then they headed on about three hundred miles northeast to Chicago without stopping to sleep, then back south into Indiana. At Rensselaer, short of cash, Zachary pawned another shotgun of J. D. Poage's that Diane had brought along "to rob people." He received $100, guilelessly giving his real name and Social Security number to the shop owner. Still sleepless, they drove to Indianapolis to shop at a mall for some music tapes. In a hospital parking garage, Zachary set about switching license plates with another car. He had detached the 4×4's plates, but his work was interrupted by someone's approach. He jumped back into the now-plateless Chevy and took off. His next stop was in Trooper Noll's cruiser.

After concluding his voluntary testimony, Zachary Wilson turned his mildly perplexed gaze up into the faces of the patrolmen who were by now silently grouped around him, staring at him, and told them that he would like his punishment to be death by lethal injection.

Zachary's confession was, in certain unmistakable ways, a Gothic travesty of Mark Twain's greatest tale. In *Adventures of Huckleberry Finn*, Huck, bedeviled by a depraved father, sets out on a great journey of escape with a companion-on-the-lam (in this case Jim, the runaway slave), leaving behind a blood-soaked cabin in a remote place to give the impression of a murder, with the "evidence" artfully tossed into the Mississippi River: "I took the axe and smashed in the door—I beat it and hacked it considerable, a-doing it. I fetched the pig in and took him back nearly to the table and hacked into his throat with the axe, and laid him down on the ground to bleed. . . . Well, next I took an old sack and put a lot of big rocks in it . . . and I started it from the pig and dragged it to the door and through the woods down to the river and dumped it in, and down it sunk, out of sight. You could easy see that something had been dragged over the ground."

Huck's great fugitive journey, of course, had been about liberation, and its telling a parable of American venality counterposed against the rough virtue of two figures on a raft. The liberating virtue of Zachary's and Diane's flight seemed compromised, at best, by the fact that the blood they left behind was not that of a pig.

· · ·

THIS WAS HARDLY the only Gothic aspect to the horror.

In other times it might have been a national news story, this confession by a small-town heartland teenager to a cold-blooded murder and cross-country escape. In other times some reporter might have dug up Zachary Wilson's familial connection to Robie Wilson and the killing Robie had been involved in. Some newspaper or network might have played up the angle of youthful mayhem in the very town where the mythic ideal of American boyhood had its origins.

But these were not ordinary times. The Hannibal/Hunnewell body counts simply had not been high enough to merit much attention beyond their local jurisdictions. Robie and Zach had claimed their victims in a season when lethally dangerous boys suddenly seemed to be swarming across America's consciousness. Robie's and Will Hill's assault on James Walker had happened in the shadow of the shootings at Pearl, Mississippi, and Zach Wilson's slaying of J. D. Poage against a freshly blood-spattered backdrop. On December 1, a fourteen-year-old boy named Michael Carneal, a baritone sax player and son of an elder in the Lutheran church, took a blanket full of guns to Heath High School in West Paducah, Kentucky. He chose a .22-caliber semiautomatic pistol from the assortment, stuffed plugs into his ears, and opened fire on a prayer circle of Christian students. He kept shooting until eight were wounded, three fatally, the bell for first classes rang, and he was finally disarmed. ("I believe there is a real demonic force that would drive someone to do this," a local minister, the Reverend Bobby Strong, was later quoted as saying. "That's why we need a saving grace now." Michael's own minister, the Reverend Paul Donner, said, "I'm firmly convinced Michael is a Christian. He's a sinner, yes, but not an atheist.")

Jonesboro, Arkansas, was a month away. Columbine, a little more than a year.

· · ·

TRIAL TESTIMONY WOULD later suggest that Zachary and Diane had more or less thought up J. D. Poage's murder on the night it happened. It was about a grievance Diane had been nursing against her step-grandfather: he had sexually molested her, Zachary would claim she told him, and that was probably why she'd lost the baby she'd been carrying—Zach's baby.

Zachary and Diane had met in the spring of 1997 on a correctional campus in St. Louis, run by the Missouri Division of Youth Services. Zachary was sixteen then and already a father-to-be by one of his girlfriends; Diane was fourteen. Both were products of broken marriages and veterans of long-term drug addictions. Zachary had been living out a stormy adolescence in Hannibal with his mother, Lana, at that time. Lana and Kirk Wilson had split up. The departed stepfather had reared Zachary from the time the boy was four until the time the marriage broke apart. Zach had been "a super-sweet little boy," Wilson would remember.

Like Robie, and like nearly half of his youthful peers in America, Zach spent his formative years in a household fragmented by marital instability. His natural father had abandoned Lana while Zach was still an infant. Divorce passed death in the mid-1970s as the leading disrupter of the family unit.

Whatever "super-sweetness" of character Zach Wilson may have been born with had not survived very deeply into his boyhood. He watched as another of Lana's liaisons deteriorated: Kirk, himself divorced and the father of two daughters, tried but failed to hold things together on the new home front. A lanky and craggily handsome man with a brush mustache, he favored aviator glasses and subtly patterned polo shirts. He held a succession of jobs, served on the Hannibal Park Board, and was a fast-pitch softball pitcher of national caliber. He had met Lana during a softball tournament in Hannibal, when he and his daughters had gone into the nearby IGA store for the air conditioning and some ice cream. Lana was selling hot dogs. Kirk and Lana talked, and one thing led to another. They managed to stay married eleven years. But marital tension, fed by Lana's drug and alcohol problems, pervaded the household, and young Zach absorbed much of the tension.

In his own tumultuous way, Zachary Wilson became something of a boyhood legend in Hannibal. With his lightning temper and merciless fists, he was the terror of neighborhood kids and their mothers. His deviousness, constant lying, and compulsive petty thievery made him the despair of teachers and ministers and priests. And yet Zachary Wilson fascinated people. No one, not even those who feared him, could deny the intensity of his intelligence or the dark brilliance of his inner world. Well before reaching adolescence, Zachary had burrowed deeply into himself, populating his *ur*-Hannibal with imaginary characters as fantastical and vivid, at least to his lights, as any in the works of Mark Twain.

"First grade, he was a good student, all A's," Kirk recalled. "Second grade, he started havin' problems with the teacher. We couldn't figure out where it was comin' from. He went from teacher to teacher after that. They tried every teaching idea: the time-outs, the individual sessions, the tutored study, everything you can do. For a while I sort of denied it: not *my* kid. Then it finally became evident to me that Zachary had serious problems."

Over the next several years, Zach was medicated, institutionalized, in and out of various schools. "We even put him in a Catholic school," Wilson told me later. "Fourth grade. After a year they didn't even want him back. I'd never seen a Catholic school turn down money. Then he got sent to Mark Twain School, the public grade school. Where he was constantly, but *daily* . . . I've told everybody, and I've told Zach this: 'You are the Babe Ruth of detention. You have records that can't be touched.' "

Zachary was put on medication at age ten to curb his anxieties, but the medication was expensive and he frequently went off it. His attention wandered; he had panic attacks. "His anger was so repressed," Kirk said. "He'd say to me, 'You don't know how I feel.' I'd say, 'Tell me. How do you feel?' He'd say, 'You don't understand.' I'd say, 'Tell me. So I can understand. Get an idea. So we can deal with it.' He'd say, 'I can't.' "

The erratic behavior intensified. "To say he has attention deficit disorder is like saying Hitler had a thing against Jewish people," Kirk said. "I mean, it was a little more widespread than that. But don't underestimate how intelligent Zachary is. Zachary is brilliant in his own way."

He made a kind of fetish of stealing. "He'd steal your tape recorder and put it in his pocket," said Kirk. "Then he'd say, '*Whut?* I didn't do that.' And you would never get him to change his story. Nothing is ever his fault. Ever. He used to break into my room. Either him or his buddy stole one of my state championship softball rings. And my softball pitching was one of the few things I did that was really important to Zachary. It was a super-big deal."

In middle school, Zachary was sent home one day for showing up in class with a gun in his pocket. (A classmate who knew him remarked on the incident to her mother in the gallows humor typical of Hannibal teens: "What was he thinking? You don't need to bring a gun to middle school. You don't need a gun until high school.") In high school, Zachary—who had grown into a pale but solidly built adolescent with a certain studied charm—stayed out of gun trouble, but he continued to steal and to menace other boys. And to take drugs and prey on his peers in various ways: he impregnated one of them.

Zachary's drinking and his use of marijuana, cocaine, and methamphetamines overwhelmed his tenuous connection with school, and he dropped out after his sophomore year, in the spring of 1997. It was then that Lana sent him to the detention center in St. Louis, where he hooked up with Diane Myers.

Diane was the stepdaughter of Ronnie Poage, J. D.'s son, a layout technician at Pace Industries in nearby Monroe City. She lived in

Poage's house in Hunnewell with her mother, the former Dee Myers, her brothers Russell and Justin, and her stepbrother Mitch.

No one who knew Diane, a small and porcelain-skinned girl with clean, youngish features, disputed that she was exceptionally bright. "Super, super, super smart," said Amanda Brown, who had known Diane since early childhood. "She counted out my money at the corner store when we were four years old." Diane's teachers recognized her intelligence as well; she was placed in advanced math classes at Monroe City High School. She was also an accomplished artist, turning out astonishing likenesses of her family members and herself, and a writer of stories and poems.

As to her relations with other people, opinions differed. "A cold person," one friend told me. Another described her as vampirish, a girl without empathy or remorse. But Amanda, who knew her well, insisted that this "weird" pose of Diane's was nothing more than a form of protection. "She really cared about me," Amanda recalled. "She would sit down and listen to everything I had to say. She loved animals, always took care of her dogs. And she was like a mother to her little brother Justin. She ran that household. She had to clean, cook, wake her stepdad up to go to work every morning. She had an innocent face, but she was very old for her age. She had seen a lot."

"She's a couple of persons," said someone else who knew her. "She can be cold, but I think that's to cover confusion about who she is and who she wants to be. I think she wants pity and she wants sympathy, but at the same time she wants everybody to think that that is not what she wants. Diane is a gigantic paradox, is what Diane is."

· · ·

IN THE FALL of 1997, Lana thought she had found a means of separating Zachary from his bad influences in Hannibal. She had begun dating a Hunnewell man named Scott Dowell. In late October she moved from Hannibal into Dowell's house and brought Zachary along. Dowell set the boy up in a trailer behind his house.

But instead of removing Zachary from his problems, Lana had inadvertently put him catercorner from a new one: Dowell's house sat diagonally across the street from the one where Diane Myers, herself recently released from detention, lived with her stepfather.

Ronnie was the son of J. D., a retired farmer and sometime car sales-man at the Poage Auto Center in Hannibal, owned and operated by several members of the Poage family. J. D. lived alone in a small house about four miles down a dirt road from Ronnie.

Unexpectedly reunited, the two adolescents threw themselves into an all-consuming relationship. They had sex nearly every day in Zach's trailer and talked vaguely about getting married and having children. They continued their drug habits. In mid-January 1998, Kirk Wilson, though long estranged from Lana's household, persuaded Zach to check into a rehabilitation facility, the Hannibal Council on Alcohol and Drug Abuse. The goal was to get Zach "cleaned up" so that he could apply for work through the Job Corps.

About six days into this, Diane arrived for a visit. She told Zach she thought she was pregnant with his child. (Zach's former girlfriend had given birth to their son some two months earlier.) But a few days after the visit, Diane telephoned Zach at the council and told him that she had lost the baby. According to later court testimony, she told Zach she could never have children; her step-grandfather had seen to that. At any rate, she was having her period again.

· · ·

DIANE AND A couple of her friends picked Zachary up when he im-pulsively checked himself out of rehab on Tuesday, January 27, 1998. She brought him cigarettes, as he'd asked her to. Their first stop was at a convenience center to pick up a better brand of cigarettes than the cheap ones Diane had bought. Then the friends drifted off, and Zach and Diane drove on to Hunnewell. Diane was agitated about the loss of her baby. Soon Zachary was agitated too.

They wandered about the little neighborhood, first to Zach's trailer, then to Diane's house, then to the house of her stepbrother Mitch, where they got high. After that, they hit a few other houses in the neighborhood, returning finally to Mitch's place.

At about seven in the evening, a weeping Diane coaxed Zach out for a walk. They strolled in the cold night along the Salt River—the same river, small and curling, whose forks had once embraced an-other nearby hamlet called Florida. It was Florida, Missouri, today submerged under an artificial lake, whose supposed potential for riches had drawn John Marshall Clemens, his wife, Jane, and their four children there from Tennessee in April 1835. In November of that year, Jane gave birth to Samuel.

Exactly what happened near that riverbank on that January night in 1998 will remain a mystery as dark and convoluted as one of Mark Twain's feverish old-age manuscripts, a latter-day enactment of "Which Was the Dream?" A series of confessions, retractions, letters, and cryptic allusions by the two teenagers would produce plausible reasons for thinking that either Zachary or Diane, or perhaps both of them in some morbid partnership, fired the two shotgun rounds that killed J. D. Poage. But the conflicting accounts did illuminate something that perhaps preconditioned the horror and countless others like it: the landscape of blankness that has steadily leached through American society. Like hundreds of thousands of their fellow adolescents—in cities, suburbs, and rural towns—Zachary and Diane moved in a muted world that had little to do with them: a world of absent or dimly connected adults, of decaying or semi-inhabited neighborhoods; a world in which meaningful work scarcely existed, and "civic" life was represented mainly by law enforcement and rehabilitative social services; a world in which the future bled daily into the present and then into the past; in which one's movement through a day consisted of infinite small, arbitrary impulses that typically culminated in sitting on someone's sofa, playing a video game, getting high, having sex, cutting one's hair, nursing grievances, in which those daily movements might easily begin with a search for a better brand of cigarette and end with a shotgun murder.

Zach and Diane were not thinking of Mark Twain, or of patterns or structures or absences, during their walk, or of anything much beyond their feelings at that moment. Diane was beside herself. Besides her distress over the presumed miscarriage, she was restless. She told Zach she wanted to steal a car, get as far away as she could, and she wanted Zach to go with her. Diane did not have a driver's license.

Zach was thinking more in terms of grabbing a little sex with Diane, but Diane was not in the mood. Brooding, the two returned to Mitch's house at around ten o'clock. Zach settled in for some Nintendo; Diane left for her stepfather's house, to wake him up for his night shift at Pace Industries. But she didn't return right away. She was gone an hour. When she opened the front door on her return, Zach saw that she had slashed her reddish hair short and dyed it black, looking like Juliette Lewis before the killing scenes in the 1994 movie *Natural Born Killers*.

Diane pulled her boyfriend off the couch for one more moody walk along a country road. She talked about wanting to get out of town. Zachary told her he would go along with whatever she decided. But what Diane wanted remained suspended for a while in a haze of indecision. They returned to the house again. At some point Zach fumbled inside the engine of a Ford LTD owned by one of the Poages, trying to hot-wire it, but he couldn't figure out how and gave it up. The winter evening edged toward midnight.

At about twelve-thirty in the morning—Wednesday, now—it occurred to Diane that it was past time to rustle up some dinner for her eight-year-old brother Justin. She told Zachary to go back to his trailer; she'd meet him there later. Zach followed Diane's advice, plopped down on his couch, and fell asleep.

He was awakened sometime later by the glare of headlights against his window. He padded outside to find Diane, an inexperienced driver, struggling at the wheel of her step-grandfather's Chevy 4×4. (Actually, the truck was a "demo" vehicle from Poage Auto Center; it bore a dealer's plate and, when checked out to J. D. Poage, showed fourteen miles on its odometer.)

"Let's go!" Diane told Zach. "I stole it!"

At least that was what Zach remembered she had said. The entire sequence of events from this point onward was muddled in a maze of confession, renounced confession, and conflicting testimony. The version that Zachary volunteered the following night in the Ohio Highway Patrol post was closer to the one that ultimately prevailed in court. In this version, Zachary was seized with the impulse to murder J. D. Poage—for what he believed the old man had done to Diane—before leaving Hunnewell. In fact, Zachary told the patrolmen, he'd wanted to kill Diane's mother and stepfather and brother as well, and to burn their house down, because he hated all those people. They all deserved to die.

Zachary and Diane set out down the dirt road on foot, Zachary carrying the stolen shotgun. Diane later remembered that Zachary had said he was going to kill Poage but that she'd thought Zachary was kidding. She thought they were just going to rob him and run away.

The glow of headlights brightened a ridge ahead of them; moments later a car appeared, heading their way. Zach tossed the shotgun into the ditch at the side of the road. The driver, a neighbor, stopped, peered into the darkness, and asked the two teenagers if they wanted a ride. Zachary and Diane declined, with thanks, and the neighbor drove on. Zachary retrieved the shotgun.

About a hundred yards from J. D.'s house, Diane stopped walking. Zach continued ahead alone. After a minute or two Diane started walking again. When Zach reached the little house, he broke the glass of the basement door and unlocked it from the inside. Diane stood waiting outside. Zach climbed the basement stairs to the main floor. He turned on all the lights in the house. Then he ripped the telephone off the wall. He didn't worry about making noise, because he knew that Poage was nearly deaf.

He found the old man where he expected to find him—asleep, "bare-ass naked," in his small bedroom. Zachary leveled the shotgun at the figure. He deserved to die. Then Zach paused, took a step or two backward, and kicked the bed. He wanted Poage to know who his killer was, he later explained.

When he was satisfied that Poage was awake enough to recognize him, Zachary squeezed the trigger.

The deafening round blew a crescent-shaped gap in Poage's shoulder. Diane flinched at the sound. Zachary surveyed his handiwork for a moment. He was fascinated by the purple design in his victim's flesh. Diane came inside the house. Zachary placed a bedsheet over the bloody and mangled body. He turned from the bed and began to rummage through the pockets of Poage's trousers, which were draped across the back of a chair, searching for the farmer's billfold. After a minute or so he was distracted by sounds coming from beneath the sheet on the bed, a kind of gurgling and snoring. By this time Diane may have entered the bedroom. Zach turned, considered the twitching form for a moment, then slipped a new cartridge into the shotgun's chamber. This time there was more purple: some of Poage's brains adhered to the wall and ceiling.

At the troopers' post in Ohio, Zachary would claim that his girlfriend was somewhere else when he fired and entirely innocent of what was happening inside the house. "He told me that Diane knew nothing about it. He hadn't told her," Trooper Noll would later testify. "He wondered if she'd be pissed—because he'd be pissed if some-one killed a relative of his.

"But he said he felt like God. He knew that he was Poage's judge, jury, and executioner."

Satisfied that his victim was dead, Zachary Wilson took Poage's billfold and the shotgun and left the house. He and Diane walked the four miles back to Zach's trailer. They got into the Chevy 4×4, the dogs in the back, and sped toward Hannibal and into the dark east. Zachary insisted on driving.

TOM AND HUCK

A bronze statue stands near the foot of Cardiff Hill in Hannibal, at the terminus of North Main Street, a block north of Mark Twain's boyhood home and about three hundred yards from the Mississippi River levee. It has commanded the town's historic district since 1926. Visitors to the town squint upward at it through their sunglasses; they put down their plastic bags filled with Mark Twain T-shirts and postcards and photograph one another in front of it. Children tend to stare at it the longest, as if it almost reminded them of something. But eventually everybody moves on.

The statue is a depiction, at once powerful and weightless, of two boys in midstride. The boy on the left wears a straw hat and grips a curved walking stick with his right hand. His face is turned toward his companion, a boy in a watch cap who has a knapsack slung over his left shoulder and who looks ahead toward some high horizon as he pushes resolutely forward off his bare left foot, his right arm swinging free. The straw-hatted boy has placed his right hand on the back of the other's shoulder. The gesture seems frozen between a comradely embrace and an attempt at restraint.

The figures are Tom Sawyer and Huckleberry Finn. The statue was struck by a Missouri-born sculptor named Frederick Hibbard; it was the first in America to represent literary characters. The bronze boys' attitudes, so disarmingly buoyant on their surface, hold deeper complexities of meaning. It took Hibbard eleven years and many conversations with his benefactor, a wealthy Hannibal lawyer named George A. Mahan, to refine a specific vision and then to execute it.

"Colonel" Mahan commissioned the work five years after Mark Twain's death in 1910, as part of a personal crusade to conserve the writer's boyhood habitat and affirm his worldwide renown, which had started to diminish under the scrutiny of a new century. (Samuel L. Clemens, as he was known before he adopted his famous pen name, moved with his family from Florida to Hannibal at age four and lived in the town until he was seventeen. He identified his boyhood house on Hill Street on a visit near the end of his life; it has since become a national shrine.) A general counsel to railroad companies by profession, the colonel was an amateur historian and specialist in Twain's life and works. His own vision of the statue provided the contours of Hibbard's finished concept.

"Mr. Mahan . . . decided that the age of the boys would be 12," Hibbard wrote in a 1926 letter to a Hannibal pastor. "Also that the statuary must convey something that would be helpful to boys and girls that viewed it."

Hibbard traveled from Chicago to Hannibal three times to brainstorm with Mahan about just what that "something" might be. He fashioned several clay models over the early years of this collaboration. Finally, Mahan was able to express exactly what he thought the statue should convey, and Hibbard got down to serious work. On May 27, 1926, before a throng of Hannibal citizens, school marching bands, National Guard companies, and troops of Boy Scouts, the resulting statue was unveiled.

It was a festive and celebrity-studded occasion. The mayor, Mahan, and Hibbard were on display, as were several clergymen, university deans, and lesser dignitaries. An elderly Laura Frazier, the girlhood model for Becky Thatcher in *The Adventures of Tom Sawyer* written fifty years before and hearkening to experiences now eighty years gone, spoke to the crowd from the dedication platform. So did Margaret Tobin Brown, a Hannibal native and "the Unsinkable Molly Brown" of the Titanic legend. She claimed that Mark Twain had once personally rescued her from a raft on the Mississippi during a cyclone and later had urged her to go west to seek her fortune. Open-air amplifiers, the first ever to be used in Hannibal, slammed the speakers' voices against the sturdy storefronts of North Main.

The "something that would be helpful to boys and girls" that George Mahan and Frederick Hibbard strove to invest in the "Tom 'n' Huck" statue (as it quickly came to be known) has lost its nuance on the rough surface of the twentieth century. The statue no longer compels the eye, much less the impulse to interpret. A dun-and-green antique now, it has long since receded into the welter of brightly colored attractions and souvenir shops that scream for the tourist's credit card: the Haunted House on Hill Street across from the Boyhood Home, the yellow Twainland Express that lugs customers around town by the wagonload, the Too-Too Twain that chugs its dismal loop a few hundred yards from the entrance to the Mark Twain Cave two miles south of town, an entrance now reachable only through a souvenir shop. Most visitors can no longer tell the two figures apart. If asked, a typical observer will likely hazard that Tom Sawyer is the figure on the left, since he is the one wearing the totemic straw hat.

Actually, that figure is Huck—the boy with the restraining arm. The proof is in the pantlegs. Tom's are cuffed and sewn, thanks to the "civilizing" attentions of Aunt Polly. Huck's are in tatters.

Tom is the boy oblivious to restraint. He is accelerating—toward maturity, toward the twentieth century—toward Pleasant Street, in a manner of looking at it.

Frederick Hibbard explained it in his letter to the minister: "A statue can only convey one moment. . . . Mr. Mahan decided that that moment should be *when Tom awoke to the world* and wanted to go out into it and see for himself all that it contained. Hence, the knapsack, the advanced foot, the gleam in his eyes, and the whole posture of his body. But Huck was perfectly contented to stay right where they were—hence, his posture with his hand on Tom's arm, the look on his countenance as though trying to persuade Tom not to venture forth, but to stay right there."

Frederick Hibbard could not have conceived what a prophetic condition he was describing. Time has encrusted his bronze forms with deeper layers of nuance to convey, whether or not the passing "boys and girls" of his hopeful vision are capable of deciphering them.

The old statue has come to represent the great sweep of American childhood itself, in its rising and descending arc.

Here is Huck, the primitive but good-hearted child of the Enlightenment, innocent and natural, reaching out to halt the flow of history. And here is Tom, clued-in, mind-tripping, the calculating grown-up-to-be, launching his trajectory away from boyhood toward eager adulthood in the Industrial Age and beyond. Alpha and omega. Huck's grasp will never be strong enough to arrest Tom's fatal glide.

· · ·

I GREW UP in the shadow of that statue and spent my childhood in a town that could convince anyone that childhood was the defining stage of a human life and that everything following it was a curious remnant of evolution, like the little toe. I was pretty far along into adulthood before it sank in that childhood was in fact a recent construct of Western society, that its rising and descending arc spanned fewer than two hundred years.

Until the late seventeenth century, most human young in the West were differentiated from adults mainly according to their capacity for work—"capacity" being a judgment rendered always by adults. Small-scale peasant and feudal communities devoted mostly to agriculture required plenty of work from everyone. There was little reason to worry about the psychological or cognitive limits of the smallest members.

And yet a rough kind of gratification underlay this harsh life. In any society whose main concern is survival, work validates its members. Nearly every community member has some worth, measured by useful labor. Individual life is short, death nearly always in evidence, but work invests one in the transcending life of community. Community in turn offers a kind of immortal extension of the self, infinite past giving way to infinite future. Its authority is seldom codified in law; the individual's obligations to it are reinforced and celebrated through ritual: seasonal festivals, communal worship, holy days, baptisms, funerals, storytelling, dance, games. Ritual symbolically conquers fundamental human anxieties (death, sex, hardship, the survival of the soul) and sanctifies place and plight and duty. Ritual expresses the irreducible value of each human life.

But the intrinsic bonds that children in Europe might have enjoyed with their communities through labor began to atrophy with the rise of cities. From the thirteenth century onward, as contact with the East stimulated trade, urban centers such as Venice, Paris, Naples,

Barcelona, and London siphoned peasants from farmland that was, in any case, growing infertile from overplanting. Yet through the Renaissance, as new systems of moral and religious thought began to focus on the nature of man and the meaning of selfhood, children remained undifferentiated from their elders: loved and valued, perhaps, but seldom treated as creatures in special need of learning, nurturing, and play.

Early examinations of childhood as a special state tended toward the cursory. John Locke, writing in 1693, held that if children were in fact different from their elders, they were different as tabula rasa—their nascent minds as blank slates, awaiting the imprint of ideas. Education was thus a preemptive process, inscribing the child with correct ideas while protecting it from its own anarchic nature.

The Puritans, with their chilly notions of the elect and the damned, extended this prophylactic view: children were "little adults," emerging into the world with the curse of fallen Eden and the mark of Cain. Inherently stunted, the young were in constant need of severe discipline and corrective moral drill.

Not until the mid-seventeenth century did history's creep accelerate and the old land-based patterns begin to fall irrevocably apart. In these new throes of dislocation, "childhood" finally gained its status as a distinct phase of life. It gained this status, ironically, from the argument that this distinct phase of life was growing meaningless as a category.

As fresh tides of displaced peasants streamed toward the cities, power and wealth replaced tillage and harvest skills as measures of human value. The great lurch from a soil-based peasantry to the modern age had begun, and with it the formation of a class system and the replacement of reciprocal service with power, coercion, and money.

Individuals now found themselves constrained by "society." But was society an exaltation of man, or a corruption? Did it promote freedom or enslavement, good or evil? No one was quite sure. Industrialized progress promised a future of marvels, but the marvels came at the expense of agrarian tradition. Human existence seemed to be separating from its satisfying textures and certainties. The historian Ian Johnston has described the cost of these dislocations as "the loss of ritual meaning to life."

How should young people be prepared for living in harmony with society? Philosophers and social critics enlivened the Age of Reason with explorations of this question.

Preparation suggested instruction. Instruction presupposed a phase of life receptive to it. A conception of childhood was the inevitable next step. And the hazy antecedents of Tom and Huck began to assume their shapes.

For Thomas Hobbes, the shapes were scarcely beyond simian. Man in his natural state was a transient brute driven by fear to destructive passions. All men were created equal—equal in their depravity. (In this view, Hobbes prefigured Mark Twain's great mordant witticism: "I have no race prejudices . . . or caste prejudices nor creed prejudices. . . . All that I care to know is that a man is a human being. That is enough for me; he can't be any worse.") Society was the great regulator. Obedience to the law was the supreme value. The education of children would amount to indoctrination in the values of the Commonwealth. Happiness lay in subservience.

Hobbes's leaden vision prevailed for more than a century—an era in which the church lost primacy to centralized states, and capitalism, ever swelling, legitimized the commodification of human beings for profit. The most easily commodifiable were children: children plucked from orphanages, bought from destitute families, gathered in off the street. A growing horror at this dehumanized "progress" started to take hold.

A book published in France in 1762 expressed this horror with historic clarity. It began with these words: "God makes all things good; man meddles with them and they become evil." This was the opening of *Émile*, the transformational novel by the social critic Jean-Jacques Rousseau. If "childhood" as later centuries understood it can be traced to a single conceptual origin, it is in the pages of this book.

Subtitled *A Treatise on Education, Émile* offers a vision of youthful consciousness contrary to all previous suppositions, from Locke's tabula rasa to the Puritans' child sinner to Hobbes's rough beast in need of constricting authority.

"We know nothing of childhood," Rousseau evenly asserts at the outset, "and with our mistaken notions the further we advance the further we go astray. The wisest writers devote themselves to what a man ought to know and without asking what a child is capable of learning. They are always looking for the man in the child without considering what he is before he becomes a man. It is the latter study to which I have applied myself the most; so that if my method is unrealistic and unsound at least one can profit from my observations. I may be greatly mistaken as to what ought to be done, but I think I have clearly perceived the material that is to be worked upon. Begin thus by making a more careful study of your pupils, for it is clear that you know nothing about them. If you read this book with that end in view I think you will find that it is not entirely senseless." Rousseau proposed a vision of distinct childhood stages of development, each inherently self-defining and self-aware. *Émile*'s five sections correspond to infancy, early childhood, youth, adolescence, and young adulthood. In each stage, Emile's father/mentor analyzes the child's temperament, skills, interests, and range of learning capacities. He devises teachings—experiential, not "bookish"—designed to steer the child toward a life of informed harmony with the world: neither its tyrant nor its slave.

Rousseau rejected Hobbes's dark visions. He saw humans as born with goodness derived from self-love and loving concern for those around them. They are born, that is, as Huckleberry Finn: noble savages, instinctively moral, able to satisfy their needs in the Eden of their natural world.

Émile awakened European society. Readers experienced the same epiphany some get staring at the statue of Tom 'n' Huck statue in Hannibal: a stirring of deep memory. The radiant profundity of childhood, the recollection of how everything *mattered*, swelled into the imagination of artists. Their work would generate historic social and political changes.

British Romantic artists such as Thomas Gainsborough, William Mulready, Francis Wheatley, and Sir Henry Raeburn turned out exquisite portraits of families, babies, and young children, often in a context of exaggerated pastoral serenity. The publication in 1744 of *A Little Pretty Pocket Book* by John Newbery inaugurated a field of specialized publishing for children, a field that expanded over the ensuing 250 years. Among Newbery's contributions were Oliver Goldsmith's *History of Little Goody Two Shoes* and a collection of Mother Goose rhymes, both published in 1765.

In 1838, in England, the twenty-six-year-old former child laborer

Charles Dickens published *Oliver Twist,* a novel that equaled *Émile* as a cry for the sanctity of childhood. The graphic saga of the urchin Oliver at large in the Saffron Hill hellscape of workhouses, thieves, prostitutes, and other plausibly monstrous adults shocked Victorian England. Through the end of the nineteenth century, an exaltation of childhood swept through Western society.

The world headquarters of exalted childhood shifted to Hannibal, Missouri, in 1876, the year Tom Sawyer launched out in his accelerating stride. The accomplishment confounded the author himself and triggered his famous ambiguities. In converting the sunniest and most delicious of his boyhood memories to literature, Twain was not even aware until informed by others that he had written a "children's classic." In a letter to his friend William Dean Howells in July 1875, announcing that he had finished the manuscript, he stipulated, "It is *not* a boy's book, at all. It will only be read by adults. It is only written for adults." Only after Howells, the editor of *The Atlantic Monthly,* had read the manuscript and pronounced it "altogether the best boy's story I have ever read," did Twain accept the designation— which he ratified by changing the word "hell" to "thunder" in a line of dialogue from Tom's friend Huck Finn.

A century's worth of purifiers and kitsch-meisters took it from there. *The Adventures of Tom Sawyer* would be translated into forty languages and by the twentieth century's end still remains in print. Twain's selectively imagined boy proved an irresistible figurehead to the most mawkish and reductive of American image makers: Tom with his pockets full of marbles and pieces of blue bottle glass to look through and tin soldier and kitten with only one eye; Tom showing off for Becky and witnessing a murder and larking like a pirate on his Mississippi River island; Tom eluding Injun Joe in the cave and bringing justice and winning the treasure and Becky's chaste adoration.

No entrepreneur, it seemed, could resist the marketability of this straw-hatted, mischievous presexual boy. The sentimentalizing was well underway during Twain's own lifetime: returning to Hannibal unannounced in the spring of 1902 for his final visit there, he found the streets filled, within an hour, with romping boys and girls costumed as Tom and Becky. An eighty-year lineage of movies, beginning in 1917, emphasized Tom's adorable naughty-boy hijinks under the long-suffering, bemused eye of Aunt Polly.

The mythifying of Tom took on a weird reality of its own. In 1935, Norman Rockwell, the illustrator-prince of exalted Americana, produced sixteen canvases of Tom 'n' Huck for the Heritage Press's commemorative editions of Twain's novels. Rockwell prepared himself by making a pilgrimage to Hannibal, just as the sculptor Hibbard had done a decade earlier. He later claimed to have "talked with several people who were boys when Clemens was a boy," which would have put them at least in their nineties. He slid down the same water pipe (or so he believed) that Twain furnished for Tom in *Tom Sawyer,* and he confessed that he'd lain in wait on Main Street, "accosting" passersby and offering to buy their "toil-worn costumes" off their backs to take home with him for his models to wear.

(Rockwell was far from the only one to conflate Twain's fiction with actual history. The mayor of Hannibal in the late 1990s liked to tell visitors to his office that he had moved to the town so that his children could walk the same streets that Tom and Huck had walked.)

The sanctification of Twain's boyhood characters has never been quite unanimous. The detractors of *Huckleberry Finn* as a "racist" novel aside, a few careful readers down through the years have tried to examine Tom, Huck, Becky, and their friends independently of the suffocating preciousness and cant.

Twain himself offered some guidance in this direction. His nonfiction reminiscences of Hannibal unveil a darker, bloodier landscape than the world of Tom. He recalls encountering two corpses (one in a slough off the Mississippi, the other on the floor of his father's law office), witnessing the beginning of an autopsy on his freshly dead father, seeing a man shot dead at point-blank range in the street and another shotgunned by a woman whom he had been harassing, watching as a slaveowner caved in the skull of a Negro with a lump of iron ore, feeling himself responsible for the drowning of a boyhood friend and for the hideous roasting, in his jail cell, of a drunken tramp who had borrowed matches from Sammy to light his pipe. In the famous despondency of his final years, Twain roughed out notes for a tale in which the two legendary comrades meet again in Hannibal as withered, defeated old men.

As early as 1920, the critic Van Wyck Brooks indicted Twain for the stunted, creepy worldview that underlay his deceptive surface drollery. Sixty years later, Cynthia Griffin Wolff slashingly extended this point of view. "Tom Sawyer," she proposed, offered nothing less than "a nightmare vision of American boyhood," set in "a phantom town inhabited by ghostly presences" where the grown-ups are anonymous shadows, the power structure built on an oppressive matriarchy, violence and treachery rampant. Even the few downtown buildings that rate description in the text are little more than "menacing fragments": two taverns, a courthouse, a jail, a deserted slaughterhouse.

And yet he called it "St. Petersburg"—paradise—in his fiction and forever longed to return.

In the end, Twain's divided consciousness of Hannibal was far clearer and more discerning than my own, which formed a century later. For just as I remained clueless—stubbornly, I like to think— about the marginality of "childhood" in human history, I remained similarly untroubled regarding any conflicting versions of the town I carried with me, through adult life, in my memory. At least this is what I was able to tell myself, for many years.

As a boy, Sammy Clemens dreamed of being a pilot on a Mississippi riverboat in an eternal summer, with the oleanders in bloom and the sugarcane green. I dreamed of being a good guy in the movies.

I'm slumped knees-up with the other kids, halfway down the dark, jujube-scented aisle of the Rialto Theater on a summertime Saturday afternoon, waiting for the cowboy double feature. Probably a Roy Rogers, the King of the Cowboys, and then a Johnny Mack Brown. Roy Rogers wore shirts that resembled Christmas trees with sleeves, and stripes down the sides of his pants. To me he looked like a saint with guns. I thirsted for pants with stripes. I wanted them so bad that I tried to glue twine down the sides of my blue jeans.

Double feature at the Rathole. And a Three Stooges, plus six cartoons and serial. It's about 1949 in Hannibal, Missouri, and there's *no problem*. Everything is hunky-dory. Nothing is wrong. Nothing will ever go wrong.

I want to be up on that screen. Not on it. *In* it. I want to get up out of my seat and walk down that carpeted aisle where the little lightbulbs at the ends of each row illuminated a few inches of purple geometric patterning on the nap, and I want to pull myself up onto the stage below the screen, and I want to walk into the movie and live there forever. That movie screen is my Grecian urn, except that

I don't know anything about Grecian urns. I just want to penetrate the geography of the movie, to be a flicker forever.

The Rialto movie screen was my first perfect place. I never made it up there with the good guys, although in a way I have been trudging down that carpeted aisle all the years since. Nothing was wrong in Hannibal in those first sunlit years after we won the war. That at least was the illusion, the hypnotic conceit that the town conferred. Perhaps it was the surface placidity of the Mississippi—all that calm, southward-drifting weight of water along the town's eastern rim. People have spoken of the curious tranquility of southern river towns. That about said it for my Hannibal.

After the matinee is over and the house lights come on, I join the kidhorde leaning forward up the slanted aisle of the Rathole toward the popcorn-scented lobby, preparing to squint as we head into the white Saturday sunlight on Broadway. I'm probably with a few buddies—stout Duly, the town rich kid, and maybe Ward, smooth and ironic, who'd grow up to run a restaurant in San Francisco. We're on our way next door, to (I swear it) the Mary Ann Sweet Shop, with its rainbow jukebox and round marble-top tables and swirly wire-backed chairs. We will leapfrog onto adjacent red-topped stools at the counter and make ourselves dizzy twirling around on them. When bald-headed Mr. Haag, a little cross-eyed and a little scary behind his foul-odored Sunday-funnies cigar, comes to wipe the counter and take our orders, one of us will growl, Longbranch Saloon–style, "Shotta *red-eye*." Our code for cherry Coke.

As we sip, satisfying pictures will replay, already fading, in our movie minds like dreams in the morning: galloping posses firing pistols that give off a windblown burst of powder smoke; the bad guy's gun flying into the air, hero-shot right out of his hand—"Why, *you*—" the sidekick doing his tobacco-juice slapstick; Roy's obligatory campfire guitar song that always makes me feel a little cheesy and, mortifyingly, a little in love; the rescued buckskin-fringed good gal, whose name is always Ann Ranson or Lynn Hinson; the climactic scene where all the good guys, having made the West safe for democracy, gather around the corral for a hearty cleansing horselaugh.

We believed it all. How could we not? The movies were real. The river was real.

I learned this fact one Saturday when the cofeature was a Wild Bill

Elliott. Wild Bill was my hero because he sported a tight buckskin jersey that was laced, rather than buttoned, across his chest; a black bandanna and a black hat that made him look like a bad guy, a highway patrolman's demeanor that assured you he was anything but; and—most wonderfully—a pair of pearl-handled six-shooters that he wore backward. This required a lot of fancy twirling when he drew and then again when he put his irons away. (The sight of Wild Bill Elliott spinning his guns remains in my mind the single most memorable image in the movies.)

On this Saturday, Wild Bill miraculously was speaking directly off the screen, ex cathedra, to me. He was squatting on his haunches with a bunch of buckaroos around the campfire, eating a slice of chocolate pie—which in itself made it seem as if he and I were soul mates—when a hard-looking cuss, suspiciously unshaven, moseyed over and asked him in a none-too-friendly voice where he planned on being later that night.

I didn't like the sound of that—I smelled "rustler"—but Wild Bill played it nice and cool. He didn't even bother to rise off his haunches as he took his sweet time with his answer. When he finally spoke, he was looking at me.

"Where I always am at eight-thirty," he drawled in his trademark dry baritone. "Asleep in my bed."

Eight-thirty! No kidding? My God, that was *my* bedtime! How did Wild Bill know that? The flickering river up on the screen and my static little nowhere town were one. Everybody in the world, the good guys, anyway, went to bed at eight-thirty. A kind of religious calm stole upon me in that moment, a fleeting sense that the world was nothing but an extremely large room—the sky the roof—and that whatever was wrong wasn't wrong. Wild Bill and I both went to bed at eight-thirty. I wanted to walk up there and melt onto the screen and shake his hand.

That is how innocent I was in Hannibal in the late 1940s. The world was a white-flickering river in the darkness, swimming with good guys. A bad place for the bad. Everything in black and white. The United States of America had just won World War II, even if Sergeant Stryker (John Wayne) had got it at the end. It was an amiable war, at least that's how it felt on the posters and the comic books and the movies. A war fought by handsome soldiers wearing these keen wide belts, and by sailors with their sharp white caps jammed back on their heads. A lot of the older boys in town had sailor caps, which they wore jammed back on their heads. Eventually the war came to the Rialto in black and white. I took it home with me in my head and refought it in color, sprawled down on my fragrant living room carpet on St. Mary's Avenue, pushing around heavy brightly painted lead figurines—a soldier, a sailor, and a marine—making the invisible bad-guy Germans and Japs eat hot lead. While my dad sold Fuller brushes and mom cooked cabbage in the pressure cooker and the orange-glowing console radio played husky duets by Les Paul and Mary Ford.

American flags were rampant in the redbrick river town. A great billowing of flags, like patriotic laundry. In front of schools and on the front wall of each classroom, and the courthouse and the armory and the police station and the public library, on front porches, on decals pasted to storefront doors. Old Glory, front and center, forty-eight stars and thirteen stripes, the red, white, and blue, one nation under God. One naked individual, with liberty and justice for all.

This is how I thought it would always be.

Uniforms too. Flags and uniforms. The Cub Scouts and the Boy Scouts, good guys certified in our thrilling gear. Neckerchiefs. Belts with complicated metal buckles. The Scout sign. The Scout salute. The Scout insignia. All those Scout pledges. On my honor. Do my best. Do my duty to God and my country. Help other people at all times. Physically strong, mentally alert, and morally straight. No problem. That was for me. Me in Troop 100, the perfect troop number, wearing the perfect neckerchief colors, red and black. Always posing. Holding the ax with a firm but not tense grip.

That Mark Twain Bridge. The oldest, most permanent object I'd ever seen or would see. Older than my grandfather Jasper the baker. Older than Jasper's black Packard with the running board. Older than the movies. (In fact the bridge was only five years older than me; it was dedicated by President Franklin Roosevelt in the summer of 1936. In 2001 it was blown up and replaced by a newer bridge.)

It stood like some ancient but still-living organism out there in the Mississippi current, all arched and humpbacked with its several elephant legs planted in the water and its long anteater snout poking down into Illinois. A terrifying yet somehow friendly nonesuch, a guardian of some kind. Certainly not the kind of edifice you would ever imagine as a conduit of escape for a boy and a girl fleeing a murder scene with a shotgun.

Hannibal's aura of childhood sanctuary survived into the years of my boyhood. "What evil . . . *lurks* . . . in the hearts of men?" snarled the Shadow every Sunday night at the beginning of his Mutual Radio serial. The Shadow, a superhero crime fighter who in reality was the millionaire playboy Lamont Cranston, had learned the ability to cloud men's minds so they could not see him. I idolized the Shadow. But his famous question never bothered me. If evil lurked in any hearts in my town, it was news to me.

· · ·

IN OCTOBER 1988 that old question took possession of my thoughts. It clouded my mind until there was nothing to do but travel back to Hannibal. The two killings were nearly a year old by then, but the country was immersed in the horror of angry children with guns. Theories and analysis and accusation filled the national discourse. None of it made much sense to me. Or it all made sense, and the sense it made was self-canceling.

I thought it was time to pay a visit to the old world headquarters of childhood and see what had gone wrong.

· 4 ·

AT HUBBARD AND HAWKINS

The white Cadillac tooling along in front of me sported a rear bumper sticker that I was dying to read, so I tapped the accelerator, closed the gap a few car lengths. I was driving north on Route 61 in Missouri, en route from the St. Louis airport to Hannibal. Only a couple of hours back in my home state, I had rediscovered the value of reading the ambient signage for information: the flat midwestern highway system, a bloated incoherence of traffic lined with franchise development, afforded a virtual *USA Today* of endless logo, news, and declaration.

I had begun to skim the landscape's editorials an hour earlier, on Interstate 70, as I hurtled west through the thick St. Louis exurban gauntlet of shopping malls, gambling casinos, Sheratons, Shoneys, and Pizza Huts. I had perused a billboard urging voters to turn down a proposed state law that would legalize cockfighting, and another one exhorting the passage of a bill to authorize the carrying of concealed handguns. The marquee of a small Christian church had fleetingly assured me that "We Care!" (Care about what? I wondered. Cockfighting? A snub-nosed in the pocket of the Thinsulated jacket? The odds?)

Now, on 61, a tar-caulked two-lane highway in my youth but now two slick slabs of divided commuter twin lane for most of its sixty-mile span to Hannibal, the messages were a shade more vernacular and less frequent. "Eternity—Where Shall I Spend It?" agonized a hand-lettered roadside sign. Mark Twain had provided the only reasonable set of choices more than a century ago—"Heaven for climate, Hell for society"—but soon a more contemporary marquee replied moistly, "Christ: With Him There's Plenty of Hope to Go Around." (Plenty of fast food, too, the miracle of loaves and fishes updated: the Burger Kings and Wendy's and McDonald's and Hardees whizzed past, on land that had supported soybeans and dairy cattle a generation earlier.)

I was edging up close now to the creamy Cadillac ahead of me. The driver, its lone occupant, appeared from the rear to be close-cropped, pink, male, and fleshily midtwenties. I shifted my gaze to his bumper sticker. Beside the intersecting curved bars that I recognized as the Christian fish logo—the Golden Arches of fast faith—was the admonition: "Caution: Driver Subject to Frequent Praise Attacks."

I heeded the warning and dropped back, out of ecstasy's range.

Forty miles south of town, the old familiar terrain rekindled the disbelief I'd felt when I heard the news of the first killing, and then the second. A big midwestern sunset was underway. This wasn't murder country. The sun hovered over the flat old horizon and fired up the sides of barns and the silver girders of the franchise logos. The prairie around me was mostly cleared of trees, but then it had been since the end of the Civil War. Good honest farmland. (No meth in those sheds!) Some sprigs of sumac poked through the thin layers of rock along the highway, bright crimson in the light. An older language, one that I understood. The language of sumac told me that nothing had changed. The sumac said that things were safe here. The sumac lied.

I passed the exit for Vandalia. Dusk was settling in now. A cluster of arc lights off in a field to my left drew my eye. I could see silvery, low-slung buildings, the arc lights towering over them. A new high school, maybe. Football tonight.

I had wanted to get back to Hannibal as soon as friends there sent me news of the killings, but no time had seemed particularly right until now. Even this trip was in some ways a false alarm: Zach Wilson and Diane Myers languished in their separate jails; Robie Wilson's trial, having been scheduled and then postponed several times, had finally been set for this week. By the time I'd bought my nonrefundable airline ticket, it had been postponed again. Still, it seemed worthwhile to revisit the old town now, if for no other reason than just to look around, talk to some people, and try to start to understand.

During my own adolescence, I had lived in a house on Pleasant Street, not three blocks from where the door of Will Hill's Bronco slammed James Walker to the ground; I could picture the spot as vividly as if I'd witnessed the impact. I had stood, on chilly November twilights, out on the pavement in the gentle curve of Shepherd Place, where Hill gunned the Bronco on his crosstown flight, playing pitch-and-catch with Bobby Schweitzer, willing the baseball season to return like Indian summer. My father had driven an annual succession of Nashes once a month or so to Hunnewell to sell his Fuller brushes there, and he doubtless sold them on the Hannibal porches of the houses where Robie and Will and Zachary eventually lived. I had crossed the Mississippi River bridge into Illinois hundreds of times and even had a recurring dream of falling off its superstructure but never quite reaching the icy winter waters below.

People simply did not kill one another in the Hannibal that was imprinted on my memory.

This at least was the myth—mine, and the nation's as well. At century's end, we seemed to require such mythic places, places that were somehow insulated from . . . well, from America, or the America that America had become. We needed places that had remained an embodiment of the America that was, whatever and whenever that was.

Hannibal, "America's Home Town," drew more than 600,000 visitors a year, even though no interstates or large airports lay within fifty miles. "People come to Hannibal just to touch the way we live," a woman had told me during a visit there in the mid-eighties, and I always thought that was a good way of putting it, even though it got harder with each passing year to reach through the "attractions" to any sort of life truly worth touching.

Most of the tourists came in the summer, to view Tom Sawyer Days in July, with its frog-jumping contest and its fence-painting contest sanctioned by Congress and its unending supply of young boys and girls with stenciled freckles, dressed up in straw hats, frayed jeans, and hoop skirts. The visitors would peek inside the Boyhood Home, perhaps glance at the Hibbard statue, round up a few postcards, and then drive the two miles south of town to file through the souvenir shop into the Mark Twain Cave. Afterward they'd slide on over to a small garish riverside theme park to drop some change and let their kids have a few turns on the Too-Too Twain, topping off the day with some "maid-rite" burgers back in town at the Mark Twain Dinette—unless the kiddies insisted on Big Macs.

In December 1997—three weeks after Will Hill and Robie Wilson took their ride—*Time* magazine, unaware of the incident, featured Hannibal as one of ten small towns that were "going strong" and triggering a new exodus of American suburbanites to the paradise of life in the heartland.

But at the same time, other visitors were combing the heartland with more clinical motives in mind.

Only a few months before the two killings, America's Home Town had been visited by a team of social researchers from Atlanta who were interested in measuring Hannibal's civic health—and thus (among other things) its capacity to rear and educate its young— against a set of standards they had devised. The research group, which called itself Health 2000, referred to these standards as "social capital" and proposed that the amount of such "capital" a community possessed was (a) quantifiable and (b) a reliable indicator of its viability as a social organism. The four interrelated constructs of "social capital" were trust, cooperation, civic engagement, and reciprocity. Health 2000 had interviewed a wide spectrum of Hannibal leaders, in politics, business, and community work, and also a random sampling of residents by telephone, to form a data pool for its analysis.

The company's president, Marshall Kreuter, had adapted his working model from his experiences as a researcher for the Centers for Disease Control in Atlanta. "The concept of human health has shifted in the past fifty years," Kreuter had told me by telephone some months before I revisited the town. "Infectious diseases have largely been eradicated in our time. They have been replaced as priorities for public health by 'chronic' diseases, such as teen pregnancies, addictions, and violence."

Kreuter went on: "Our country has a problem with violence that a decade ago was not being seen as a public-health problem. But the rationale is compelling now. It shows up so dramatically in our hospitals. And so we have seen physical-injury prevention and control come into the scope of public health. It's sort of analogous to the function of finding a causal agent for an illness and developing a vaccine."

Kreuter had not fully processed his data when we spoke. But his early impressions of the "intervention" were not optimistic.

"You get a strong sense of 'us guys and those guys,' " he said. There are strong differences among people neighborhood to neighborhood. There are a lot of physical dividing lines, including a highway that cuts right through the middle of the town.

"And there are differences of opinion between the people in the neighborhoods and the decision makers. There's a level of governmental chaos that is hard to explain."

I had already grown aware of some of the dread and suspicion down at the neighborhood level. Well before the two episodes of violence that brought me back to Hannibal, old schoolmates and other friends had been writing and phoning me with ominous hints of a new kind of dread taking shape in the Home Town, half glimpsed on the night streets, a blur of defiance and then gone, pairs of eyes following you: kids in chains and spiked hair and pierced noses, a far cry from Tom 'n' Becky; kids who gave off vibes that made your short hairs go rigid. Gangs were operating in the town, people swore, druggy franchises of the West Coast Crips and Bloods that coalesced in the still-distinct black neighborhoods, but newer, more regionally defined ones as well: white racist gangs with names like the Cowboys and the Rednecks; and at least one murky, homegrown outfit called the Grace Street Gang. (Missouri, I later learned, was the seventh leading state in the nation in the number of youth gangs reported, with 740. California led the way with 4,927; Texas followed with 3,276; then Illinois with 1,363; Colorado with 1,304; Arizona with 974; and Florida with 793.)

Packs of teens stalked the downtown business district on weekend nights, my friends said. They drank beer and smoked weed, they were high on meth, into drag racing, and taunted the passing traffic. The editor of the town's daily paper, the *Courier-Post*, wrote to tell me about an elderly man who had apologized his way into her office one recent morning to report that a group of teenagers had repeatedly tried to run his delivery truck off the road. I'd heard stories about friends' children being insulted, threatened, roughed up.

And the area's teens were clashing with law enforcement at about the same escalating rate as teens in the rest of the country. The low-slung arc-lighted buildings I'd passed in the dusk at Vandalia, I later learned, were not a new high school but a new prison.

• • •

A GREAT POOLED wetness of logoed yellows and oranges and reds and blues around the descending curve, a stalled convoy of white Wal-Mart semitrailers, their brake lights burning for the red to turn to green: Hannibal, or the franchise encrustation at Hannibal's edge, the hot, stale energy of colonizing commerce. I inched through the glut, turned right at the light, and slipped free into the older town, its loaves of hills and sturdy bungalows. I stashed my suitcases at my lodgings and got back into the car. As it happened, my route took me a short distance down a leafy little avenue and then to Pleasant Street. I turned left, crested the hill, and almost immediately passed the point of impact. I'd bicycled past there a thousand times. I continued on down to the bottom of Pleasant and turned right onto 61, as Robie Wilson said Will Hill had done. Unlike Hill, I didn't immediately turn again; I kept on going. I had something to do.

I was headed several blocks north to Hannibal High School, to watch my first Pirate football game there in forty years. Homecoming in America's Home Town. The redoubtable Mexico (Missouri) Bulldogs were going up against the Black and Red.

The high school's main building had stood facing west across a graceful lawn since 1934, a classic old learning cathedral of red-brick, with gothic spires towering above its main entrance. HHS had hardly changed since my graduation in 1959, but the vicinity had changed. Where once the high school had formed part of Hannibal's grassy western perimeter—looking across to woods and farmland on the far side of the street—it now served as a kind of reflecting facade for another battery of franchise wattage. A McDonald's, a Long John Silver's, a Taco Bell, and a frozen yogurt outlet poured out their yellows and oranges in a long bright wash. Beyond them, the mother colony sprawled, its macadam spreading northward toward Hannibal–La Grange College on what had once been the pastures of a local farm family—one of the boys had been a star fullback for the Pirates when I went to school—and now was the inspirationally named Huck Finn Shopping Plaza, with its Wal-Mart, Penney, Pizza Hut, Blockbuster, and grocery emporium. A great pustule of concentrated corporate commerce far from the old business center of town. It was as though Hannibal had leapfrogged over the high school in a mad dash west that had begun at the riverfront. There was some truth in that, as I would find.

The scene at the football field restored some sense of the town eternal. The school parking lot was crammed to spillover. The October night air lay balmy on the skin, the pep band drums tatted out school spirit and the PA system crackled with pregame bulletins. Well-upholstered boosters in black-and-red regalia jammed the walkway from the ticket booth to the stands, hawking programs and caps and pom-poms. Volunteers in mobile concession vans strung with yellow lights ladled out Cokes and forked up hot dogs. Doc Porter Field was a midway of small-town cohesion and pizzazz.

Perched on a high tier in the crowded concrete bleachers, watching as the quarterbacks fired warm-up passes to echelons of acrobatic receivers, the coaches on the sidelines coiled their headset phone cables, the gleaming cheerleaders chewed their gum and counted the house and absently shook their booties to the rattle of the snare drums, it was easy to dismiss the months of dire news and rumors from Hannibal. Here was excitement, optimism, community, the feeling that life was going on. No killers here.

I looked at the munching families clustered around me, mostly white but sprinkled with Asians and African Americans; the football moms wearing their kids' jersey numbers, the dads natty in their pressed jeans and shades beneath their squared-away ball caps. I followed the blurs of children doing fast giant steps up and down the concrete steps, trailing popcorn. The arc lights bathed all our faces, making our eyes glitter. A massive marching band took the field in geometrical rows, led by a drum major in white, his plumed hat nearly touching his posterior, and issued forth a National Anthem that left no doubt what country we were in. At its conclusion, from behind the flagpole on a high bank above the east end zone, an eruption of red-glaring rockets issued skyward. We certainly hadn't had this kind of firepower during the Eisenhower administration. When I was spotted by an old fellow Boy Scout, who greeted me after four decades with, "Are you retired?" I reached the high-water mark of my conviction that Hannibal was beyond the taint of evil.

At halftime, the home eleven's prospects bolstered by a dazzling end zone touchdown grab, I wandered down to the running track that encircled the football field, where kids were milling, and looked around for somebody who might be willing to talk about Robie Wilson and Will Hill.

I got a few blank looks and snorts of "what sumbitch wants to know" derision, as I'd expected, but at length a lanky boy silently pointed me toward a lively cluster of kids, two or three each of boys and girls, who had the elusive but timeless aura of "headed for college" about them. Their good nature and thoughtfulness were equal to the aura.

"No, not like that," one of the boys quickly answered when I asked whether he would have expected Robie Wilson to get into this kind of trouble. "His older brothers are kind of known for getting in a lot of fights and stuff. But it shocked me when I found out. Of the four brothers, Robie was pretty much the one who stayed out of trouble the most."

Another boy agreed. "His older brothers are really big. Really big guys, muscular builds. But when you looked at Robie, you just saw this average kid. Good-looking. Dressed clean-cut."

What kind of circles did Robie run in? I asked.

"Pretty rough," a kid in the cluster ventured. "People around town know the name Wilson. Lot of his friends got in fights and stuff. But people don't mess with Robie because they know Chris and Eddie would back 'em off if anything happened."

I asked the group at large what was it like when they heard the news of the killing of James Walker. "Shocked," several of them said at once, and then the first boy continued: "I was shocked. Everybody at school the next morning was shocked. Nobody could believe it. And they hadn't got caught yet, the first day, either. Kids were just standing around talkin' about it, but they didn't want to say too much, 'cause they hadn't got caught. It was a kind of outrage, really."

But no one had named Robie or Will by then, I prodded. The group exchanged quiet glances. "I heard the day after they did it what had happened, and it was them," a boy finally said. "And it was three or four days until the police caught 'em."

"Will talked about it," put in one of the girls. "He was kinda braggin' a little bit. And that might have been what got him in trouble."

I asked what kind of a guy Will Hill was.

"I think Will is a nice person," the girl said. "He was in my sculpture class. He's really nice. I never really knew him much, I'd just heard about him. We made mobiles to hang from the ceiling. I made a helicopter that has a little hinge that makes the propeller spin. He made a clown that had a big nose and eyes and a smile."

She thought for a moment. "He's a big talker. Not real deep. He doesn't talk about deep stuff, he just talks a lot. In sculpture class he kinda liked to tease people. But he really did want to know things. We had a foreign exchange student from Germany, and he was always asking her a lot of questions, like about where she was from. Do you like America? In Germany, how did you live? And he really wanted to know. He wasn't just hitting on her. He really wanted to know."

The kids in the group recalled how Will had returned to school the day after the accident, but Robie hadn't—he was attending class in a separate building, a class for kids with discipline issues.

"Will had some tough times," one of them said. "The problem was that Will and Robie were best friends, and then Will decided he was going to plea-bargain and testify against Robie. And so all of Robie's friends got really mad at him because Will had just moved back to the area like last year. Robie's friends accepted him. But since they were Robie's friends first, they got really mad at Will."

"But then came baseball season," said another, and everyone gave off knowing smiles.

I changed the subject. I wanted to know what habits or traits, if any, had separated Robie and Will from any other Hannibal teenagers before the collision with Walker. What kind of stuff would they do, say, on a typical weekend? I asked. Shrugs, all around.

"Just stuff that everybody would do," said one. "If somebody was havin' people over, they would go there. Drive around some." Added one of the girls: "There's not a whole lot to do, really, in a town as small as this. Pretty much sit around Robie's house."

So were Robie and Will different? Several heads shook.

A boy spoke. "I don't think they're a whole lot different. I don't think they meant to do it at all. It all just got way out of proportion, just the impulsive—I mean, there's a lot of impulsive people out there. And other than that, they've never done anything really wrong. They try to act tough, put on the impression of don't mess with them. But there's a lot of people out there that are like that. They just got carried away one day."

The gala halftime show had begun just a few yards from where we stood, a vast thundering surge of precision marchers flashing their tubas, trombones, and bass drums, American flags advancing at a hard-nosed tilt, all under the baton of the majestic drum major bestriding a scaffold tower. In that moment the timeless town cast its spell on me. I wondered whether these teenagers felt it too.

Life in Hannibal, I asked them—wasn't it supposed to be special for kids? America's Home Town, and all that? I could almost hear the answer before one of the girls gave it. If anything, it was phrased a little more kindly than I'd expected.

"I like Hannibal," she said, choosing her words carefully with a scrunched-up kind of expression. "But you know, when people come here, they're like, oh, wow! 'cause it's got all this tourism stuff. But once you live here for what, fifteen years of your life, it's just like, it's not—cool. You just get tired of the same old things. Same old things to do, same old places to go."

I thanked the kids and edged back through the milling crowd to the bleachers. I hung around for a few minutes of the third quarter. And then I left.

It had hit me that here was a chance to prowl the nighttime town while the stadium was full and the streets nearly empty. In my rented car, with my elbow propped on the open window jamb, just like the old days, and the radio tuned to an oldies station, I grabbed it.

Hannibal at night looked as it had looked nearly half a century ago, or at least great portions of its interior did. Someone had figured out how to spin off the lucrative Christmas-decoration market, and several neighborhood front porches glowed with illuminated Halloween regalia—shimmering creamy ghosts and strings of small orange pumpkins. I knew these plump old bungalows. I had mowed these lawns and thrown newspapers onto these porches. I drove and felt the cool October air on my arm and tapped my fingers on the outside of the door in time to the oldies. In the dark, and suffused with the football stadium's homecoming buoyancy, it was still possible to cling to the myth of the town eternal, the safe place of other Americans' dreams.

Before turning in, there was one place in Hannibal I had to visit. It wasn't on any tourist maps, and none of my relatives had ever lived near there. It was nothing special, just an intersection, an intersection in a neighborhood of tidy white bungalows and overgrown trees whose roots had long since lifted up some of the concrete slabs of the sidewalk. But if I'd had to pick one place in Hannibal that was the distillation of every habitat, every experience, and every dream that formed my happy memories of the town, it would have to be the intersection of Hubbard and Hawkins streets, a block north of Mark Twain School. My Patrol Boy corner.

Our official collective name was the Schoolboy Patrol, but everyone called us Patrol Boys. We formed an elite corps of kid guardians; membership was restricted to boys in the sixth and final grade at Mark Twain. Our duty was to stand on an assigned neighborhood street corner that children crossed on their way to and from school. When schoolchildren approached the corner and a car was coming—a Packard, a Studebaker, a dreaded Whippet—our job was to hold out our hands, scarecrow-style, until the car had passed and it was safe for the children to cross.

Each Patrol Boy was identified by a special three-pointed badge pinned to his shirt and by a heavy white canvas belt strapped around the waist and supported by a diagonal sling that looped over the shoulder. The "BadgeandBelt," as they were known in Patrol Boy lore. The badge was great—I loved wearing the badge—but it was the white belt that moved me to gooseflesh: the sacred white belt and, in particular, that diagonal sling. Frozen lightning across the chest. Purity, authority, responsibility. I endured five years, five slow grades up the ladder, to reach the moment when I could drape that sling over my shoulder. Five years of being just another measly little kid who needed to be protected by pretenders to my regalia.

On the first day of school in September 1952, a couple of weeks before Richard Nixon gave his "Checkers" speech to save his candidacy on the ticket with Dwight Eisenhower, I stood in assembly, in a row of my fellow male sixth graders, our right hands raised, while the school principal administered the oath to honor the BadgeandBelt. I remember doing funny things with my mouth to keep a poker face. I couldn't risk a grin. This was too serious. I was prepared not just to honor the BadgeandBelt. I was prepared to die for it.

I had become a part of a continuum that ended at Wild Bill Elliott or even Roy Rogers up on the movie screen at the Rialto. Or John Wayne in *She Wore a Yellow Ribbon* in Technicolor at the classier Tom Sawyer. Now I was a part of the world whose values had been imparted to me from the movies, radio, comic books, church, Boy Scouts, the Hannibal Pilots minor-league baseball team, the living presences of all the Kiwanis dads and apple pie moms in my holy town. I was a good guy.

Scouts and Patrol Boys had responsibility for people's safety, for their lives, though I'm not sure that any of us ever saved a kid from being crushed under a car's wheels. The point was that we believed we did. Maybe that was the whole point of Patrol Boys—not safety so much as belief.

I made a right turn off darkened, silent St. Mary's and negotiated my car up the narrow incline of Hubbard Street, where parked cars created a zigzag single-lane maze. It was almost midnight, but when I reached the intersection with Hawkins, I could see things as clearly as on a bright morning forty-six years before.

My domain was preserved exactly as I had left it. The three little white bungalows that separated my corner from Mark Twain School were still perched atop their rounded banks, looking down upon the facing three across the street. The two opposing houses nearest my station each sheltered a girl whom I loved, though at different stages of my boyhood.

And the sycamore was still there—the sycamore that towered over me when I reported for duty each morning, fifteen minutes before school began, my belly still hot with my mother's oatmeal. So was the Japanese maple that grew on the corner diagonally across the street, in front of Edie's house, where I stood after classes let out. The house that Jean moved into had a Japanese maple as well, so there was a lot of leaf cover in the vicinity.

I never wanted that sixth-grade year to end. But it started ending, it seemed to me, as soon as I reported for duty. Late summer deepened quickly into autumn and the sycamore and maple leaves above me flared up. Then, over many languorous Missouri weeks of Indian summer, they fell into deep drifting piles on the sidewalks and pavement. Winter was coming, and then spring and a new, unimaginable life for me, and the locus of my Patrol Boy ecstasies shifted a little. I still loved the BadgeandBelt, and I loved saving kids from traffic, but gradually I came to love that corner almost as ardently. Even as it started to recede, it became my corner. And then it became not so much a neighborhood street corner as a kind of room, my room, with the white houses as its walls and the interlocking tree branches its ceiling. I didn't exactly have to deal with a steady stream of schoolkids who needed my protection, and not too many cars to protect them from either, for that matter, and so I spent a lot of my on-duty daydreaming. I would fantasize saving kids, diving and rolling to scoop up one of them in my arms just out of the path of some crazed dentist late for work. For my heroism I would be awarded a medal in a special assembly, with Roy Rogers himself there in person. It was Roy Rogers's adopted kid I'd saved. Roy and Dale happened to be in town for some reason I never bothered to work out. Roy was so grateful that he offered me a special movie contract. I'd get to make movies with Roy in Hollywood. I was his kid sidekick, right up there with Gabby Hayes. But I'd get to keep on living in Hannibal. I'd travel back and forth on a high-speed train, a Zephyr, specially equipped with a regulation-size movie screen and a limitless stock of jujubes. . . .

But then my kid brother Jimmy would come sloshing along the sidewalk through the fallen leaves, on his way to school, and it would all fade. Jimmy, inevitable in his real-world horn-rims and starchy short-sleeved shirt. He would walk right up to where I was standing on the corner in my BadgeandBelt and shoot me a look as if he were waiting for me to save his life or something, and the imaginary world would evaporate in the glint of his glasses. Roy's kid, the special train, all the chambers of the room I'd built. All of it would wash back into a street corner for another day.

The child psychologist Robert Coles has observed that it is exactly in moments of solitude—in moments that might easily be mistaken by adults for boredom—that the child forms its personality, through a kind of radiant daydreaming. Richard Hawley, the headmaster and author of *Boys Will Be Men,* insists that, surface evidence and received opinion to the contrary, "Every boy . . . longs to be a knight, a questing, adventuring, fully realized man."

To Hawley, the boy eternal is Percival, the quester after the Grail. Percival emerges into consciousness "a high-spirited little fool," naive, a mama's boy whose father and older brothers have been slain in chivalric warfare. The mother, Heart's Sorrow, withdraws with Percival into a forest, hoping to protect him from the same fate. But the boy's questing future is annealed when he encounters a group of knights on the road. "The child is so immediately taken with the sheen and beauty of their presence," Hawley writes, "he mistakes them for angels." He learns everything he can about their origins and their sacred mission; then, armed only with his small javelin, he sets forth blindly onto the journey that will lead him, after many trials and mentoring by virtuous men, into knighthood in King Arthur's court, a chivalric encounter with Blanche Bleur, entry into the enchanted realm of the Fisher King, and the search for the Grail and for a transcendence beyond merely human knowledge.

I suspect that I was not the only Patrol Boy idly improvising his Percival myth while woolgathering on a street corner. I suspect that Coles and Hawley have it exactly right: Children form their dreams in a kind of holy protected solitude, and the dreams of boys are chivalric.

What happened, then, to the dreams of Robie Wilson and Zachary Wilson? And of Will Hill and Diane Myers? What happened to the dreams of a generation of children, several generations, to the dream of childhood itself?

I drove away from the darkness of my old Patrol Boy corner and toward the house where I was lodged. A few hours of my own fitful dreams of Hannibal, and the next day I would begin a quest, in my middle-aged foolishness, to transcend knowledge. To find out where Tom and Huck had gone.

5

THE WIDOW

Jim and I were never ones to set around," Virginia Walker was telling me. "We had so much fun. We loved country music. I used to have a fan club, the Helen Cornelius. She's a Hannibal girl. Her first husband and Jim went to school together; they were buddies. That fan club kept us busy for ten years. I mean, we traveled all over. We did wonderful, wonderful things."

We sat in her small living room on State Street. The room was simple and tidy. Little ceramic figurines decorated the walls. The drapes were pulled against the morning sunlight, reinforcing an aura of faded things. Since her husband's death, Virginia had been living on his life-insurance policies and Social Security. She wasn't destitute, but she wasn't on top of the world, either.

State Street was not quite the "great street" that its name implied; it was in fact a two-block stretch off Pleasant, bordering an incongruous little meadow where cattle fed—a vestige of farm in the middle of town. A couple of blocks to the west, nearly in the epicenter of Hannibal, gently rising Pleasant reached its peak elevation, crossing an old ridge line that formed the spine of Country Club Drive. The intersection was guarded by an ancient, rusting water tower. Less than half a mile west of there was the spot where James Walker had been struck down.

"Jim and I both took an instant liking to her," Virginia was saying about Helen Cornelius. A pale willowy woman in her early sixties, she kept her white hair in a neat perm. Her eyes were quarter-moons behind old-fashioned glasses whose frames slanted upward from the bridge of her nose, and her voice seemed filtered through decades of lace-curtain Sunday afternoons, a fried-chicken-and-lemonade voice that took me back. She was a recent denizen, and just now a kind of prisoner, of a Hannibal that no longer existed.

"Jim was their best man at their wedding," Virginia went on. "She just asked me one time if I'd like to take her fan club over. She wasn't too pleased with how it was being handled." Virginia smiled and her voice went dreamy. "I thought, yeah, that would be a good challenge. And I really enjoyed it. There was a lot of mail, there was a newsletter that had to be issued every other month. Membership kits to be mailed out. It was a lot of work. Course I was into it."

I had come reluctantly to Virginia Walker's house. I knew this would be the hardest of a number of hard conversations I wanted to have. When Jim was killed, the Walkers had been married forty years and had lived for thirty-eight of them in the tiny green house where we now sat—a house so small that it seemed almost hidden behind the thick blue spruce that grew in the postage-stamp front yard. "We planted that tree; it was a little $2.98 shrub from Kroegers when we bought it, and that's what it's become," she'd said as we talked on the doorstep.

The blue spruce, in a way, had symbolized Virginia's and Jim's residency in the town that no longer was: a thing growing from the soil that needed tending and expressed loving generational memories. There were thousands of people like the Walkers still in Hannibal—hundreds of thousands, millions, in towns and suburbs and cities like that around the country: people of a certain age who had not seen it coming; people who lacked the wherewithal, the right magazine subscriptions, the money, the curiosity perhaps, the elasticity of youth, the simple enabling catharsis of a bad encounter, to understand that the world they thought they inhabited was a phantom one. It had given way to a world scarcely detectable by their accustomed perceptions until one day it lurched suddenly into the foreground and crushed them.

"We went through school together," Virginia Walker was telling me, in answer to my question of how she and Jim had met. "He lived out on Vermont Street"—she pronounced it *Vermont*—"was raised up there, and went to Eugene Field School. He was just a year ahead of me. We probably knew one another since he was in eighth grade."

I asked Virginia what Jim had been like. "*Wail . . .*" she began, her voice far away, and paused to think about it. "He was fun-loving," she said finally. "He went to work at an early age. Filling station on Market Street. Probably as soon as he could. Possibly"—she gave a chuckle—"*before* he could. But he loved working around cars. His father was a railroad man."

The phantom world that most distorted the Walkers' perceptions of life was the lost world of "the country." Not "country" as in United States of America so much as "country" as in country roads, or country people, or country music, as expressed by the likes of Helen Cornelius. Like many town people of her generation, Virginia had been brought up on a farm north of Hannibal—"I was raised in the country," was her way of putting it. "My folks had horses, pigs, cows." Jim's family had made the move to Hannibal a couple of generations earlier. Their marriage had been a typical fusion of town-and-country Missouri: an interrelated land-based society, deep-layered in its agricultural traditions and intensely local in its rituals and values and etiquette, a rural society whose influence extended well into the state's small towns and, for most of the century, its big ones as well. Kansas City, after all, had long been an overgrown cowtown, a marketing center for cattle driven up from Texas along the Chisholm Trail. St. Louis, a manufacturing and river city, produced most of the goods that the state's German and French settlers took with them out to the prairies.

Farming had created and re-created generations of this Missouri folk culture. A broad-beamed squarish midwestern state—vaster in area than all of New England and the eighteenth largest of the lower forty-eight—it had, virtually since it achieved statehood in 1821, ranked second among all states, behind Texas, in the number of farms. (This despite a population a third that of the Lone Star State, or five million in the late 1990s.) Missouri's peak years as a family-farm state were the 1910s and 20s. Fifty million pounds of butter was a routine annual production back then; the state ranked fifth nationally in corn yield. As for poultry, the hen, known as "the mortgage-lifter of the Ozarks," generated more eggs than any other state but five.

Mark Twain, farm born and town bred, reflected late in life on his powerful associations with sacred place. "I can call back the solemn twilight and mystery of the deep woods," he wrote in Vienna near the beginning of his autobiography, in a reminiscence about his uncle's farm that seemed a meditation on the formation of his soul. "The earthy smells, the faint odors of the wild flowers, the sheen of the rain-washed foliage, the rattling clatter of drops when the wind shook the trees, the far-off hammering of woodpeckers in the remote forest. . . . I can call back the prairie, and its loneliness and peace, and a vast hawk hanging motionless in the sky. . . . I can call it all back and make it as real as it ever was, and as blessed."

Generations of children, in Missouri and elsewhere, would call back similar memories of sacred place and draw on them to reinforce their identities and sense of connection to a meaningful world. Paradoxically enough, the psychic value of place for children depended on many of the same social conditions that obtained in the eighteenth century, before industrialization forced "childhood" into view as a distinct and endangered phase of life.

Place presupposed a localized society in which nearly everyone in a region at least vaguely knew everyone else, or had relatives who did. It presupposed an economy of useful work that conjoined the efforts of adults and the young and gave structure and intimate purpose to young lives. ("I drove a tractor as soon as my feet were long enough to touch the pedal," an academic scholar at the University of Missouri told me. "That was about the age of ten.") Place leavened the harshness and danger of work with a rich inventory of rites of passage, ceremonies, celebrations, and myth. And place assured that violence was nearly always personal, rarely random; a man could see his enemy coming in time to negotiate, prepare for a fight, or run.

As recently as 1935, Missouri boasted 278,000 farms and a pervading down-home flavor of conservative politics, Bible-believing Protestant worship, hard work, and Main Street democracy. (Black Missourians would have good cause to dispute this last; those same pockets of yeoman virtues remained laced with racism well beyond the era of "desegregation.") The state would soon produce a president, Harry S Truman, with a sodbuster twang in his voice and commonsense roots in the farm-town ethos. Fifteen years later, with the postwar suburban surge in full force, the falloff in farms (20,000) was hardly noticeable. And yet something had begun to change. A momentum had formed. Illusion was already encroaching on reality.

Jim Walker enlisted in the army in 1953, and he and Virginia were married four years later, after he got out. Jim found a job as a mechanic at the D. B. Gray Company of Hull, Illinois, a few minutes on the far side of the Mark Twain Bridge. In 1960 he took a job closer to home, at what was then Mills Auto Parts (later renamed Car Quest). He worked there until he was killed. The couple had one son, Michael, who grew up to be a telephone company worker in St. Louis and did not marry.

These were still times when the continuum between farm and town still felt nearly seamless. Local radio stations wrapped John Philip Sousa march music around their noonday livestock reports and broadcast the homilies of circuit-riding preachers on weekday mornings ("Looking Through the Window of Life," with "The Old Ridge-Runner," the Reverend Johnny Golden, was a staple of my childhood). Gene Autry in the Saturday matinees was nothing if not a farmer-king to us kids in his rolled-up blue jeans and his earnest nasal inflections, defending the land from men in pencil mustaches and tweed coats. Everybody I knew listened to the Grand Ole Opry and ate "dinner" at noon and "said their howdys" to relatives at family picnics. Farmboys made up a good third of our high school population in the late 50s, rawboned, serious-faced kids in complicated pompadours combed back to tapered DAs, or ducks' asses. They sported zippered denim jackets that bore exotic sewn insignia: 4-H or the Future Farmers of America. We town kids might have whispered about them as "aggies" or even "shitkickers" (high school cliques were hardly an invention of the late century), but we felt an awe at their unknowable skills, their loamy brotherhood, their sheer aura of *capability*.

In late autumn of every year, the farm literally invaded Missouri towns in the form of the Fall Festival. In Hannibal, six blocks of Broadway, sloping down to the riverfront, were cordoned off and turned into a midway of big-top tents held in place with sandbagged ropes. There were Ferris wheels and cotton-candy stands, all peripheral to the bins of homegrown produce, homemade pies, jams, and prizewinning cattle, pigs, and mules.

By the early 1950s, the yellow lightbulb strings of the Fall Festival were diverting attention from a fissure that had opened up between appearances and reality. The folks strolling the Main Street midway in their bib overalls and straw Stetsons were looking ever more distinct from their necktied and high-heeled town neighbors. A massive postwar farm exodus had begun. Small-scale rural Missouri withered over the next two decades. By 1974, less than half the farms of the 1930s—116,000—remained. Equally significant, the scale and concept of the "family farm"—the defining social unit of Missouri culture since pre–Civil War days—had begun a historic shift. The surviving operations of the mid-seventies were bigger, wealthier, and more professionally run: the average size of a Missouri farm expanded from 169 acres in the early fifties to 258 in 1974.

The Missouri farm exodus was hardly unique in America. The great national suburban push had begun in the early postwar years, as wealthy speculators paid top dollar for land no longer bringing wartime crop and livestock prices. Soon came new roads and highways to access the row houses built on good topsoil. President Eisenhower's historic interstate highway program cut directly across Missouri's middle with I-70, the principal east-west link. Franchise development followed the roads and highways: Stuckeys, Shell, the Golden Arches. Shopping malls followed the franchises; in the vast exurban circles the malls bled together. Each new spillage of macadam diminished the farm acreage a little more, pushing the old town culture a little farther back toward the margins. Hotels and corporate office buildings followed the malls.

In the 1980s, what was left of Missouri's founding farm-based society came apart. The upheavals sent shock waves rippling through the state's towns and cities.

The now legendary "farm crisis" of the early Reagan years hardly spared Missouri as it tore through the cattle and grain economies of the Midwest. Farmers, advised by federal and academic economists to invest in equipment and plant "row-to-row," found themselves overleveraged as the newly opened "global economy" revealed a world awash in debt. Bankruptcies vitiated the wheat and corn and soybean homesteads on the state's northern flatlands and cut into the poultry and hog and cattle farms southwest of the Ozark Mountains, where the terrain began to resemble that of the Great Plains. Farms went under. Traditional farm-centered villages (such as Hunnewell) dried up or became what one rural sociologist described to me as "rural ghettos"—clusters of decayed housing stock that attracted welfare mothers and other low-income denizens.

By 1997, the number of farms in Missouri had shrunk to 100,000. But many experts believed that number to be highly inflated, an artificial construct of political bureaucracy. "Our census definition of a farm is a place that sells a thousand dollars' worth of agricultural output, *or has the potential to sell a thousand dollars' worth*," said Daryl Hobbs, a professor of rural sociology at the University of Missouri. "But only ten percent of those 'farms' are producing eighty percent of the total output. I'd say that in realistic terms, the number of real working family farms in Missouri is closer to ten thousand."

Heads of households—capable young men who had inherited the land from their fathers and assumed a life in which stress and unending labor were normative—slid into depressive anger. Hard drinking, family abuse, fights, and even suicides increased. Many rural families simply left the state: At decade's end more than sixty-five thousand people had left, many of them from the richest agricultural areas.

Replacing this vitiated family-farm culture was agribusiness. As small farms failed, large corporations took possession of the land, corporations such as Cargill, Koch Industries, ConAgra, and Farmland Industries. The transition left deep imprints. In 1996, the *St. Louis Post-Dispatch* warned editorially that "Mega-Farms Are Polluting Our Land," in part by constructing massive waste lagoons for hog manure, some of which spilled into streams, causing large-scale fish kills. A typical "big-pig" farm in the state, owned by a corporation such as Premium Standard Farms, would hold between 2,500 and 17,500 hogs.

The environment was not the only casualty of the megafarms. The economic and social integuments of heartland society were weakened as well. As William D. Heffernan, professor of rural sociology at the University of Missouri has pointed out, agribusiness mergers have excluded many diverse local businesses from participation in the farm-to-market economic chain. Thus, an entire traditional network of rural and town entrepreneurs found itself ostracized from the sustaining work it had developed over several generations.

Meanwhile, a similar usurping economic force was expanding through the heartland, this one attacking the cohesion of small- and medium-sized towns. This force exploited the economics of scale and the perennial human attraction to "a bargain" to drain many towns of their fundamental reason for being towns.

Wal-Mart discount stores began to appear in 1969. The nation's first Wal-Mart Super Center opened in rural Washington, Missouri, in 1988. A decade later there would be thirty such centers in the state. The total number of Wal-Mart outlets reached 109, one for every ten towns in Missouri.

The Wal-Mart phenomenon was hardly incidental to the reengineering of heartland society, in Missouri and throughout America. The discount chain had been conceived by Sam Walton of Bentonville, Arkansas, specifically as a thrust into rural communities that were underserved by retailers. Hard times made the chain's massed inventories and low pricing even more attractive. One consequence of Wal-Mart's success, perhaps unintended at first, was the withering of the small-town mercantile class: the latticework of family-owned dry-goods and hardware stores, pharmacies, booksellers, furniture dealers, and "notions" shops. Through two centuries, enterprising local merchants had provided cohesion and vitality on American Main Streets. They had generated long-standing jobs for local people and career apprenticeships for adolescent boys and girls. They had been reliable donors to community charities and volunteer drives. They had sponsored athletic teams and parade floats and decorated their store windows for seasonal holidays. They had supported a compacted, thriving downtown universe of office buildings, banks, libraries, restaurants, coffee shops, movie houses, barbershops, news vendors: a hive of human commerce and companionship. They shaped and animated the town counterpart of rural "place."

With the supplanting of local merchants by corporate retail colonies at century's end, place had lost most of its morally regenerative force in heartland American life. The distinctive textures and the nuances of country and town life had stopped growing more separate. In fact they had largely reconverged: subsumed into a larger, encroaching culture dedicated to the leveling of distinctions and the allegiances and exaltations that such distinctions fed. "Place" had been supplanted by "venue."

Increasingly, venue was manufactured to imitate and exploit the nostalgic value of authentic place. The 1990s saw a mushrooming of rustic theme-park and "attraction" centers around America, where icons from the receding past re-created their wholesome songs and attitudes like glittering aboriginal specimens on a reservation. Not three hundred miles from Virginia Walker's house sprawled Branson, Missouri, to which six million visitors a year, most of them senior citizens arriving in tour buses, deployed to patronize the thirty-six "country" theaters in the town, featuring faded celebrities like Tony Orlando, Bobby Vinton, the Lennon Brothers, and the Lennon Daughters.

One indicator of vanishing place, paradoxically, was the *increase* of rural residents in Missouri in the 1990s. Between 1990 and 1996, the "open country" population increased by 163,626, a growth rate of 9.3 percent. The paradox lay in the fact that most of these new "country people" were not moving to farms or small towns. Rather, they tended to be urban and suburban refugees intent on building or buying suburban-style houses on isolated tracts that once had been farmland. Now the acreage simply provided physical and psychic distance from other people. This new population, then, was neither exactly rural nor exactly urban. It was something else—a kind of anticommunity that owed its allegiance not to neighbors and local places but to the abstractions of income earning (which often involved lengthy commutes), recreation, and the standardized phantom images of television, the movies, and the Internet.

The rural young and the town young melted into this great subsuming. Connected neither to country nor town by usefulness, extended family ties, ritual, or adult mentoring, they struggled to figure out where they fit in—or who, in fact, they were. With ever greater frequency their mothers had left the household to join the commuter workforce. ("It became not a matter of too few jobs," said an observer of rural life, "but of too many. Too many jobs, and not enough income.") Often, the household simply lacked a mother or father— nearly 20 percent of the state's 1.4 million children (a quarter of the population) lived in single-parent families; one in ten was born to a single teen mother. (Overall, the time that American children spend with parents dropped by a third since the 1960s.) Twenty-one percent lived in families whose income was below the poverty line.

The indices of disconnection grew ever more dire. By the late

1990s, the high school dropout rate had reached 27 percent—"unconscionably high," in the words of Daryl Hobbs. In 1995, a survey showed that one in four teenagers had carried a weapon in the past thirty days; one in eight, a gun. More than half had used alcohol; 22 percent had smoked marijuana. One in five had made suicide plans; one in ten had made an attempt.

More disturbingly still, behavioral scientists in the late nineties were picking up on a "quantifiable" increase in the number of young people experiencing psychological distress—at a time when in-patient admissions for other age groups were on the decline. "Attachment disorder," or a decline in the capacity to feel empathy, gained prominence in clinical discussions and studies. An emphasis on peer attitudes (often oppressive) as a factor in behavior replaced earlier assumptions about the primacy of parental influence.

Bad news, all of it, for a man jogging by the side of a small-town road. Or a man sleeping peacefully in his rural bed.

· · ·

IT HAD BEEN near the beginning of the great reconvergence—in 1968—that Jim Walker took up the urbane sport of jogging.

Jogging was an imported fad in the heartland back then. Like the mushrooming spread of health clubs, it was a way of facing a fact that city and suburban folks had long since acknowledged: that life liberated from physical stress was an unnatural life.

Looking back on it, Virginia Walker shrugged off any deeper associations. "He never was one to just set around," was her way of explaining it.

Jim's route never varied, summer or winter. He'd start out on nearby Lincoln, then head along fashionable Country Club Drive and shortcut across the golf course, loping parallel to the long leafy arc of Palmyra Road, past St. Mary's Cemetery and the new Hannibal Middle School to McMasters. After that he would head down that straight stretch past the high school where he and Virginia had graduated, to Pleasant Street. He would turn left on Pleasant and begin the long uphill chug toward home.

"He was so hoping to make a thousand miles last year," Virginia told me. "He had it all planned out. I think he had a little over a hundred miles left. I've kept the running books. I've still got all of them. He knew the distance. He'd get in the car first and see what it was."

Virginia Walker paused for a bit, took off her glasses, and then put them back on. "I thought I'd run with him too, at first," she said, "but I've got a bad left knee."

The Walkers lived a life of refracted flash and glitz during Virginia's reign as president of the Helen Cornelius Fan Club. They were admitted to the periphery of the hermetic world of country entertainment, a world that grew ever more stylized in its self-conscious folksiness as the authentic culture of country receded. On weekends and when Jim could get away, the two would set out by car to follow Helen and her singing partner Jim Ed Brown around the midwestern county fairs and jamborees and hoedowns where the two were booked. They thrilled as Helen, in her big platinum hairdo, and Jim Ed sang popular duets such as "I Don't Want to Have to Marry You," "You Don't Bring Me Flowers," and "We Still Sing Love Songs in Missouri." They socialized with other Helen Cornelius fans—nice, dazzled people like themselves, taking Polaroids and exchanging home-cooked treats and celebrity anecdotes and mailing addresses. "We'd kind of have our little get-togethers," Virginia said. In this charmed, illusory little world just outside the sodium beam of glamour, it was possible for a couple of starstruck Hannibal folks almost to believe they were a part of the magic. Jim, who'd always been an ardent country-western fan, bought himself a guitar and took lessons for about three years. When Helen was splitting off from Jim Ed Brown's tour and forming her own band, she brought her musicians to the Walker house a couple of times, and Jim had sat strumming along with them while they noodled around in the basement.

But by the mid-nineties, Helen Cornelius was long gone from the rural Missouri sawdust circuit. Just when life in her slipstream was proving all so exciting and wonderful for Jim and Virginia, she took her band and headed south to seek her fortune in the big time, in a place whose concentrated energies of faux homespun glitz and non-stop consumerism epitomized America's wholesale replacement of authentic culture with mass-marketed replicas. She went to Pigeon Forge, Tennessee.

Five miles from Gatlinburg, Pigeon Forge was one of the proliferating "rustic" venues in America. Pigeon Forge was a mélange of outlet stores (two hundred of them, including a Mountain Man Military Supplies), God-bless-the-U.S.A.-type dinner theaters, Hill-Billy villages, Comedy Barns, a mind-reading pig, Western-wear stores featuring vintage Roy Rogers bedspreads from the 1950s, and many high-voltage theaters offering nonstop country-music revues. Its crowning attraction was Dollywood, the world-famous amusement park owned by the legendary hometown girl Dolly Parton.

But not even Dollywood was beyond the range of ambitious competitors. In 1997, a country music impresario from Pigeon Forge named Howard A. Knight, Jr., got the notion in his head to top Dollywood by building a theme park dedicated to God. God's Wonderful World, Knight promised, would be a $400 million biblical extravaganza, featuring a hell fueled by propane jets of fire, a David and Goliath venue where kids could fire real slingshot pellets at an animatronic giant, a David's Diner (the number of stars wasn't specified), an animatronic Jesus Christ who walked on water, and roboticized disciples kibitzing with one another over the Last Supper.

Howard Knight found that making his vision a reality would consume considerably more time than required by its namesake to create the heavens and the earth. By 2001, the only attraction around Gatlinburg with "God" in its logo was God's Corner, a sort of Supreme Being boutique in a mall called The Village, that featured gospel music CDs, inspirational videos, and a selection of Precious Moments dolls whose black beady eyes reminded one of the more secular-humanist Beanie Babies. But Pigeon Forge as a whole was doing just fine. By the late nineties, the former cow-pastureland on U.S. Route 441 was sucking in eleven million tourists and $615 million tourist dollars each year.

Jim and Virginia didn't let any grass grow under them after Helen Cornelius went away. They got into antiques. Virginia gave a musical laugh at the memory. "We loved to take off weekends and go antiquing," she said. "Illinois, Iowa, wherever we could find antique auctions. Jim was always interested in railroad items. I collect this Frankoma pottery," she went on, gesturing to the figurines on the wall—little cowboy-boot flowerpots and horses and bears. "It's from Sapulpa, Oklahoma. It comes in about twenty different colors. It's just always fascinated me, and in fact the first piece I bought was when a friend of mine and I went to Unionville to hear Helen and Jim Ed. We stopped at a flower shop at Shelbina because she knew the people that owned the shop. This was back in seventy-eight."

We admired the little figures for a while.

"The horse was Jim's mother's," Virginia told me.

I asked her about a birdhouse that lay on a coffee table. Virginia choked before she replied. "It's one Jim made. It was in the backyard on the post, and the post was just about ready to fall down. So my yardman took it out one day, and I said I want that birdhouse. Jim had a workbench downstairs and one out in the garage." She paused and breathed deeply, collecting herself. "He was always—he didn't set around; he was not one to set."

I asked Virginia how she'd heard the news. Her answer came straight from the old predictabilities of the phantom world.

"I knew the times," she said. "I could always depend on the time he'd get back. He'd come home from work, get into his running gear—you know, it was chilly then, November, so he was into the jogging suit. He'd leave here ten, quarter after five. And I could bet money on it. He'd walk in that back door six o'clock. Five after at the very latest.

"On that afternoon he wasn't in by then. I started watching the clock; I was getting very jittery. I had heard a siren at about ten minutes till six. But I hear 'em all the time. I always worried when Jim was out running." She paused. "I know now that's what it was.

"Finally, quarter after six, I called my neighbor next door. And I told him, I said I'm quite concerned. At that time there was all kinds of construction on Pleasant Street. They're all workin' around over there, they were diggin', and Jim was one to climb over fences and one thing and another. So I thought, oh, my, he's fallen." She fell quiet again for a moment. "You know, someplace.

"So I asked Michael, my neighbor, if he could go out and look around. He said sure. And he gave me his truck phone number.

"And half an hour, I hadn't heard anything. I called him. He says, 'I'm here talking to the police right now, we'll be there' . . . and, uh . . . and it wasn't two minutes till they were here. And that's—" Virginia cleared her throat. "And so I went out to the hospital."

She thought for a moment, looking down at her folded hands, and then glanced up with a kind of smile. "Jim and I, we kinda argued sometimes 'cause he didn't always carry ID with him. Would you believe this was one of those times I had just washed his running outfit? And course his ID was downstairs on the washing machine."

What was next? I asked her.

"I have an attorney. I've been subpoenaed to appear at this trial. It surprised me. I really didn't want to face . . . I didn't want to know who these boys were. I still don't, but now I have to."

So you'll have to testify, I said.

For the first time, I heard something wild and dangerous in Virginia Walker's voice. Her reply was two words. The first was "terrible." The second was so choked with guttural rage that I could not understand it. I have since played it back dozens of times on a variety of tape recorders, and it remains indecipherable still.

Virginia took a minute to collect herself in the drape-darkened room. Then she said, "I'll do this if it will help the judge and the jury. If they give them the punishment they deserve."

The full force of Virginia Walker's loneliness struck me just then. Here was a woman cut off not only from her husband but also from her past—from any kind of history, personal or cultural, that could help her make sense of what had happened to her. The world had changed while she and Jim had been absorbed in Helen Cornelius. The old world had drifted off into space, leaving only a fragment anchored by Virginia's blue spruce tree. That fragment was now surrounded by the unknowable.

I drove away from Virginia Walker's house on State Street, past the incongruous little slice of grazing land that bordered it, and into a daylit Hannibal filled with more mysteries than my childhood self ever would have believed, all coalescing into the overwhelming one. Why—by what perversion of history—were children killing people here now?

Ahead of me was an appointment that might take me closer to the answers, in intimate ways, than the more generic evidence of social breakdown I had been gathering. Kyle Wilson, the father of Robie, had agreed through a mutual friend to meet with me and talk about his son. (My efforts to contact members of the Hill family had gone nowhere. As far as anyone knew, the Hills had left Hannibal, destination unknown, and the adolescent friends of Will's whom I asked for interviews responded with stony silence.)

I wanted to talk to Kyle Wilson, and yet I didn't want to. I kept putting it off, kept finding other things to occupy my time. As difficult as the interview with Virginia Walker had been, the prospect of talking to the father of a boy who had killed—the prospect of asking him any question that would not be automatically self-profaning—seemed forbidding at best, at worst, a vile kind of invasion.

And so I circled around that encounter for several days. I made Hannibal itself my focus and allowed myself only gradually to contemplate the layered weight that generations of fathers, fictive and real, imposed upon their sons in this shrine to boyhood.

6

FATHERS AND SONS

One dinnertime, I could not have been more than six, my father came home from a day of selling Fuller brushes, received a report from my mother of some misbehavior I'd committed, whipped off his belt, and laced me a good one across the backs of my legs.

"That's just a *sample* of what you're gonna get if you don't behave," he told me.

As much as the slash hurt and shocked me, I was for some reason preoccupied by the nomenclature. "You mean . . . like in your sample case?" I blubbered absurdly through my tears, as I rubbed my legs.

My father carried a slim black case with him on his Fuller rounds, like a suitcase, only smaller. He called it his "sample case." I never knew what was inside it as a small boy, and he never thought to show me. At some point in my childhood I learned that the case was full of cheap little trinkets that he offered to housewives when they answered his knock on the door. There were wire brushes and tin-foiled grains of sachet—peace offerings, so that they wouldn't think he was going to rob them. (Rape was a depravity too exotic even to merit denial in those days.)

Now he had just given me a "sample." The mystery of the adult language overwhelmed my humiliation and pain, just as the mystery of what sin looked like would later overwhelm my guilt. Was this what he carried in that case? Was this what happened to housewives who refused to buy his brushes? It was a winter evening, and he was still wearing his long black topcoat, as he called it, that wrapped around his body like a tube. (He'd unbuttoned it to grab his belt.) He still had on his dark fedora. He always wore a fedora, and he wore its brim at an extreme tilt across his forehead; it gave his face a shadowed private-eye kind of severity and offset his shining eyes.

All I could think of just then was whether the sample he'd just given me had come out of his sample case. What it was about fatherhood that he liked was a question that would not surface for many years. Ever, actually.

He was as much mystery as menace. His speech, for example. He was a font of secret grown-up language, of phrases that made no sense to me, or seemed to make no sense. He had a way of talking under his breath in a soft southern Illinois drawl that made comprehension tough.

I kept trying to figure out his language through my early boyhood. I might have thought that if I could understand it, I could understand him. But he seemed to talk in some kind of unfathomable code. For instance, he kept referring to the "iced paper." Every evening, upon coming home from work through the front door (and provided I did not need a "sample" that day), he would ask my mother, first thing, where the "iced paper" was. What did he want with iced paper? Was that where he kept his cold cuts? (Dad was always asking Mom whether we had enough cold cuts; he'd bring home brown-wrapped packages and hand them to her—"Here's some cold cuts for lunch," he'd murmur in that low conspiratorial drawl—and she'd hustle the package into the refrigerator. I yearned and dreaded to see what an actual cold cut looked like; the phrase reeked of dried blood and human flesh. But all I ever saw come out of the packages were round slices of bologna and squares of boiled ham.)

I never could figure out this business with iced paper, and I never saw him actually doing anything with iced paper; he always ended up slumped in the blue easy chair with a drink, frowning at the *Hannibal Courier-Post*. I may have been into my adolescence before it hit me that what he'd been asking for all these years was "tonight's paper."

Then there was the coded mystery of the "nash." Dad talked a lot about his nash. After supper, he would frequently tell my mother that he was going out in the nash. My mother never looked very pleased at this news. I quickly came to associate "going in the nash" not with traveling in a car but with an unsavory, if not outright nasty, activity—especially given that "going" was a euphemism, in our family, for using the toilet. One winter, as a very young boy, I caught a virus and came down with diarrhea. I came down with it so suddenly that it filled my pants before I could make it to the bathroom. Locked inside, hopelessly soiled, knowing I was in for it, I peeled down my trousers and gazed glumly at the reeking yellowish discharge.

As I looked at it, I suddenly recognized it for what it must have been. It was *nash*. No word could more perfectly describe it. Now at least I knew the vocabulary for what I had done; I could explain it to my mother, and if she didn't like it, at least it was not a new story to her. I had gone in the nash. I knocked on my side of the bathroom door, and called out, and when my mother answered, I opened the door a crack and confessed.

To my astonishment, she found it a scream. She laughed out loud for a while—it was odd how rarely my mother laughed out loud—and when she got control of herself she called to my father in his easy chair. "Ronnie went in the nash," she told him when he had put down his paper and, making noises of inconvenience, slogged down the hallway to the bathroom door. She invited him to peek inside, where I was still half barricaded, and take a whiff. Eventually my father got the joke. When he did, he signaled his enjoyment of it by taking off his belt and favoring me with another of his "samples."

I see another figure, sometimes, when I dip into memory and call up the image of my father and his whistling belt. Sometimes, my mind's eye replaces him with the ghostly contours of Pap, swinging his cowhide.

Pap Finn, Huck's father, is maybe the least appreciated of all Mark Twain's dark minor characters—underappreciated even, perhaps, by Twain himself. Pap lurks on the shadowy borders of the two great boyhood novels, peering out through his hair "long and tangled and greasy," with his eyes "shining through like he was behind vines." Pap, progenitor of violence, sorrow, and every son's long downriver flight.

No actor ever plays Pap Finn in the little summer pageants that amuse tourists in America's Home Town. No interest group has ever honored him by forming to damn him as a stereotype. His creator gave him the most minimal exposure; he appears only in four short chapters near the beginning of *Huckleberry Finn* and is mentioned in only a few others. But in the few strokes of description and language allotted him, Pap Finn lives as convincingly (and as much outside time) as a boyhood nightmare. Twain's Huck knew him well: "There warn't no color in his face, where his face showed; it was white; not like another man's white, but a white to make a body sick, a white to make a body's flesh crawl—a tree-toad white, a fish-belly white. As for his clothes—just rags, that was all."

Grooming was the least of it. A drunkard, a vagrant, a racist prince in a culture of racists, a boozy railer against "govment," a lowlife resenter of "frills" and "airs" and schooling, and especially of offspring who show evidence of being tainted by these, Pap Finn rules his son with threats, curses, the back of his hand, the leather strap, the hickory switch. Had Samuel Clemens been less Victorian in his sense of public decorum, Pap perhaps would have harbored some deviant sexual impulses as well. As matters stood, he was loathsome enough: "But by-and-by pap got too handy with his hick'ry, and I couldn't stand it. I was all over welts. He got to going away so much, too, and locking me in. Once he locked me in and was gone three days. It was dreadful lonesome. . . ."

Pap inhabited a lot of Hannibal fathers in the years of my childhood, and before, in *their* fathers, and after, in their sons. He is without doubt a more representative daddy—in Hannibal and in the nation—than the more celebrated Judge Thatcher, Twain's softened fictionalization of his own father. John Marshall Clemens glowered at his offspring, beat his few slaves, and kissed his wife only on his deathbed, but this educated, icy pauper with his frustrated aristocratic pretensions never approached the outlaw luster of Huck's old man.

Neither, to give him his credit, did my dad, although he came a lot closer than the judge. Paul Powers liked his beer—he especially liked drinking it out of a skillet gripped with his left hand while driving the Nash down some dirt-top road after a Sunday barbecue at somebody's cabin on the river. He liked a good honky-tonk tune. He hated "airs" and would have hated frills if there had been any frills to hate in Hannibal. His handiness with a belt or switch in punishment might have fetched him a court summons in later decades. But he never really had the long-term dedication to match Pap's level of depravity.

Basically, he was just an ex-farmboy who sold Fuller brushes door-to-door all of his adult life. I never heard him tell a story about his roots, or speak with any feeling about Hannibal. He didn't seem to belong anywhere particular, although his face might well have been the most recognizable one in town; he was the Fuller Brush Man. If he had an irreducible place, it was probably the bowling alley. I went with him there sometimes, sprawled myself across the wooden bench behind the lanes, listened to the pins explode, and watched the blue-jeaned lower legs of the pinboy hanging down from his invisible perch above the pins. I watched the legs jerk out of sight just as the ball reached its targets and always hoped to see what would happen if the legs were a little late, which they never were.

Dad had been born in the tiny town of Nebo, in southern Illinois. The Depression had forced him off his father's failing bean farm and out on to the road to find work as soon as he graduated high school. That exile, I think, shocked him deeply, and the shock never went away. For the rest of his life he clung almost obsessively to the meager income he earned selling brushes and to the mostly drab, cut-rate things he grudgingly allowed his meager income to buy.

He portioned out things in halves. Even small things. He'd pull a package of Doublemint chewing gum (he called it "chun' gum") out of his shirt pocket, thumb a stick partway out and say, in his toneless murmur, "You want half a that?" (I often pondered what half a Doublemint would equal.) At the dinner table, if he saw something on your plate that he craved, he'd lean toward you, clear his throat, point his fork, and ask, even more sotto voce, "Can I have about a half a that?"

This parsimony by half informed his entire worldview. Nobody of whom Dad disapproved was ever completely crazy; he was always about half crazy. The drunks in his anecdotes were about half crocked, or about half loaded. He always had about half a mind to do this or that (which he seldom did). When I'd committed some offense that activated his dark temper—fight with Jimmy, say, or break a basement window firing rubber balls against the wall—he would advise me, as he pulled his belt free from its loops, "Ah'm own 'bout half kill you." And frequently it half felt like he was going to.

I never saw my father buy more than a dollar's worth of gasoline at any one stop. The thought of handing over a five-dollar bill to anyone shocked him. He loved it when he thought he was getting a bargain. Only he didn't call it "a bargain." He called it "cut-rate." He'd drive clear out of town and across the river to buy his cigarettes "cut-rate." (He smoked Pall Malls, which were pronounced the British way, "Pell Mells," but which, for Dad, were always "Pawl Mawls." Which meant using more gas. But who was counting?)

The other way he had of saving money was his network of this-soleboys. Need a repairman? Tailor? Lawyer? Don't check the Yellow Pages. Ask Dad. "I know thissoleboy who'll do it cut-rate." Thissoleboy usually turned out to be some scary-looking clueless phantom inhabiting a seemingly abandoned farmhouse so deep in the country that the rattlesnakes were inbred. But we saved money. *Cut*-rate!

I guess he'd been a pretty good sports prospect, once. His best sport was the sport of his time and place, baseball. He used to tell me he was pretty good, but it wasn't until his funeral that I learned how good. His brother Carl told me the night of the visitation, right there in the funeral parlor, that Dad had had a baseball nickname as a kid: "Peg" Powers. "Peg" in honor of his throwing arm. My uncle said that he'd even been scouted a little. I never knew that.

• • •

HE'D BEGUN HIS exile from the farm by working on road-construction crews in the state of Washington, part of Roosevelt's WPA program. After a couple years of that, a boyhood friend hired him into the Fuller ranks and gave him the Hannibal territory. Paul arrived there in 1936, a nineteen-year-old boy driving a secondhand Model A Ford with no brakes. He took a room in a boardinghouse across from the public library, learned to stop his car by aiming it at light posts and trees, and began his long Fuller trudge.

It took him another couple of years to meet my mother, Elvadine Toalson. She answered his knock one day on the door of her father's house near the top of Union Street Hill, the highest hill in Hannibal. (How he got back down that hill is still a part of local legend.) I was the firstborn, in 1941. Then came Jimmy in 1945 and Joyce in 1950.

I don't think my father cared much for being a father. I don't think he knew what to do with fatherhood. I don't think he was ready to stop being a boy himself when the Depression hit and his own father had to stop being a father. In a way, Paul never did get out of his lost boyhood. I used to catch him staring at me sometimes as if he didn't quite recognize me, or as if he couldn't quite figure out how he, still a boy himself, had come to have a grown son.

I knew he couldn't figure me out. Once it was clear I was not willing to enter the world as he understood it—become his partner in Fuller Brush sales—the gulf between us would be permanent and vast. This recognition came to him early in my teen years, and it darkened him further.

My choice of a life's profession—writing, even though it was mostly journalism—meant only one thing to my father: "airs." But he did the best he could to cope with it. Once he even tried to engage me in literary badinage. It happened a few years before his death. I was at home visiting him and my mother. We were seated in the living room, trying to surmount the silence that had set in after the initial burst of small talk. After a while my father leaned forward on the couch and squinted intently at a book that lay before him on the coffee table. He cleared his throat and tapped it with his forefinger. "Is this one of them that you wrote?" he inquired.

In my adolescence, though, Dad attacked my "airs" in less subtle ways. One way was by goading me to go out for sports. "What've you got to be afraid of?" he'd ask, encouragingly, at the dinner table, as the rest of the family sat silent and I stared into my mashed potatoes and gravy. Other times he'd flatter my physique: "Big ox like you." I wasn't an ox; I was skinny.

The irony was that I loved sports. Loved to play ball. But my father's wheedling only made me think of "going out" as a guarantee of being scrutinized, failing in public, dropping the goddamn ball, maybe getting carried off the field with a broken leg. Sports were for my pal Duly, the town rich kid who could do anything.

Playing pickup sports, out of view of coaches or crowds, was a different thing entirely. On a sandlot I could be the center fielder of my dreams, unafraid, taking care of business in my easy outfield lope. "High fly out to right-center. Powers drifts over, says, 'I'll handle this one,'" I'd drawl, drifting over, doing Mel Allen doing me.

One perfect moment occurred that way, when I was eleven. It was on a hard-clay playground field at the foot of the massive Union Street

Hill on the south side of town. The hill rose steeply above the playground's screened outfield fence, anchored with high wooden posts almost flush against a redbrick house, from where the terrain seemed to accelerate upward. (That screen still stands.) This was a brutal hot July afternoon, probably 1953. Firemen dozed in their tilt-back chairs at the hook-and-ladder company across the street. The only two moving bodies in sight were me and Skeeter Stewart.

We were playing Indian ball. Skeeter wiped the sweat out of his eyes, tossed the softball in the air, and fungoed a towering fly ball toward the screened fence, well over my head and behind me. I spun around, put my head down, and dug as hard as I could. "Powers back, back, *back*—" I grunted as I ran. When I turned at the screen and looked up, the ball was suspended just above my head, a beautiful grapefruit waiting to be plucked. I stretched my arms and gathered it in. Stan Musial and all my Cardinal teammates in their white uniforms patted me on the back as we loped gracefully toward the dugout. In all the years since then, I have never done any single thing as perfectly as I timed and shagged that Skeeter-fungoed fly. The playground, in that moment, became a sacred place-within-a-place, floating free from the world.

My father never knew about that catch, of course. I never told him.

As for Pap Finn, the "respectable" world of St. Petersburg/Hannibal soon gave up on him as well. A "new judge" in town had a go at reforming him—"took him to his own house, and dressed him up clean and nice, and had him to breakfast and dinner and supper with the family, and was just old pie to him, so to speak"—and even got Pap to sign a temperance pledge with his mark. "Then they tucked [him] into a beautiful room, which was the spare room . . . and in the night sometime he got powerful thirsty." He slid off the roof and climbed back in a while later with a jug of forty-rod and got drunk as a fiddler. "And when they come to look at that spare room, they had to take soundings before they could navigate it."

The new judge's amended strategy for dealing with Pap had resonances into Hannibal's violent past, and its future as well: "He said he reckoned a body could reform the ole man with a shot-gun, but he didn't know no other way."

7

MARKET STREET

The morning after my talk with Virginia Walker, I began my re-visitation of Hannibal. Before I talked to anyone else, I wanted simply to look at the town, to examine it as I'd never been able to as a child, or even as an adult during other visits home. This time, I wanted to see it not simply through the prism of personal memory but as it might look to a young boy fifty years beyond my own childhood and a century and a half beyond Twain's.

He had stopped in Hannibal for three days in the spring of 1882, one of his seven return trips there, and wrote in *Life on the Mississippi* that "I woke up every morning with the impression that I was a boy—for in my dreams the faces were all young again, and looked as they had looked in the old times—but I went to bed a hundred years old, every night—for meantime I had been seeing those faces as they are now."

Not faces for me just yet; buildings. I began my exploration with a visit into the strip of old honky-tonk commerce that had drawn Robie Wilson and Will Hill to it in their panicky flight from Pleasant Street and that once had winked at me through the night like a carnival midway. This was Market Street on the southwestern border of town. Doglegged Market with its hot black strut. At least that was how I recalled it from my youth. From a boy's point of view in the 1950s, this narrow, jagged old thoroughfare, with its frontier-style storefronts, had throbbed with intimations of sass and sin.

White and black Hannibal gingerly mingled on Market, if not in the same taverns and drugstores and "beauty shoppes" and cafés, then at least in the same neon-lurid neighborhood. My great-uncle Jesse Toalson ran his storefront Dan-Dee Bakery on the eastern, or "downtown" edge of Market through the 1930s and 40s; his son Clyde was elected mayor in 1957. I remember the heavy scent of sweet warm dough inside the place. Pale Jesse and his wife in their white cardboard hats, white flour on their hands, and always a collection of cautious black children out front on the sidewalk. Sometimes they'd venture inside with nickels in their fists, savoring the distant warm whiteness.

In the 1870s, when Mark Twain was writing *The Adventures of Tom Sawyer* in Elmira, New York, twelve mills were hauling logs out of the Mississippi, logs that had been floated down from the northern forests, and slicing them into lumber. Market Street grew into a gaudy midway of taverns, lunchrooms, cheap hotels, pool halls, and dance parlors, where rivermen, railroadmen, and Negro laborers drank beer and ate pickled eggs and got happy.

Hannibal had been a slaveholding town until the Civil War, and a permanent population of African Americans had formed afterward, mostly in the floodplain on the southwest side of town between Bear Creek and Market, an area known to white Hannibal as "the Bottoms." Circuses pitched their tents there in the mosquito-ridden summers. One August night as a small boy I sat with my parents in the bleachers laughing so hard at the horde of clowns pouring out of a small yellow car that I pitched backward through the opening between the planks and fell to the grass below; my mother was there an instant later, terrified that I would be carved to pieces by a Negro—*"they always carry knives!"*

Black Hannibal had lived in hand-built wooden shacks and shanties along the Bottoms, most of which still stand, and Market Street was their Harlem, which they grudgingly shared with white folks out for a good slumming time.

I remembered drinking it all in, that blurry stew of sound and shape and odor, from the passenger window of my father's beetle-shaped Nash when he took me with him to make Fuller Brush deliveries at night on Market. I always sensed that Dad knew more about

Market's pleasures than he let on. Nighttime deliveries made a convenient opportunity for him to "stop in" for a couple of cool ones at some tavern while I waited in the car, hearing the crash of women's laughter and jukebox music. I remembered smelling the beer and fried food on the night breeze and studying the intense "colored" men who glided past in their trimmed mustaches and narrow-brimmed fedoras, their unfathomable cliff-side faces illuminated for a second or so by the burn of a Schlitz sign.

One summer night while Dad was "stopping in," I opened the door of the Nash and felt the actual pavement of that street underfoot for the first time. I was wearing my new Cub Scout uniform and felt impervious to peril, the same as I did with my Patrol Boy BadgeandBelt. I ventured half a block to the most opulent-looking storefront on the whole strip, the Rexall Drug Store at the corner of Market and a side street whose name I'd since forgotten. Its glistening entrance seemed reassuringly aloof from the night under the proprietary wash of the blue-and-orange Rexall sign.

Instead of crossing inside, I lingered on the sidewalk, absorbed in my own daring and in the displays of new White Rain Shampoo and Wildroot and Preparation H in the plate-glass window. And then the night street suddenly stole upon me. A passing black man cradling a brown paper bag in his beefy arm halted his stride directly at my back. I stood stock-still and held my breath, suddenly alone and naked, feeling on my scalp the once-over he was shooting me.

"*Cuuuuuhb* Scout," I heard him mutter as he accelerated into the night, a terse indictment that thrilled me with its surgical disdain and, for just that second, opened up the true contours of a world beyond my own. I dived back into the Nash, halfway wanting to follow him.

· · ·

BUT NOW, IN this broad daylight, I saw that that world had faded. The carnival had long packed up and left. The old storefronts leaned against one another under their peeling paint, either vacant or claimed by transient businesses, shot-and-beer joints and bait-and-tackle shops. Everywhere was soot and sawdust. Empty windows showed the curling traces of hand-painted signs. An occasional stack of the most improbable debris lay on the sidewalk: rusted turbines, upended soft-drink machines, broken sleds, scraps of children's clothing. And not a high-stepping pedestrian in the whole universe. Much less a wondering Cub Scout.

Hannibal "is no longer a village, it is a city," Twain wrote in 1882, "with a mayor, and a council, and water-works, and probably a debt. It has fifteen thousand people, is a thriving and energetic place, and is paved like the rest of the west and south—where a well-paved street and a good sidewalk are things so seldom seen, that one doubts them when he does see them."

I was letting myself wonder whether the old town boy had made it out to Market Street on this visit. And then I spotted it. Wedged into the guts of this ghostly detritus—between a bar called the Picadilly and a corner sporting-goods store that billed itself as the Huntin' Hut—was the place I'd come to see: the Water Hole, where Robie and Will had fled after smashing down James Walker.

It took a few minutes for me to realize that the Huntin' Hut occupied the shell of the old Rexall. And that the side street I'd forgotten was named Hope.

I sat in my rented car across the street from the Water Hole (feeling even more reluctant than ever, after forty years, to hit the pavement) and stared at its facade. It redefined "dingy." The chipped white lettering on its small windowpane—the whole place could not have been more than twelve feet wide—misannounced itself as "The Hole in the Wall." (The phone book confirmed the new designation.) Through the dirty glass I could make out a few shapes in plaid work shirts. Hours before noon, the regulars were already in place, drinking. This was the safe haven that Robie and Will had sought after their deadly misadventure. This was their idea of sanctuary.

Where was everybody else? Other than the shapes inside the Water Hole, the area looked evacuated. If this was where two panicky teenage boys would come for refuge, what did that say about their everyday world?

I craned my neck up and down the block and saw nothing but remains, archaeology. Near the old Rexall was a yellow-brick facade that bore the traces of an ancient "Customer Parking" script. Not far from that, a disintegrating billboard proclaimed, in black and white, "Need Help Call Dodge Bail Bonds."

Beyond it, a gray building, a kind of Quonset hut, that declared itself an Animal Hospital. Cutouts of cartoon cats and dogs were taped to the window. Across the street was an abandoned brick two-story building with a marquee that read, "Electric Motor Company, Sales Repair Used Motors." It appeared to be abandoned. On an exposed wall beside it I could make out the remnants of an old painted legend: "You'll Like Bluff City Dairy Grade A Guaranteed Milk Products." The paint had been fresh in my boyhood.

"Welcome Harleys," said the hopeful window sign in an Auto Trim and Upholstry shop, though no hordes of bikers appeared imminent. I saw Budweiser signs in the shape of electric guitars, some out-of-place bungalows, and row houses. No people.

My gaze came to rest on a Smiley's Live Bait and Tackle, a blue storefront with the signage in yellow and brown. A Dr Pepper machine squatted outside the entrance; a pickup truck was wedged between the sidewalk and the store. As I peered at the shop's window, I could make out the only other traces of humanity in this universe: a couple of little kids, or perhaps a very small mother and her child, huddled on the inside next to a Coke machine.

I briefly considered moseying inside the Water Hole. That led in an even briefer interval to my next thought, which was about the likely impact my entrance was likely to make. (My big-deal trench coat doubtless would have drawn an admiring chorus of oohs and ahs.) I decided the hell with it. Market Street in the late 1990s was not what you would call a tourist's paradise. In fact the only edifice that looked remotely approachable by an outsider hulked a block away, an impersonal little fortress of redbrick: the Juvenile Justice Center. ("WATCH YOUR STEP," warned a sign at the center's entrance, probably oblivious to its double meaning.) That, and a mecca-in-progress, a sharply angled new Conoco convenience store, its macadam plaza being gouged out by yellow backhoes and graders.

Somewhere in the interstices of the vanished Rexall and the emerging Conoco, a small civilization had formed, flourished, and then withered, a demimonde at once rude, gaudy, vulpine, and exuberantly alive. Where had it gone? Where was everybody? Where were the kids? I pulled my rented car away from the curb and into Market Street—no traffic to speak of—and began a meandering cruise around my old hometown, to see if I could figure out the answers.

· · ·

WHEREVER I DROVE, the atmosphere was about the same—vacancy, withdrawal, absence, a town of phantoms. Not every neighborhood was a squalid as Market Street, and some were solid-seeming, even graceful. But they all seemed curiously uninhabited. Where were the leaf rakers, the bicyclists, the knots of children playing on front lawns? Where were the football players, the crowds, from the night before? Shouldn't they still be visible, somehow, taking the morning sunlight, replaying the victory? Driving Hannibal's streets was like exploring a movie location after the movie had been made. The cast and the crew had left the premises, but the set and the props hadn't been struck.

I knew that it wasn't true, of course, that I was in fact surrounded by humanity. Car traffic moved; large white-painted eighteen-wheelers with blue Wal-Mart lettering trundled along arterial streets; the parking lots of shopping plazas were filled. The single-shot .12-gauge shotgun that Zach used on J. D. Poage had been bought by the victim's son, Ronnie Poage, in 1990 at the Wal-Mart. Yet individual human beings—just plain ambulatory people, as distinct from motorists and consumers—were a rarity. The thought occurred to me how startling, how out of the ordinary, it must have been for Robie and Will to behold that lone jogger that November twilight. It had been so jarring to expectations, perhaps, as to invite an extreme response of some kind. Then I put that thought away.

My sense of disconnection was reinforced by the car radio. I had it tuned to Hannibal's AM station, KHMO, but the programming seemed to come from everywhere and nowhere. A serious-voiced reporter named Suzanne somebody from Los Angeles was delivering a capsule celebrity profile of someone named Bob Wilcox. Wilcox, it seemed, was learning how to be a better parent. "His three oldest children range in age from seventeen to twenty-four," Suzanne informed her listeners, "while he also has two sons, ages three and five." She forged on, crunching her syntax a little in the interest, I supposed, of brevity: "He made some mistakes early on, he admits, pushing too hard for achievement, particularly his oldest boy." (She pronounced it "pertikerly.") "But he's taking a more understanding approach now."

Then the voice of Bob Wilcox himself came on, in husky sound bite: "What you do is support and be a stable background. You love.

You look deep in people's eyes when you talk, instead of just talking to 'em. Um. You touch. And the rest, let them do it. You know, they don't need merit badges on their forehead, they don't need credits. They need you. And, uh, hopefully, I'm getting better about that."

Suzanne then revealed that something involving Bob Wilcox would air October 27 on TNT. She signed off: "Suzanne Somebody, Los Angeles."

What made this scrap of broadcast babble eerily appropriate to the moment was that its perfect disjunction from any sort of context corresponded, in an astral kind of way, to the formlessness of the physical town that passed before my windshield. Rather than flow in a kind of municipal logic, as in my boyhood recollections—residential neighborhood giving on to shops, then to downtown business, and then to the riverfront and its Mark Twain attractions—the town seemed stitched together, and badly at that. Out-of-scale service stations, with their assertive franchise logos and colors, their "mini-marts" and convenience stores, squatted on macadam rectangles that had been gouged out of property with no apparent regard for context or neighborhood cohesion. The logos saturated the townscape, their overripe oranges and reds and blues bleaching the life out of tree and lawn and garden.

I headed for the northern border of town and a long thoroughfare that was the economic opposite of Market. Hannibal's municipal boundaries form a cone that widens rapidly from the Mississippi riverfront to the west. Market Street runs along the southern border of that cone. Its corresponding rim to the north is leafy Palmyra Road, bounded not by decaying taverns but by apple orchards, spacious houses, and the country club golf course, where I'd caddied some forty years before. And where Jim Walker used to jog.

I saw that the apple orchards of my boyhood had been thinned out considerably. The land on which they'd lain—high, rolling terrain that extended for nearly a mile northward between the road and the steep dropoff to the Mississippi—had largely been cleared over the past quarter century. Behind a remnant of apple trees that served as a concealing buffer now spread Hannibal's small colony of wealth. Here was the sort of ostentation that my Fuller Brush Man father had liked to refer to, admiringly, as "them prom'nent homes."

Here, in subdivisions with names like Oak Ridge Point, Woodland

Acres and, inevitably, Orchard Point, tastefully invisible to the passing traffic on the thoroughfare, the lawyers and the doctors reposed. Lots out here sold for $60,000; the "homes" they eventually contained went for $300,000 to $400,000—big money indeed in Hannibal's economy. Some were local legends, though rarely glimpsed: the doctor's house with its six-car garage that some said resembled an entire condominium complex and was worth $1 million; the others with their carpeted dens and wrought-iron interior details and remote-controlled windowshades and blinds. A view of the Mississippi was the prevailing status mark in this little society. I wondered whether Zach or Robie had ever glimpsed the river from these bluffs. The question answered itself.

Hannibal, as I learned, subdivided itself according to degrees of affluence nearly as severely as it divided itself between affluence and poverty. Even as the doctors competed to claim the best custom-built house with the best view, salaried workers at companies such as the chillingly named American Cyanamid chemical plant struggled to secure beachheads for their $120,000 trophy homes on the farthest frontiers of the town's westward expansion—just then delineated by Head Lane, a mile west of the old bordering road, McMasters.

It was a little like looking at a rubber band that had gradually been stretched, then stretched some more, stretched beyond its normal tolerances, until holes had begun to appear and grow in the elongated fiber. More accurately still, it was like looking at a miniature model of an aging metropolis, its industries defunct and its central city vitiated by strip development and flight—nearly all of it white—toward its receding suburbs.

"In the small town of Hannibal, Missouri, when I was a boy everybody was poor but didn't know it; and everybody was comfortable and did know it," Mark Twain wrote in his autobiography. "Everybody knew everybody and was affable to everybody and nobody put on any visible airs; yet the class lines were quite clearly drawn and the familiar social life of each class was restricted to that class . . . you perceived that the aristocratic taint was there."

Except for the claim that "everybody knew everybody," that description pretty much obtained a century after Twain had recalled it.

I headed my car back east, toward the riverfront. The Folklife Festival was going on, and I wanted to see it.

· · ·

THE FOLKLIFE FESTIVAL had replaced the Fall Festival many years ago. It was a sleeker, more packaged updating of the folksy old street fair. No Ferris wheels, no merry-go-rounds, no house of mirrors or target shooting or Fool the Old Guesser, no carnival attractions of any kind. There were no strings of yellow lights for nighttime meandering—the Folklife was strictly a daylight affair—and no livestock, no pie-judging contests, no arrays of the summer's harvest. The venue had been moved from Broadway, the wide main thoroughfare that ran perpendicular to the riverfront, to a tidy little two-block stretch of North Main Street, which paralleled the river and encompassed the Twain tourist shops.

I parked my car on Broadway near Main and walked north and into the crowd.

Everybody seemed to be eating fried dough. A cluster of people had gathered at Main and Center, all sunglasses and cowboy hats and beards, to watch some teenagers doing an old-fashioned step dance to recorded music. The girls were in black bonnets and black skirts, the boys in white shirts and suspenders. Most of the dancers looked as though they had sent their minds somewhere else. So did most of the spectators.

Both sides of North Main were lined with booths. Between these lines people strolled and munched. Trinity Episcopal was offering roasted ears: hot corn with the husk still on, dipped in a can of melted butter. Other booths, operated by women in bonnets and long gingham skirts, featured "Victorian parlor dolls," watercolored canvases, strands of jewelry, pottery—all of it looking suspiciously unhomemade. The bonnet-and-gingham women wore name tags that said, "Just Ask." They hawked wind chimes, old-timey teddy bears, mint fudge, cheese soup, and German-style knockwurst. Holy Family Parish was offering applesauce donuts.

This festival had a detached, transient consumer flow feel to it that was different somehow from the comfy old Fall Festivals of my boyhood. This feeling didn't quite take hold in my mind until I spotted a car parked behind one of the booths. It bore an out-of-state license plate and a bumper sticker that read, "Single Women Don't Fart. They Don't Have an Asshole Till They're Married."

I studied the bonnet-and-gingham women briskly dealing out

goods and making change inside the booth and wondered which of them might be the owner of that car. I decided to ignore their name tag suggestions and not ask.

Adolescents were scarce. Among the handful I did see were two suited up as the inevitable Tom and Becky. The boy was outfitted in the regulation straw hat, frayed overalls, and starched white collar; he gripped a fishing pole, its string wrapped tightly around it. The girl had on a long turquoise dress—gingham, naturally—and pantaloons. She was feeding anachronistically from a bag of popcorn. They were both part of the ambient munching and strolling, munching and strolling.

In front of the Pilaster House, a historic building where Sammy Clemens's father had kept his law office and young Sammy awoke to find the corpse of the stabbed man, a woman named Cindy was offering oil portraits on commission for $250. The price included the plastic bag for carrying away the portrait. Cindy's work, displayed behind her easel, ranged from studies of jumping trout to turquoise waves crashing against a shore to the heads of lions and deer and wolves, and the stars and planets. Next to her booth, an artist named John offered pen-and-ink renderings of Charles Lindbergh, Mark McGwire, and a Mississippi riverboat.

The Hannibal Folklife Festival was nearly entirely given over to the souvenir-and-kitsch-mongering of salespeople from someplace else. Judging from the license plates, many of the ambling munchers were from someplace else as well. The Folklife Festival was largely a gathering of strangers: professionals on the American small-town folk life circuit and their faithful consumers. Not all that dissimilar from, say, the roving Helen Cornelius and her fans.

· · ·

AT AROUND ONE o'clock I had lunch with a man who had thought a lot about the correlations between Hannibal's air of detachment from itself and the growing remoteness of its young. "One of the things that really intrigues me about this Robie Wilson story," Don Nicholson remarked to me as we sat in a small restaurant on the western outskirts, "is that few people in this town, or any other town nearby, really even think about it. Not the grown-ups. Not the kids.

They're not really aware of it at all. Most don't even have a recollection that it occurred."

A friend had told me about Nicholson, a big open-faced man born in Montana who performed community work in the area, mostly with rural kids and their families, for the University of Missouri Extension Service. He supervised 4-H club programs, offered nutritional advice, and kept in touch with school administrators, mental health workers, and probation officers in four counties.

I asked Nicholson how the Robie Wilson incident could possibly avoid dominating the town's consciousness. His answer drew upon the "diagnostic" visit, a few months earlier, by the Health 2000 research team headed by Marshall Kreuter.

"One of the things that came out of the discussion with Marshall that was particularly interesting to me," Nicholson said, "was that he found a sense of fatalism in Hannibal. There's a feeling here of, 'Well, whattaya going to do?' I've always noticed that, but it was interesting to hear it from someone else."

What did Kreuter mean, exactly? I asked.

"One of the things that he found that has been real telling for me," Nicholson replied after a considered pause, "is the lack of a ministerial alliance. There are a couple or three kind of *sort* of ones. But that is compared to some of the other communities we work in, where there is a very well-defined ministerial alliance. Hannibal was just noticeably absent on that front."

I remarked how surprising that sounded to me, given the almost constant presence of churchly slogans, references to God in conversation, and Jesus chat on the radio I'd been aware of since arriving here.

"The churches are fairly visible," Nicholson conceded, "but I'm wondering to what degree the churchwork is mostly *inwardly* focused—as opposed to a spirit of 'Here we are and what can we do for the greater good?' My sense is that they're pretty highly inwardly focused, each church on its own congregation. 'This is us and this is our people and that's who we work with.'

"And I think that spills over into the community. And I guess one of the things that I keep going back to in my mind over and over again is that kids don't belong to a community so much anymore."

Nicholson laced his fingers together and stared at them. "It's not just Hannibal. It's everywhere. People may be identified by where they live, but they don't feel a part of that community. Where we live, outside of town—out there in a kind of cow pasture heaven, along with the other people in their pretend five-acre ranches—even if that's where they live, they don't belong to a community. There are people that live one, two houses away from us that I don't know. Wouldn't know 'em if I saw 'em in town. And I think that has a real profound effect on kids."

This withered sense of community hardly stopped at the town border. "There are a lot of 'Hannibals' in this town," Nicholson said. "A coworker of mine contends that there are seven or eight, depending on how you count. They're divided up by roads and highways. So there isn't a lot of activity that brings young people from different parts of town together. Kids spend a lot of time in front of the tube. They don't do much playing in their neighborhoods, even. When we worked with kids in some of the areas, you'd think they'd know the kids on your own block, or about your same age. Not really.

"I have a hunch there are a lot of kids that have no expectations of them, either from their family or from the community that they live in. There are no expectations. If you ask them, 'What's expected of you?' a lot of them may come up with, 'Well, I'm expected to stay out of trouble.' But that's it."

Casting around for a hopeful thread, I recalled for Nicholson a remark from Marshall Kreuter to the effect that Hannibal took measurable pride in its school system. Nicholson sat silently in the booth for a moment, his chin on his interlaced fingers.

"I've not sensed that there was a lot of strong pride," he said finally. "The community doesn't feel much of an investment in the schools here. It's like, 'Those people' run the schools. And I think the people in the schools talk in similar ways: 'Those people out there.' Part of a project we have going in the Hannibal Middle School is we're hiring a person full-time to do nothing more than try to attract more parents to get involved with Friends of the School. Now, the other side of that is teaching the school how to work with the community so that they would want to get involved."

Professionals, hired by the community to teach itself how to be a community. It was my first encounter with a concept I would revisit with unnerving frequency in my travels around America's Home Town. But now Don Nicholson was on to another topic.

"There's the distance between the home and the workplace," he was saying. "In some parts of this county, between forty and sixty percent of the workforce leaves every morning to go work somewhere else. If Mom and Dad are commuting thirty, forty, fifty miles one way to go to work, it just sucks the life right out of the community— in terms of energy for time to be on the volunteer fire department, the Little League ball games. When Highway Sixty-one between Hannibal and St. Louis is finally all four-lane, I think we're gonna see more and more of it. We've already got families around here driving to Wentzville, to the automotive plant down there. When they get that last little piece of four-lane done through Frankfurt, you can get to Wentzville in sixty, seventy minutes. Less time if Smokey isn't out. And some of those jobs are pretty high-paying. These are not folks that, just say, 'Please, God, give me a job.' These are people that are electricians, high up in the trades."

I asked Nicholson when he thought the effects of all this blankness and busyness began to show up in a child's developmental cycle.

"I have a hunch you should go to the day cares," he said. "The preschool day cares. Take a look at how kids interact. I would have a hunch you'd see some things there." He gave me the name and address of one, and I promised him I'd go there.

· 8 ·

A SPIRIT GOIN' ROUND

On Sunday morning I put on a jacket and tie and went to church in Hannibal for the first time since the Eisenhower administration. To be specific about it, I went to St. John's Lutheran Church, a satisfyingly heavy and darkly steepled house of worship built in 1897, the very year that Mark Twain began work in Vienna on "The Chronicles of Young Satan," as it happened. St. John's sat in an old neighborhood on Lyon Street, two blocks south of Broadway near the western edge of Hannibal's downtown district. I flipped on the radio during the drive over, expecting to hear a bit of inspirational programming, and was not disappointed.

"*Yeah,*" a breathy man's voice was saying on KHMO, "how you have to *ignore* so much reality in order to doubt *Gawd's* reality for your life! I hope these words can speak to you. I feel in a very musical mood right now and I'm going to ask the choir to just come and sing another song for us this morning in this festive and beautiful fall day. Choir? Could you help us out?" The choir was only too happy to oblige. As "We Will Gather at the River" kicked in over the chords of a trip-hammer piano, I decided to cruise a bit and let the spirit overtake me, if that were possible. The old familiar cadences had just begun to work their spell on me. I was starting to conjure up old memories of women in flowered hats, singing and fanning themselves in the sanctuaries of my First Christian youth, when the broadcast of the service gave way to, of all things, a commercial.

It began with tinkly music and the voice of a woman singer: "There's a feeling/over the land/Open up your heart/And give someone your haaaand . . ." Here she was gently interrupted by a deep, resonant, anchormannish narrator: "There's a spirit goin' round. And you can catch it. You know, Jesus said, 'Love God and love your neighbor as yourself.' United Methodists find their neighbors among the rich and the poor. Among the street people of the inner city and the migrant workers in the country. Among the walking wounded in suburbia. All those who struggle for survival across our nation and throughout the world. United Methodists believe that our relationship to God has a lot to say about our relationship with people." The tinkly music swirled upward again, and the singer resumed her jingle: "Feelin' Ga-ha-*haaad* in everything we do/*Woo-hoo-hoooo!*/Reach out your hand and catch the spirit *tooo!*" And then the anchorman, nailing the tag line: "Catch the spirit! The United Methodist Church."

The spot was so slickly done that I felt a quiver of sheepishness at being on my way to consume a competing brand name. I parked my car on nearly empty Broadway in the heavy yellow penumbra of the Broadway Shell gasoline plaza, a mighty temple of octane and "BUSCH 12-PAK, $6.19." I hurried south toward the somewhat less majestic St. John's, past the Holy Family School, its marquee advertising a "Big Beanie Baby Sale, Nov. 14, K.C. Hall."

St. John's was among the several churches hanging on to their traditional locations in the heart of Hannibal. Several others had abandoned their old neighborhood sites to follow the westward flight of younger, somewhat more upscale families. I suspected (though I did not know it for a fact) that St. John's was one of the churches that Don Nicholson had implicitly criticized as being insular, as opposed to community-minded in its outreach. But there was no denying the ruddy warmth and intelligence of its pastor, the Reverend Richard L. Ingmire, who rubbed my hands between his as he greeted me at the entrance.

A mutual friend had spoken highly of Pastor Ingmire and urged me to take in one of his services. A merry-eyed man with thinning hair, a lilting voice, and a pinkish neck that bulged a little above his clerical collar, the pastor welcomed me inside and proceeded to conduct his well-attended service with an easy intimacy—not from behind his pulpit but strolling back and forth at the foot of the altar.

(I later learned that this departure from tradition had scandalized some of his parishioners.) From my back-pew vantage point, I felt the curiosity of those around me. And the attention: when I fell a little behind the pace in locating a hymn or switching from my printed prayer sheet to the hardbound liturgical book, a kindly usher would appear instantly and help me back up to speed with the service. If I were not such a dyspeptic soul, I might almost have said that there was a spirit goin' round.

But as much as I admired Pastor Ingmire's stewardship at the altar, it was a postservice activity that had drawn me there: a Bible class for young adolescents in the church basement. I squeezed into a rear chair in a low-ceilinged room, behind a dozen or so brightly clothed twelve- and thirteen-year-olds arranged in a semicircle and jiggling their knees, hunching their shoulders in giggle fits, and aiming wisecracks at one another when the pastor swept briskly into the room.

"All right, let's do a little quick review here about what we've been talking about on the Apostles' Creed," he began with the air of a man who is certain that the so-called generation gap is vastly exaggerated. "How many creeds do we have?" He darted his eyes right and left, brows raised. "All right, let's hold up hands." He paused again. "All right. Maxine? Which three are we studying?"

Undaunted by the absolute silence he'd inspired, the pastor retreated smoothly to a fallback poser: "What *is* a creed?" And then, after another split second, prompted, "It's what you believe!

"It becomes for us, as people of God's church, a symbol," he went on. "What's a symbol? Can you think of a symbol? It makes a statement. A symbol is something, uh, that tells you what it is. Or stands for. Can anyone think of a symbol?"

As the children ruminated, I studied them. Middle-class Hannibal kids, mostly girls, shiny and squirmy inside their Fashion Babe and Chillin' Dude clothes, on the brink of deep adolescence. What did the Home Town look like to them? What did they make of this sweetly hovering pastor? Of me? Of their futures in the town and nation around them?

One of them spoke up that the flag was a symbol, and Pastor Ingmire pounced gratefully. "The flag! What does the flag symbolize for us? Eric?" ("Uh, the freedom that we got from England," said Eric.) "Anything else?" ("Patriotism.") "What's patriotism?" ("Uh, it's the way you believe. It's how you feel about your country.")

"All right!" Pastor Ingmire rubbed his hands together in a now-we're-cooking sort of way. "All right! Symbols. Symbols. That's what we're talking about." And now the sly transition: "We have symbols of our *faith*. They stand for loving Jesus. Right? What good is a creed or a pledge or whatever—what does it do? Any ideas? What makes it worthwhile?" ("Belief!" This from the pastor himself, after a moment.)

As the lesson progressed, "talking about the greatest things in the creed today," the topic turned to angels, or rather the pastor turned it that way. How does one know anything about angels? Is one supposed to believe in angels? What kind of angels are we talking about?

"I remember there was evil angels," spoke up one boy with a certain connoisseur's interest.

The pastor shot him a sidelong glance but was game: "Tell me a situation in the Bible about them."

The boy thought a moment. "Oh, yeah. Satan. He was the angel that thought he was better than God. And so God made him into a devil."

"All right!" The pastor seemed to be looking for a way out of this line of thought. "Uh, let's just try going around here a little bit here, so we can move along."

Crystal said that angels are invisible. Someone else mentioned wings.

"Things that describe good angels?" the pastor prompted.

"Evil ones have a tail," someone volunteered. Pastor Ingmire held up a finger. "Those are sometimes artistic perceptions. That's what artists, over the centuries, way back in the days—" he foundered.

One of the girls volunteered that angels were protective, which seemed to rally the pastor a little.

"I think the whole point we want to get today is that there's good in the world, and we have to also accept the fact about what?"

"Evil!" chorused several voices, way ahead of him.

"Evil. Then we want to talk about what happens with us."

"The devil made me do it," someone muttered, to giggles.

"All right. Now, the Bible tells us in the creation that God created man. A little below the angels. In what way would man be a little below the angels?"

"We don't have wings." This from the kid who observed that angels had wings.

Everyone else seemed stumped.

"We can solve problems. We are made in God's image. We can learn. But that's not what makes us just below the angels. At our house we have a dog that goes to the back door and rings the bell when he wants to go outside. So other creatures are capable of learning besides man. Right? Okay?"

No argument there.

"All right, let's talk about—" the pastor appeared to be improvising just a little now. "God has given us something that he has asked us to use in everyday life. A conscience. You have a conscience. Have you ever had to wrestle with your conscience?"

This brought several mutters of, "*Oh*, yeah."

Pastor Ingmire tumbled on ahead. "Would you be willing to share with me some of the things you wrestle with? Kinda personal, I know. Try to think back in your life to a time when you have had to wrestle with your conscience."

One girl recalled an episode involving her best friend. She'd told the girl she was coming to her house, but then was invited to a party, and the best friend wasn't invited. Pastor Ingmire was overjoyed. "You had to wrestle with your conscience? Whether you had to keep your word to go to that friend's house or go to a party? That would be a wrestling situation. What do you think would be the right thing to do?"

"Take your friend *to* the party," a bored wise guy voice intoned. The pastor, avid for dialogue, ignored this. "Remember, we talked about reason? Maybe sometimes we can reason our way through these things. All right—what else has your conscience had to wrestle with?"

A hand shot up. "Oh! I wrestled with *my* conscience!" It was the wiseacre, a good-looking Tom Sawyer with his white blond hair carefully combed. Under Pastor Ingmire's beaming attention, he unloaded: "I saw a baby duck swimmin' down the river! I didn't know if I would shoot it or let it live and shoot it when it was older, or shoot it now. I just went ahead and shot it. And then I didn't feel bad afterwards."

The kid could not have prayed for a more satisfying reaction. Pastor Ingmire froze in his tracks, his Socratic aplomb knocked lopsided. He did a classic double take and gaped at the boy.

"You shot . . . *a baby duck?*"

Shrieks from the chairs. The boy calculated his triumph and rode it a little.

"Yeah. And my uncle made me feel really bad. He told me, as I was pullin' it out into the boat, that there was still eggshell on its head."

Groans now from the girls; even the pastor released an involuntary *"Awwwww."* He strove to regain control of the moment. "Well, how did you feel about that?"

"Well—" the kid appeared to mull this over, then delivered his zinger. "That was okay, 'cause it tasted pretty *guuuhd.*"

Another round of giggles. Pastor Ingmire appeared to be locked helplessly inside the straight-man role. "You mean you actually *ate* it?"

The latter-day Tom Sawyer was in full show-off mode now: *"No, I just shoot 'em and let 'em float down the river.* Of course you *eat* it. I mean—"

Pastor Ingmire redoubled his hold on the structure of the day's Bible lesson, albeit by his fingertips. "But you didn't wrestle with your conscience about killing that baby duck?"

The boy relented a little. "Yeah, I did, because, you know, it was just a baby—"

Not quite enough repentance, and the pastor regained the offensive. *"Did you feel bad about killing that baby duck?"*

". . . Yeah."

A limited victory, but Pastor Ingmire appeared relieved to accept it. He reassumed something of his brisk interlocutor posture. "All right. Anything else? Let's talk about choices, people. Choices. What about choices? Sit and think for a moment about choices people make in their lives. I'll try not to be judgmental."

It was a goal that not everyone in the room could attain. *"You murderer,"* one girl hissed at the boy as the class fell into Christian contemplation.

STORED CHILDREN

The Children's Station, one of the day-care facilities Don Nicholson had suggested I visit, turned out to be a squat little outpost of pale brick in a lawn sprinkled with swings and plastic slides bounded by a chain-link fence. It sat facing a gravel lane near the intersection of Market Street and U.S. 61 on the southwest tip of town. Diesel gas plazas and terminally unfinished budget motels wedged into bulldozed, grassless earth commanded the landscape. It was a minimecca of "stations." Farther down the gravel lane were McNally Plumbing Supply, an Auto Glass Parts Shop, Basford Pool & Spa, the United States Army Reserve Center, Williams Electric Motor, a lighting showroom, Bleigh Ready Mix Concrete, Peters Heating and Air Conditioning ("It's Time to Get Your Furnace Serviced!"), Hannibal Testing Laboratories Inc., and Bates Bearing and Transmission Co. In this setting, Children's Station seemed to fit right in: a spot where busy parents could drop off the spare parts.

The mood of industrial bleakness receded, though, as soon as I pressed the buzzer beside the locked, glass-windowed front doors. Someone materialized almost at once: a striking woman in efficient makeup and a cheerfully colored pantsuit, her blonde hair cut in a practical shag. She had a cell phone pressed to her ear. Without hesitation, though I was a complete stranger, she pressed the release button and let me inside, not missing a beat of her conversation.

Her name was Jill Whitaker and she ran the Children's Station.

Without interrupting her phone conversation, she took in the purpose of my visit, agreed to an interview, and led me down a hall raucous with children's voices and decorated with cartoon cutouts of clowns and animals ("Only Positive Attitudes Allowed Beyond This Point!" a cardboard sign warned). Seated at her desk in her small office, surrounded by balloons, ribbons, more color cartoons, and an ambience of pinkness, Jill Whitaker finally clicked off the phone and turned her full attention on me.

"I always laugh, 'cause I got to take my vitamins every day," she replied when I asked her how she managed to focus on any one thing. "But it's the love of kids that keeps me goin'. I have a staff here, but runnin' the place is pretty much a one-woman show."

Children's Station had been around for fourteen years in Hannibal, the last six of them at its present location. Jill Whitaker had been involved with it for ten years. The center's license provided for the care of 89 children at one time. Its total clientele just then was 113.

"Our mission when we started was to provide child care for working parents," Whitaker told me. "But now lately we see a lot of single moms. They're either going to school or working. We get into scheduling dilemmas when it's not just a nine-to-five job, but different hours—evenings, weekends, whatever. But most of the kids that we have here, their parents are working. Both parents. That total number, one hundred thirteen, takes in kids that come before school, like from six A.M. to eight A.M., and kids that come after a full day of school, three-thirty to six P.M."

Why, I asked her, would a child come to the Station from six to eight in the morning?

"The parents have to be at work like at seven or seven-thirty," Whitaker answered. "They live out in the country. Or they don't want to leave the children by themselves. They come here till eight, then the school bus picks 'em up and takes 'em to school, and drops 'em off here again at three-thirty in the afternoon."

Children's Station was conceived as a community-volunteer effort—to provide a day-care facility for parents who were not necessarily affiliated with a church. A practicing Christian herself, Jill Whitaker signed on because she felt that the local churches' centers were not reaching everyone who needed help.

"We're probably unique because from the beginning, up until

about four years ago, we served the handicapped and disabled population," she told me. "We had a preschool program for that. But now the schools run that program.

"And we've always kind of veered toward, you know, the lower socioeconomic class, because they don't have the ways and means. I right now have twenty-one kids who are funded through the Department of Family Services. The state pays for them to be here."

And the other kids, the families pay the full freight? I asked.

Jill Whitaker hesitated a moment before responding with a measured, "Mmm hmm. Sixty-five bucks a week for a preschooler, eighty-five a week for an infant-toddler."

Something told me that those payments did not always get made. Does that budget allow you to do what you want to do? I asked.

"Well," she admitted, "it's always nip and tuck every month. If we break even we're happy. And usually we don't." A phone rang down the hall and Jill Whitaker craned her neck toward a volunteer near her office door: "Can you git that, Grandma? Thanks!" She beamed at me. "My grandmas are wonderful," she said. "They instill manners, politeness, respect your elders . . ."

What happens when you don't break even? I wanted to know.

Whitaker's cheery smile went a little flat. "We hope that next month it evens out.

"It's expensive," she added after a moment or so. "We have a staff of eighteen. But then, you're in Hannibal, so you cannot charge what needs to be charged, because people can't afford it."

A nonprofit operation, the Station operated on fees, bank loans, and an occasional donation. "We don't get much support from business groups," Whitaker acknowledged. "We used to be able to go to United Way, as long as we had the handicapped program, and they always would give us some money. But after we had to stop that program, they didn't—well, it was more or less said, quote unquote, 'We don't want to step on other day cares' toes.' "

Exactly which day cares' toes, Jill Whitaker was too tactful to stipulate. But she went on, with more passion than she had shown up until then: "But we're not *like* other day cares. We are not-for-profit, we are not church affiliated. We embody Christian values. You know, we do unto others, and we teach values and stuff like that. But we just are not a church denomination. We always make it a point to serve everyone. We don't turn anyone away."

I asked Jill Whitaker what kind of stresses she observed in her young clientele that indicated the realities of their family lives.

"They are not, typically, with their families," was her instant response. I heard indignation in her voice. "We *are* their family. An average day for my kids is ten or eleven hours here. Five days a week. And if we were open on the weekends, they'd be here then too. I've had some kids up to six, seven years. Parents wonder why they cry when they come to pick them up. To them, we are their family."

How young do you get them? I asked her. Jill Whitaker lifted her shoulders in a sigh before replying. "We had one as young as two days old," she said. "It was a single mom, nursing school. She had no choice."

Jill Whitaker read the surprise in my face. "The kids love it here," she assured me, as if I might draw some Dickensian implications from this. "You know, the parents can't always help it. Everyone is so busy. Myself included. You just—everyone's trying to make the extra buck, make ends meet." She shook her head. "It's even my professional parents. Those are the ones whose kids are here the longest. Those are my engineers, the degree people. I've noticed through the years that my lower socioeconomic parents—they are the ones that leave work as soon as they can and come right here to pick their kids up. The other ones, the degree people, they'll go to the Y, they'll work out, they'll go do their little extracurricular thing, and then they'll pick the kids up, about five-thirty or six. You'll hear 'em: 'C'mon, guys, hurry. Gotta do this. Gotta do that.' And then, the children are in bed by nine-thirty or ten. Of *course* they're not keepin' up as a family."

The fact was that I had picked up a Dickensian whiff. The Children's Station was beginning to sound a little like a proto-orphanage. I asked Jill Whitaker about the effects on the younger children of these prolonged stints outside a family's care.

"It's real funny," she replied. "I mean I think all my kids are good kids, but after they've been home, it always takes like all of Monday to get 'em back in the routine. And then part of Tuesday. And then the rest of the week is wonderful. And then we always laugh and say,

'Well, it's Friday, here we go again; we'll start all over on Monday.' 'Cause it's just like two different worlds. I don't think—in fact I know—that in most of their homes there's no routine, there's no structure, there's no following through with discipline or anything. You can just see it. The parents will come to me and say, 'They won't go to bed. You know, we have trouble with 'em goin' to bed every night. We put them in bed, kiss 'em good night, tell 'em to say their prayers and that we'll see 'em in the morning. But they'll cry.' "

Jill Whitaker shook her head and widened her blue eyes. "Well, yeah, they're *gonna* cry. I have parents calling me at home—and you know, the funny thing is, I don't have children. I have two stepchildren, but their father and I have only been together four years. But these parents are *clueless*. You know, they think they have this—I don't know what, this experiment they don't know what to do with. It's just that the basic parenting skills are not there."

Before I left, Whitaker led me on a brief tour of the Station. I saw playrooms, art and activities areas, and the small kitchen with several chipper "grandmas" at their pots and pans. A sight I recalled quite vividly, afterward, was the nursery room: cribs lined up in rows, their slatted sides pulled up, with several very small inhabitants asleep inside them.

But the nursery room was not the most arresting image I took away with me from the Children's Station. That distinction belonged to my last glimpse of Jill Whitaker as we waved good-bye. On the other side of the locked, glassed front doors, she was talking again into her cell phone. I could not hear the conversation, but something told me that it was not an especially encouraging one.

• • •

THAT AFTERNOON I went to look at the feral children.

The feral children were kept in a wing on an upper floor of the former St. Elizabeth's Hospital, near the center of residential Hannibal. The squarish redbrick building, erected in 1915 by the Sisters of St. Francis on what had been a small dairy farm, had long since been overtaken by neighborhoods and had long since ceased being a hospital. (Its replacement, Hannibal Regional Hospital, where Jim Walker had first been rushed, lay a mile or so beyond the expanding western rim of town, on something called Clinic Road just off Highway 36.) I carried strong memories of St. Elizabeth's. I'd been admitted there at least twice as a boy—once to have my tonsils removed, when a terrifying nun in a flowing black habit swooped down on me, clutching a pre-ether bottle of orange soda pop, and again as a fourteen-year-old, when I accidentally kicked my right foot into the rotary blades of the lawn mower I was using on a neighbor's lawn. I'd left two badly mangled toes in an operating room somewhere inside St. Elizabeth's. I felt a certain attachment, as it were, to the place.

The feral children in a sense represented the next-higher age group of displacement above the kids of Children's Station. They were not necessarily Station alums, of course, and they were not called "feral children," not officially. They were "disruptive" or "abusive" or "violent"—or had been so designated by the Hannibal public school system. As their behavior had "exhausted" the schools' capacity for disciplinary action, they had been removed from the school premises and redirected to a ward in this half-empty institutional building, where they pursued such curricula as "contemporary living" under the supervision of clinically trained social workers. The official name for their place of sequestering was the Alternative School. The implied "alternative" was long-term suspension or expulsion, with a loss of credits. Or jail.

Robie Wilson had spent time in the Alternative School.

The school had opened about a year earlier, one of about 150 such emerging facilities in Missouri's 525 school districts. Funding came from a grab bag of state grants linked with the Department of Education and the Division of Youth Services. The facility accommodated an average of thirty-eight students in a given semester, twenty-four at any one time. Some kids came for half a day, while others were involved in school-to-work programs. Since its opening, it had produced three graduates. One had joined the marines. The other two had moved out of town.

I had wanted to visit this place since I'd first heard about it, shortly after arriving in Hannibal, although I had my trepidations. "Disruptive" and "violent" were not the kind of adolescents I looked forward to hanging around with, even in a controlled setting. I was braced for an atmosphere of hard stares, complicated razorings of the hair, tattoos, body piercings, big muscles, and tight leather. But I wanted to see them. Maybe they would lead me to a way of comprehending the inevitability of Robie and Zach.

St. Elizabeth's had changed surprisingly little from my boyhood. Its space had been subdivided down from an integrated hospital to a series of social-service warrens. But once past the glass security doors, I was struck by how intensely I remembered the geometric patterns on the linoleum floors and recognized, at least in my imagination, a familiar old whiff of disinfectant. I recognized a few familiar recesses carved into the pink plaster walls of the lobby: alcoves into which the nuns of the early postwar years had placed vases of bright flowers.

St. Elizabeth's had nearly made it to the century's end as a community hospital. In 1973 it had enjoyed its fifth and last enlargement, a six-story, $2 million new addition that increased its capacity to 173 beds. But in 1993 it had yielded its function to the new Regional Hospital west of town. Its rise and decline thus reflected the shifting self-identity of the town. Now, as a catch-all hive of service agencies, it was known by the leaden designation, Hannibal Regional Office Center, and more commonly by its jagged diminutive, H-Roc.

Michael Richardson greeted me off the ancient caged elevator in H-Roc's North Wing. A thoughtful-looking man in a trimmed salt-and-pepper goatee, dark-rimmed glasses, and a green knit shirt, he was a clinical psychologist who administrated the Alternative School. (His wife, Teresa, also a psychologist, was director of the state-run Mental Health Center, with offices downtown.) It was Richardson who had used the term "feral children" in a phone chat a few days earlier. He'd acknowledged that his staff's teaching obligations went to levels far more basic than the officially designated ones, such as cooking, balancing a checkbook, managing money, and "job preparation."

"These kids are 'feral' in the sense that they have essentially raised themselves," he'd told me. "They've had very little exposure to civilizing norms. They've come from homes so broken that no one has bothered to teach them how to control their emotions, much less etiquette or manners. They have suffered incredible abuse. They are among the most abject victims you're ever going to meet."

Now, as we walked toward the Alternative School's quarters—a converted emergency room—Richardson filled me in a little on his personal history. "My real job is as a substance abuse counselor," he told me. He'd taken his counseling degree in Maine in the late 70s and arrived in Hannibal in 1980, met and married Teresa, and now served in a variety of counseling capacities around town.

Inside the school's cubicle of an office space, as I kept a wary lookout for the first sign of a menacing feral child, Richardson sketched out the brief history of the project. "It was created by the Missouri Safe School Act of 1996," he said. "That was a legislative response to violence in the public schools. Supposedly, separating the really violent ones would make schools safer for other kids." He sighed. "We used to scold kids who were acting up," he said. "Now we call the police and haul them away."

Does that mean you don't think this school is a fair response? I asked him.

Richardson raised his dark eyebrows and spread his hands. "We're helping them survive," he said. "Look, the term 'disruption' has taken on a whole new meaning. These kids are so alienated that fairness is no longer even a concern. Their way of communicating with their teachers is to say, 'Fuck you.' You slap them, and their response is instantaneous and escalated. Their attitude is, 'You hit me and I'm going to take your head off.'

"Their anger is incredible. Everyone in their entire lives has done them harm, or at least they perceive it that way. And it's usually true. Their parents have harmed them, the schools have harmed them, the police, the courts—everybody. A lot of them have been on methamphetamines, which is an anger *potion*. Missouri currently leads the nation in the number of meth labs out there. I'm talking total numbers, not per capita. We even surpass California.

"These kids have no home life, so they do their meth and hang out on the streets together. There's a dairy on the south side where you can see them every day, every night."

That accounts for the boys, I remarked to Richardson. What about the girls?

His answer was inflectionless. "Ninety percent of our female substance-abuse population here has been sexually abused at home. It's so bad that Jerry Springer once did a show with people from here. A mom and her thirteen-year-old daughter were said to be having an affair with the same man."

Courting rituals in the Home Town had intensified since Tom Sawyer did handstands for Becky Thatcher. For some reason I thought of an old wooden sign posted near the entrance to the Mark Twain Cave two miles south of town, a sign that had been erected who knew when and had existed into my own adolescence. "No Spooning," it had warned, in blocky, wood-burnt script—whether seriously or ironically my friends and I were never quite able to figure out. Some of us were low-down enough to consider carving a little addendum to the sign: "And No Forking, Either." But we weren't quite low-down enough actually to do it. Eventually the sign was replaced by that larger addendum, the souvenir shop attached to the cave's entrance.

I told Richardson that I guessed I was ready to meet the feral children.

He arose and walked through a door into a larger room beyond his office. I stood up too, the better to fend off some escalation of anger, if nothing else.

But when Michael Richardson returned, he led a procession of ten or eleven creatures whose appearance baffled any possible expectation I could have conjured. Far from being heavy, buffed, and menacing, they seemed almost translucent. They reminded me of nothing so much as the emergence of the thin, glowing, large-headed aliens from the giant spacecraft in the final minutes of *Close Encounters of the Third Kind*.

The feral children—pale, small, thin, and dreamy looking—filed past me and obediently held their hands out for a shake, each in turn. When that was done, they stood motionless or took seats in Richardson's small office and looked at me in the most solemn silence I could recall experiencing. I found that it was difficult to return their gaze. I'd come prepared with a few questions to ask them, but in the lingering shock of their abjectness, any attempt at conversation seemed profane. There was nothing to ask of them. Nothing to say.

"After breakfast they went whooping and prancing out on the [sand]bar, and chased each other round and round," Mark Twain had written of the wild children of his Hannibal memories, "shedding clothes as they went, until they were naked, and then continued the frolic far away up the shoal water of the bar, against the stiff current, which later tripped their legs from under them . . . and greatly increased the fun." But even as they plan their exotic murders and abductions on their river island, and eat turtle eggs, and depend on rattlesnake bracelets to ward off evil, these youthful hellions are never far from the call of home. "O, boys, let's give it up," moans Joe Harper as the afternoon lengthens, "I want to go home. It's so lonesome."

The difference between Joe Harper and the thin kids sitting motionless around me was that they had no home to go to. An address, perhaps. But no home.

The silence in the room drew out for a few minutes, and then I managed something about having to get going. At Richardson's nod, the children stood and filed silently through the door and into wherever it was that they passed their time in the Alternative School.

When Richardson reemerged, his thoughtful detachment had given way to something hotter. "They wouldn't have known to shake hands with you if I hadn't told them to in there," he said, reseating himself. He shook his head. "I teach them to brush their teeth. Wash their clothes. Seventy percent of them are addicted to drugs. Am I helping them? Is justice being done here?" Again, he shrugged.

"The taxpayers are happy to have 'em here. Costs 'em seven thousand a year per kid, and I can give these kids personal counseling for a hellava lot less, but people think: At least they're off the street. The Alternative School came out of the Governor Ashcroft administration, and our current governor, Mel Carnahan, followed suit. It's a response to what people believe, what they want.

"People are afraid of their own kids. They're afraid of their neighbors' kids. But is anybody out there trying to solve the problem? The people in the neighborhoods?" He thought about it. "Well, I guess they're trying. But it's hard to get going. At some point, people think, Well, it's a problem, but it's not my problem. And this whole grassroots idea, which is wonderful in theory, it just keeps butting up against institutions. Institutions are not going to solve this problem. It's personal."

I asked him what he meant by that.

"A few days ago a young man showed up here with a bruise over his eye," Richardson said. "He told me he and his uncle had been horsing around, and they kind of got into a fight, and then his dad got mad and hit him.

"Now, I'm mandated, when something like this happens, to call the Department of Family Services. Their one eight hundred number.

So I did, and this caseworker shows up, visits the family, and now the family's torqued off at me. They won't talk to me anymore.

"And then last Tuesday, the uncle—a twenty-two-year-old man— was killed. Got run over by a boxcar on the railroad tracks. So I call the young man to try and console him, and he hangs up. Won't talk. Doesn't trust me. So I can't counsel him.

"The public schools aren't helping these kids. Schools are inherently enclosed institutions, which is what the kids don't need. And they're getting more insular, more closed off every year—more procedure-driven, more responsive to lawyers, more control-freakish. It's just about inevitable that these kids get alienated. Any kid, but especially these. They're pushed around, then they're pushed out, and they feel they have absolutely no control over any facet of their lives. And we wonder why they're so angry."

I asked Richardson whether he thought the Hannibal school system had any particular skills in dealing with deeply alienated children.

"This is one of the more rigid school systems I've ever seen," he replied. "I know of no other system outside Missouri where teachers and administrators are still allowed to use corporal punishment. They do here, despite not one iota of evidence that says it works. It just adds to the humiliation, the sense of being put down, the feeling that the teachers are against them.

"And eventually they will end up in this place here, or at the Department of Family Services, or in jail. DFS is well intentioned, don't get me wrong. But it can't fix what's broken. We have DFS handling more complaint calls this year than last year. But is that a success or a failure? In bureaucratic terms, of course, it's a success. Bureaucracies are geared to function toward their own survival. It's easy for them to lose a sense of what it was they were originally set up to do. Which in this case is save families. They can't save families, ultimately. But we're looking at a culture that is growing further and further apart from any basic understanding of how to raise its children. I have a group of batterers that meets on Tuesday nights . . ." His voice trailed off.

We sat there for a couple of minutes, and then I said again—meaning it this time—about having to get going.

At the elevator, Michael Richardson cocked an eye at me. "You know who's the biggest new employer in this whole area of northeast

Missouri? New in the past year? The prisons. We have two new ones—the one at Vandalia for women and the one at Bowling Green for men, with a wing for boys. This is our big business boom: nine dollars an hour to be a prison guard."

I drove away from the old St. Elizabeth's—now H-Roc—with a completely new and utterly chilling vision of Hannibal taking shape in my mind: a kind of cultural battlefield, on which the forces of something that used to define me, and still did, had been routed, and on which, amid the smoke and debris, social-service agencies had sprouted like Red Cross stations, trying in vain to teach the survivors how to be functioning members of a community.

· 10 ·

FAMILY SERVICES

Pap Finn would not have cared much for the Children's Station, or the Alternative School, or any of the other agencies that existed in modern-day Hannibal to improve the lot of children on the edge. "Who told you you might meddle with such hifalut'n foolishness, hey?" he demands of his son when he gets wind that the boy has learned to read and write. When Huckleberry answers that it was the charitable Widow Douglas who'd put him in a school, Pap comes unhinged. "I'll lay for you, my smarty; and if I catch you about that school I'll tan you good. First you know you'll get religion, too. I never see such a son." Later, Huck explains, Judge Thatcher and the Widow "went to law to get the court to take me away from him and let one of them be my guardian." But the "new judge" who had just arrived in town "said courts mustn't interfere and separate families if they could help it; said he'd druther not take a child away from its father. So Judge Thatcher and the widow had to quit on the business." Later still, the widow discovers where Pap has locked Huck in a log hut on the Illinois side of the Mississippi while he "traded fish and game for whisky and fetched it home and got drunk and had a good time, and licked me." She sends a man to try and rescue the boy, "but pap drove him off with a gun, and it warn't long after that till I was used to being where I was, and liked it, all but the cowhide part."

A hundred thirteen years after publication of Huck's book, local attitudes toward do-good meddling in a child's plight had not changed all that much.

If a troubled or unwanted Hannibal child managed to avoid long stretches in day care and consignment to the Alternative School, there remained one final possibility (besides conviction of a crime and criminal incarceration) for separation from the daily world of family and community. This was the enforced removal from the household by the Department of Family Services. DFS was an option cherished by exactly no one, as far as I was able to tell, including the administrators and caseworkers for the agency itself. In fact, of the many varieties of social alienation I encountered in Hannibal, none matched the virulence of the alienation nursed by afflicted families toward DFS and other social-service agencies that had been designed to help them.

To such families, DFS's powerful imposed statutory "services" amounted to nothing more than a textbook demonstration of Pap's hated "govment" gone amok. DFS, to them, was a bureaucratic predator that snatched people's kids and taxpayers' money.

Neither Robie nor Zachary had ever attracted the concern of a DFS caseworker—a fluke of probability, given that each had spent a good deal of his childhood away from the direct supervision of parents or stepparents, and that each had gained a certain reputation for waywardness. But Hannibal is a small town, and in my searches for people who might have known the boys, I stumbled across a family that epitomized the broiling fury that DFS could expect almost any time its fieldworkers telephoned a troubled household, or knocked on a household door.

Butch and Kitral Chaplin, when I visited their carefully waxed and polished rural home in the rolling countryside several miles south of town, were still seething from what they viewed as a nightmarish battle with DFS, waged the previous summer. The agency had seized their fifteen-year-old daughter Abbey after the girl had run into trouble on a church outing.

The Chaplins had waved good-bye to Abbey one June morning as she left on a trip to the Mall of America in St. Paul. The trip was organized by Tabernacle of Praise, an Assembly of God church whose large youth program was frequented by, among others, Robie and Zachary Wilson. The chaperones were the youth pastor, Kevin Blase, and his wife, Lynne.

Abbey's sojourn extended well beyond the mall. Within a week, she was a ward of the state of Missouri. Arrested on a shoplifting charge at an Abercrombie & Fitch outlet in the mall, Abbey had returned home with her parents, who drove to Minnesota to pick her up. A few days later, in the midst of negotiations with local DFS agents over how best to deal with Abbey's behavior, Kitral Chaplin answered her doorbell and was horrified to find a clutch of men and women seeking entry to her house. Among them were a county deputy sheriff, a highway patrolman, a juvenile deputy officer, a woman from DFS, and a man and woman whose identity she never learned. The juvenile officer produced court papers authorizing him to remove Abbey from her parents' custody.

The authorities escorted Abbey out of the house and shipped her to a center specializing in the treatment of emotional and behavioral disorders in Columbia, nearly one hundred miles away, then transferred her to a foster home on the outskirts of Hannibal. Over the next several weeks, DFS caseworkers repeatedly interviewed and evaluated Abbey and placed her on prescription drugs as the Chaplins scrambled frantically for the legal means to regain custody of their daughter.

The interventionist power of the Department of Family Services was itself a function of the anxiety that swirled about the well-being of children in the aftershocks of America's social revolution. DFS had been created in 1974 as a branch of the new Missouri Department of Social Services, a $3-billion-a-year retooling of the old Department of Welfare. Similar shakeouts were happening in every state. The activism that had transformed civil rights, women's rights, and the prosecution of the Vietnam War now turned its energies to the eradication of domestic pathologies both real and imagined. Near the top of this list was child abuse, which by some accounts had reached epidemic proportions. Accounts of a "battered child syndrome," popularized by books and media coverage, inspired a national wave of abuse and neglect reporting laws. (In the mid-sixties, no American state had such a law. Within twenty years every state had one. And the number of children placed in foster-care homes for reasons of abuse and neglect had vaulted from 75,000 to 300,000.) To facilitate these complaints, state government agencies demanded and received bigger operating budgets and reorganized themselves for direct action.

In Missouri, the new Department of Social Services continued to perform its original welfare functions: awarding public assistance to needy people and families, offering rehabilitation services for the blind and shelter for the elderly. But to discharge its new powers of enforcing relations between parents and their young, the legislature created a subbranch called the Department of Family Services. Although its stated mission was to provide prevention and treatment programs for needy families, DFS came ever more to be perceived collectively as the people who knocked on the front door and demanded the handover of children.

A retired social-service caseworker of twenty-seven years' experience in Hannibal recalled the priority shift quite vividly. "After the reorganization, DFS became essentially a twenty-four-hour abuse-neglect investigative agency," he acknowledged. "We were more and more in contact with families based on allegations they had mistreated their children. Many of those reports were found unsubstantiated. But the policies of Family Services required immediate, within-twenty-four-hour contact with the family. And just the nature of that contact contained an adversarial sort of overtone. We were out knocking on people's doors saying, 'We've received a report that you've hit your child with a belt.' And because there really was no screening possible in terms of the legitimacy of the report, we had pretty discretionary power to award that child to someone with care-taking responsibility. In fact that became acceptable investigative practice. And it created a tremendous amount of resentment."

"Resentment" was a word so inadequate to Butch and Kitral Chaplin's emotions as to seem a part of another language system. ("Pure evil," was Butch's phrase of choice for the department and everyone he'd dealt with in it.) By the time they had regained custody of their daughter late in the summer, the two of them had tapped deeply into a loosely affiliated national network of right-wing anti–"family services" groups and individuals, a force that in many ways matched the energies of the leftist sixties advocates themselves.

Abbey Chaplin did not easily vindicate either side's position in this deep schism. Certain particulars of her emotional development, as volunteered by her parents themselves, suggest the complexities of deciding when a government agency should and should not intervene to separate a child from her family. If DFS's attempts to protect Abbey were heavy-handed and perhaps excessive, they were hardly without foundation. In her brief years of adolescence, Abbey had already acted out a range of symptoms that strongly indicated a troubled girl. And her home environment was not completely beyond reproach. Butch Chaplin, a large, barrel-chested man with a ringing voice that he always seemed to be struggling to hold in restraint, had, by his own admission "an overwhelming and dominant personality. Very abrasive." A "time line" kept by Kitral of Abbey's DFS ordeal alluded twice to "an incident down at the bank" about eight years earlier, a confrontation that had raised questions as to whether Butch had been armed with a gun. Butch denied to me that a gun was involved.

Butch described himself as a self-taught exporter of hardwood logs to markets in Japan, "sourcing" them via telephone and computer contacts from Missouri, New England, and the far West.

Butch and Kitral had met in the mid-seventies when Kitral—a small, tidy, dark-haired woman—was waitressing at the Mark Twain Dinette. "He was working across the street at the gas station," Kitral recalled of their first encounter. "He came over to get something to eat."

In the first years after their marriage, the Chaplins lived in Hannibal. But like many American families with the means to do so, they gradually sought insularity. They left their neighborhood to live in the sparsely settled Ralls County south of Hannibal, first renting their quarters, then building a handsome brick ranch-style house and detached office that commanded a sparsely traveled gravel road in the semiforested backcountry. Abbey thus reached her teen years in a place several miles removed from any of her friends. Shortly before her high school years, her parents removed her from public education in the small town of New London and began to home-school her.

"We started noticing behavioral things going on with Abbey when she started going through puberty, about 1996," Kitral Chaplin acknowledged to me. "She was like thirteen. She was getting into the style, I mean really into the style, the fashions, of today. The Tommy Hilfiger clothing, the Calvin Klein."

"Right off the streets of downtown Manhattan," put in Butch. "Right to the very edge of the classics. I mean, the black cocktail dress, the stiletto heels. She loves all of that." These affectations, Butch mused, were an abrupt transition from Abbey's "vanilla" childhood: Barbie dolls, armloads of books from the library, poetry writing. "She was not given to anything unbalanced, up to that point." Kitral agreed, but she chose a subtly different emphasis for her memory of the younger Abbey. "She wasn't real vocal as a little girl," the mother mused.

The Chaplins' time line conceded that there had been some other disturbing behavior shifts as well: depression, episodes of bulimia, disobedience, and a suicide attempt the previous October.

As to the sources of these problems, the Chaplins had some pretty good ideas. One source was a murky set of doings in Abbey's classroom in the Ralls County public-school system, a set of doings that, to the Chaplins' alert senses, smelled of questionable morals, smelled, in fact, of witchcraft.

"We had felt that, you know, God had given us this kid that we had," Butch explained, "and that we're responsible for her, and then we send her to school eight hours a day, and we don't know what she's bein' told, we don't know the morals she's bein' taught, and just a lot of things along that level. And then over the summertime one year, I'd heard that they had brought in a new reading curriculum. And that it was very controversial as far as witchcraft being entered in."

The Chaplins' suspicions were backed up—not by close friends and neighbors, of which there were none, but by a figure from the surrogate community of media.

"I don't know if you know Dr. James Dobson," Kitral said, naming the ultra-right-wing Christian activist, radio broadcaster, and founder of the Christian-right organization Focus on Family. "He had mentioned this reading program, and I heard him talk about this reading program, and then after that, I heard that our school had brought in a new reading program. So I called one of the teachers to ask her what the name of it was, and unfortunately it was the same reading curriculum that Dr. Dobson had just talked about."

One of the things that Kitral was horrified to hear, she said, "was that in the classroom setting they would sit in a *circle*, and they would have the teacher hold a candle. And all the kids were to watch the candle, and she would tell them to watch the candle and to drift off—"

"*Transport!*" Butch interjected.

"To transport—" Kitral resumed.

"*With their friend!*"

"Of course, she didn't use that word—"

"They was supposed to conjure up their mythical *friend!*" Butch fairly shouted. "That they privately have, and transport to—wherever!"

"Then," said Kitral, "when the teacher would get through with her story or whatever she was going to present to the kids that day, then she would blow out the candle, and then it was time for everybody to come back to their bodies."

Kitral paid a visit to the school principal to express her concern about this practice. The principal, apparently, failed to appreciate the crisis through the same lens as the Chaplins. "He said, 'I can tell you that my teachers will never do anything like this because I will make sure that they don't.' But I said, 'Well, how can you monitor six classrooms?' He said, 'I can assure you that they're not gonna do that. Thank you *very much* for bringing this to my attention!'

"That," said Kitral, "was the—"

"Straw that broke the camel's back," finished Butch.

Abbey was removed from public school.

(Months later, I contacted some present and former teachers in the Ralls County system. None could imagine what Kitral and Butch had been talking about in those pre–Harry Potter days. One recalled a Canadian-based series of children's stories that featured a frog casting a magic spell. Another observed that teachers occasionally conducted relaxation exercises that might involve sitting in a circle and envisioning a safe place, such as a pond or a forest. To a person, none of the teachers could imagine themselves or their colleagues employing a prop as controversial—as potentially career ending—as a lighted candle.)

I was surprised to learn, considering these rather emphatic citations of God and the Christian faith as underpinnings of their vigilance against idolatry in the classroom, that the Chaplins had no strong affiliation with a church. Kitral had been "brought up in the Baptist denomination most of my life." As for Butch, "No one on either side of my parents' families, in either direction, through either family tree, has ever been any sort of religious or aware of their spiritual state for five, six, several generations." Yet Kitral, who'd had no experience as a teacher, steered Abbey into her home-school regimen with the serene conviction that a divine light would lead her.

"I felt like if that was something I was gonna be doing, then God would show me that that was something that I needed to do and a direct way to go," she said.

I was further surprised to learn, given this confidence in the Christian light, that the Chaplins named, as the second major source of Abbey's emotional crisis, the Tabernacle of Praise.

"That was very disturbing to me as I look back on it now," Kitral told me, "because I thought she was in a good place. Tabernacle of Praise had a large youth group. Abbey wanted to go there. But through this youth group we have honestly had nothing but trouble."

As examples of "trouble," the Chaplins cited the Wilson boys. "They were part of the group," Kitral said. Hard feelings surfaced about a stereo stolen from the car of Abbey's older brother Trent. The Chaplins suspected the Wilsons: "One of the boys approached my cousin's daughter and wanted to sell it to her. And she said, 'Is this Trent's stuff?' And he backed off and, you know, started talkin' about something else."

The problem with the tabernacle, in short, was that it tended to attract sinners, or at least potential sinners.

"I really think that these kids were just there because of the happening thing, and the place to be," said Kitral carefully. "I don't know that it was Lynne and Kevin Blase's intention to just have it be the happening place to be, because I believe that they wanted to teach spirituality to the adolescents. But *they* weren't there for that. The kids—"

"Part soda shop, part pool hall," interjected Butch. After a minute, he confided that it might have been even worse than that. "I noticed a gradual, it seemed to me like, gravitation by Abbey toward a looser, darker something. A deep-seated, at this point uncorrectable personality and attitude change, combined with a cocktail of adolescence and immaturity. And I was like, *keep aware* of this, *monitor* it, watch it and be on guard and not be surprised at what's going on. And I definitely was not surprised at any of it."

The Chaplins were surprised, however, to learn that their daughter had been arrested for shoplifting at the Mall of America.

Kitral Chaplin kept a minutely detailed log, which she called a time line, of the travails that ensued. In the months following the family's ordeal, she and Butch pressed the document on newspaper editors, lawyers, law-enforcement officials, and others whom they hoped would sympathize and somehow lend support to their grievance against the Department of Family Services. A "Dear Friend" preface to the time line read, in part: "Please pray for us to have strength to endure this battle. Also, please pray that things like this will never be inflicted on other people. Today it is us, tomorrow it could be you. This is a tragedy and has taken every waking hour for us to fight this. This country is in peril because freedom, liberty, and the pursuit of happiness is not present anymore."

Alerted by Abbey's obvious state of near-hysteria following her arrest ("Abbey had told me not to bother to come and get her," Kitral's log read, "that she would either be dead or in the hospital. Lynne said she would sleep with her, and watch her continuously"), the Chaplins sought a treatment center for their daughter even before they began the return trip home. Kitral learned of a "Christ-centered program" in Columbia, Missouri, called the Rapha Center—a branch, actually, of a nationwide chain that advertised "medically and biblically-based treatment programs" for people in crisis. The couple reserved a bed and brought Abbey directly there, arriving off the road from Minnesota at midnight on Thursday, June 18, 1998: "Abbey was assessed and met criteria for an inpatient stay."

Conflicts began almost immediately. From their home the next morning, Butch and Kitral found themselves in a telephone argument with a staff doctor who asked permission to place Abbey on the antidepressant drug Prozac. The Chaplins resisted, asking instead for the nonprescriptive herbal remedy Saint-John's-wort. The staff doctor stood fast, warning that treatment would be withheld if the parents did not comply. The weekend began with an edgy standoff between the family and the center.

Partly to distract herself from her anxiety, Kitral threw herself into housework. No solace there. Part of her log for Saturday read as follows: "I found Abbey's journals while cleaning her room. Devastating information within them."

Monday brought yet a new crisis. It seemed that the Chaplins had misread the terms of the $2,500 fee they had paid to the center upon Abbey's admission. Butch had understood that it would cover a stay of five to seven days. Now, someone in the business office was telling him that that payment had been merely a "deposit," and that the family now owed an additional $2,285.

Things accelerated at this point into a kind of manic series of cross-country showdowns. The Chaplins hit the road for Columbia and arrived around nine P.M., intent on retrieving their daughter. They encountered a nurse, who soothed them with the news that the center would "really like" to keep Abbey, would like to keep her so much that they'd be willing to waive the additional fee. The Chaplins were mollified and drove home. But they were back the next day, after another center operative told them by phone that the inpatient billing would click in again at midnight.

More frustrations awaited them. Abbey herself said she did not want to come home. Butch informed her that she had no choice. But then he found himself face-to-face with the staff doctor who had insisted on Prozac for the young girl. "[The doctor] said it was against medical opinion to release Abbey," Kitral later wrote. Butch, whose outrage was soaring, declared that Abbey was going home anyway. The staff doctor, according to Kitral's journal, responded, "If you take Abbey out of here, I will call the DFS Hotline." Butch stormed out of the center. He returned with a Columbia policeman in tow. Things settled down a little after that; the Chaplins signed a release-of-information form with the center and returned to their Ralls County home with their daughter. And then the serious trouble began. A DFS caseworker was on the phone the following morning, summoning the parents to a meeting by noon.

The department itself refused, as a matter of policy, to comment on what transpired at that meeting, or on any other aspect of the Chaplins' case. Kitral's time line showed no such restraint. It depicted a caseworker bristling with reprimands directed at Kitral and her husband over their past handling of Abbey's problems—reprimands apparently based on the girl's version of these events. The caseworker extracted a promise from the Chaplins to obtain a psychiatric assessment of Abbey.

Kitral Chaplin claimed that by the end of the day, she and Butch had agreed to accept a therapist's suggestion that they petition for ward-of-the-court status for Abbey as a means of securing state funding for her therapeutic care. "Butch must have reiterated that at least three times," she wrote in her log. But by then an irreversible momentum had overwhelmed all negotiations.

It was the following afternoon—Thursday, June 25—that the DFS caseworker, flanked by the highway patrolman, the deputy sheriff, the juvenile officer, and the two unidentified people, knocked on the door of the Chaplins' home and departed with Abbey in tow.

The next three weeks amounted to a pitched battle between the Chaplins and DFS. Kitral's time line became a dense compendium of affronts suffered, threats exchanged, calls made, letters written, experts sought out, muscles flexed. Butch vented his anger to the Ralls County sheriff's department. The DFS caseworker announced that Abbey was receiving both group and individual therapy, which she manifestly needed. Kitral reported her outrage that it had taken five days for her daughter to receive some clothes Kitral had sent off. Kitral petitioned to speak to Abbey by phone; the caseworker responded, Kitral's time line entry reported, that "there was nothing in the file about Abbey being able to talk to us." Finally the caseworker relented. The Chaplins were indignant to discover that a continuance hearing had been held without them. The caseworker complained that the Chaplins had passed up a continuance hearing. Much was made on either side regarding which interested parties "knew" one another apart from the case.

On July 7, DFS placed Abbey in a foster home. Kitral telephoned DFS to find out where her daughter was and "got cut off." More calls, more negotiations to get Abbey back home. A meeting was held, with many attendees. Rules and conditions (medications and therapy) were presented and agreed upon. An agreement-signing meeting was scheduled; attended. The agreement went unsigned. "We were compliant with all the terms . . . except the one that stated, 'We as parents of Abbey neglected or refused treatment,'" Kitral noted in her time line.

But there was another unacceptable request as well. A DFS agent pressed for Abbey to be returned to public school. This was out of the question for the Chaplins. Agreeing to it would have required them to release their daughter once again, at least for part of each day, into the treacherous precincts of community. Never mind that twentieth-century behavioral science fairly rang with insistence on participation in group life as indispensable to the construction of the childhood self and mind. This is not where the Chaplins were coming from—nor a vast, withdrawing portion of the American public, for that matter.

"Social interaction," Kitral maintained, "is where we have had a problem with Abbey."

And so yet another hearing was set. And the tension mounted again.

By this time, Butch Chaplin was going around to churches in a ten- or fifteen-mile radius of Hannibal, handing out drafts of Kitral's time line and trying to stir up a wave of grass-roots passion for the case. "We have received a whopping two phone calls this morning regarding our situation," Kitral glumly noted in her log.

Butch had also probed deeply the national network of anti–family-service individuals and advocacy groups. He had sought and received a pledge to secure legal help from the Rutherford Institute in Omaha, a powerful Christian-right organization that specialized in funding and advocating its agenda through court actions. He had contacted Richard Mack, the former Arizona sheriff who had gained brief national fame in 1997 by successfully petitioning the Supreme Court to overturn a provision of the Brady gun-control law requiring local police to determine whether buyers were qualified to own handguns. Mack, by then a consultant for various libertarian clients, agreed to "investigate" the Chaplins' case from his Provo, Utah, headquarters and eventually mailed back a seven-page "investigative report" that concluded, among other things, that Butch and Kitral were "responsible and loving parents" whose "concerns were not respected by the professionals and bureaucrats involved in this affair." He ended by decreeing, "The bottom line is that government assumed a role that they *do not* properly or constitutionally possess."

(Curious about the extent of this network, I did some surfing of my own upon my return home. I found Web pages warning, "The State of Utah is stealing children for money. Will yours be next?" The reference was to the state's Department of Human Services, as it intervened in reported cases of child abuse. I found The Witchhunt Information Page, which announced that in North Carolina, an "Appellate Court endorses bizarre satanic ritual abuse conviction." I found the Fathers Rights Helpline, similarly aligned against a court system seemingly dedicated to the forcible disintegration of family households. I found VOCAL, a national organization of "innocent people who have been victimized by child-abuse laws and are asking for justice." I found several others, their rhetoric saturated with the almost unrestrainable anger that coursed through so much of America's public discourse. As I surfed, I recalled a warning issued several years earlier by the social historian Robert Bellah to the effect that individualism, a national trait so admired by Tocqueville in the 1830s, "has in our time grown cancerous, and threatens to destroy the integuments of our society." It struck me that anger—anger from a variety of ideological sources—had, since Bellah's writing, become one of those very integuments. And that children had superseded "society" as the entity most threatened with destruction.)

Abbey Chaplin was restored to her parents' care on July 10. A few days later Kitral made an appointment for family therapy—with Michael Richardson, as it happened, at his private clinic. She, Butch, and Abbey met the following day with Richardson "to discuss details," but Butch turned up in an uncooperative mood: He felt as if DFS "was twisting his arm" to participate, and "for him to be honest in therapy was an impossibility at this point." The Chaplins proposed a less "arm-twisting" alternative: therapy for Abbey. "And whatever came out of that, should it be family therapy or whatever, so be it."

Meanwhile Abbey, whose depressive symptoms remained under scrutiny, was assigned a daily dosage of Luvox, supplemented, according to Kitral's log, by Prozac.

The meetings, calls, and negotiations regarding possible treatment and medication for the young girl continued daily. Abbey more or less retreated to her room, where she held long telephone conversations with a boy of whom the Chaplins did not approve.

Butch Chaplin, who had resisted the "arm-twisting" of family therapy, embarked on a little arm-twisting of his own. He photocopied and distributed copies of Richard Mack's investigative report to anyone who would accept them. Appended was a page of Butch's own writing. A compendium of labels, catchphrases, and appeals to piety and patriotism that were standard issue in the right-wing Web page universe, it detailed how a consortium of agencies had "contrived to kidnap our daughter and did so." It disclosed how "armed officers" had "placed our entire family in a potentially life and death situation" and had been "needlessly rude" in the bargain. It railed against "LE-

GALIZED THUGS" who were "hell-bent on their personal agendas of destroying any functioning family group, any followers of Christ, any home-educated children, any independent thinkers or patriots." It inveighed against courtroom star-chambers headed up by dictators more interested in inquisitions than justice. It alluded to crimes against humanity. It requested money.

Among all the principal actors in the drama that swirled about Abbey Chaplin, the character who oddly remained the least defined, the least engaged, and perhaps, in the end, the least relevant to the struggles undertaken in her name was Abbey herself.

She seemed to hover, imprisoned and ignored in some abstracted half life, while the adults on all sides of her case loudly unburdened themselves of expert opinions, prescriptions, legal formulas, self-justifications, and varying positions on "therapy." Whatever insights her various caseworkers, counselors, parents, or law-enforcement escorts might have developed about her remained unarticulated or embargoed in confidential files. Not once, in my reviews of interview transcripts and available records, did I encounter evidence of acute curiosity regarding Abbey Chaplin beyond her symptomatic labelings as a problem to be solved. "Depressed," "disobedient," "suicidal," "down," "a problem," "having a problem," "upset," "mad"—these characterizations ran through nearly everyone's allusions to her, but these were about as far as it went. No one seemed to have asked her about her dreams, her own wishes as regarded her education, the nature of her fears and passions, what kind of food she liked. (Although here and there a tantalizing hint of some inner life flared and quickly faded, unpursued: Kitral's time line of June 30 noted, "Abbey said they had her on Prozak and another antidepressant but she didn't know the name. She said the first night she was on it she started laughing and couldn't stop.")

Her parents had told me a little: of the "vanilla" girl who loved Barbie dolls, kept quiet, and consumed books—"an entire double arm of library books in one week," Butch had said—and who eventually took up poetry. "Unbelievable poems," said Kitral. But still, this did not coalesce into a distinctive human portrait.

I felt this stunted sense of Abbey as an abstraction even though I met and talked to her. Before I left the Chaplin household, I asked Butch and Kitral whether I might spend a few minutes alone with her, and the two readily agreed. Abbey emerged from her room into the kitchen and sat opposite me at Kitral's Formica table.

I would recall her only vaguely in succeeding months—a pale and pretty blonde girl with straight, lustrous hair and a manner that seemed to define "unobtrusive." Kitral provided us with glasses of Coke, and then she and Butch left the room.

We talked for perhaps twenty minutes, but I later found that I could not reconstruct the conversation. Abbey's voice was so soft and hesitant that it did not register as audible on the cassette recorder I had placed on the table in front of her.

I did, however, retain one remnant of Abbey's voice. It is preserved in a copy of one of her poems, which she gave me upon my request. She had written it a few months earlier. Whether or not it was, in her mother's words, "unbelievable," it seemed to cry out for some kind of credence. Untitled, it began with Abbey sitting down to write to an unnamed "You," who had taken over her heart and mind, and "robbed" her of self-esteem and dignity. The poem ended, "I simply can't find/one good thing about me/my worth is gone/my words are goodbye/why live?/When I long to die."

· 11 ·

JIMMY

My thoughts floated around as I drove through the deepening rural countryside on the road leading away from the Chaplins' house. There was nothing much on the radio to break the solitude, except for the companion solitude of a public-radio station over in Illinois, in the death throes of its spring membership pledge drive.

"We need your call," a woman's voice was pleading. "Don't be a member of what Jesse calls the Procrastinators' Club. If you haven't called, please call. We don't want to lay guilt trips on you, but if you don't call we're gonna feel really bad." She and Jesse, her male colleague, recited the 1-800 number in unison. Jesse said, "I notice, Marian, when we say that together, we do it slowly, and that's good, so the listeners out there can hear that and, uh—give us a call."

Marian said, "All three phones are silent, silent again. It's very quiet in here. We've run out of things to say to one another, and we're starting to bicker." Jesse said, "If you love music, if you love dogs and cats . . . or how about this—if you *breathe*—pick up the phone and call this number." At that point I turned the radio off and flipped another switch on, this one inside my head. In a minute or so the voice of my brother Jimmy was coming in across the decades.

"In the small town everything seems lazy. Even the radio announcer sounds relaxed and more sincere than the announcers on big city stations. Traffic seems just to drift along, as do the people browsing in the old stores. At the park, old men and mothers watch the

boys play ball with teams from nearby towns. No one is in a great hurry; anyone is glad to help a stranger find a street or a good café."

This was not his speaking voice, to be sure, but his adolescent writing voice—a voice that I didn't know existed at the time. How different the tone of it sounded from that of Abbey's poem.

"In towns along the Mississippi, boys hike or ride bikes to their secret forts on the bluffs, where they explore faint trails. Sometimes a barge comes laboring by, so near that a far-thrown rock would hit it."

Whereas Abbey's poem was dolefully inward-looking, unfixed from time or locale, and suggestive of a morbid wish, Jimmy's essay—written when he was sixteen and submitted for a statewide school essay contest—was expansive, elegiac, and gently loving toward his sacred place.

And yet it would be a mistake to assume that either piece reveals the true heart of its young writer. That was certainly true, at least, of Jimmy.

The true heart of any adolescent is notoriously elusive. Adolescents are nothing if not conditional—improvising moods, attitudes, and alternate personas almost from moment to moment. Still unendowed with the developmental tools necessary to predict, much less analyze and master, their intense range of emotions, they are often as surprised by their shifts of temperament as anyone around them. In a sense, they are the perpetually amazed audiences of the movie of their own lives—yearning, perhaps, to walk down the carpeted aisle and penetrate that screen, to be a flicker forever.

I have long recognized the distortions I am capable of—the alternate screenplays—when trying to reconstruct the movie of my Hannibal childhood. I can convince people, including myself, that things were perfect. I can achieve this state of mind even while recalling vividly clear scenes suggesting that things were not perfect.

Mark Twain was prey to the same treacheries of recall—his famous "duality." Twain's Hannibal was by turns heavenly and evil. The two versions of the town seemed to occupy separate chambers of his reverie, each utterly unaware of the other.

He was capable of writing about the universe of his boyhood with such fraught reverence that the town began to imitate Twain's vision of itself even before his life was over. The white town, drowsing. St.

Petersburg. Heaven. A heavenly place for a boy. And yet not everything was perfect in Sammy's town. Lethal danger and violent aggression were part of the fabric. We know from Twain's own works
that he lost two chums to drowning and blamed himself for the death
of one. At nine he saw a man shot down on the street and then
watched him die on a table in a drugstore. At ten he witnessed the
murder of a slave by his owner. A few years after that he saw a
drunken lout shotgunned on Holliday's Hill by the woman the lout
had been abusing. He saw the corpse of a mutilated runaway slave
heave up before him in a slough off the Mississippi. He looked on
helplessly as a drunk immolated himself in the town jail after trying
to light his pipe with a match that Sammy had given him earlier on
the street.

We know, too, that it was not the town alone—not just "social
conditions"—that generated the traumas of violence and alienation
that formed Sammy. His family was implicated as well. He endured
the deaths of two siblings before he was seven and blamed himself
for the death of one. (His mother Jane took his hand and pressed it
against the small body as it lay on its deathbed.)

He witnessed the death of his father before he was twelve. Much
of the anger he experienced in later years derived from this disap-
pointing figure. John Marshall Clemens, the spectral "Judge," was at
once a cold, imperious patriarch and a perpetually desperate ne'er-
do-well. Grimly aloof from displays of affection, at times a slave-
beating tyrant, John Marshall inspired mainly caricature and
contempt in Mark Twain's writings.

In short, Sammy Clemens experienced enough mayhem and
wrenching separation as a boy virtually to guarantee a violent career
of his own, according to such current theories as "violentization."
That he did not pursue such a career may be due to his great gift, his
habit of mind of converting sorrow and horror to humor. It was a
gift to which precious few other sorrowing, horrified boys have had
recourse.

"What evil lurks in the hearts of men?" the Shadow asked, chillingly, on the radio of my boyhood days. As I've said, I always had
the feeling that he was talking directly to me. And from across the
chasm of decades, I sometimes feel tempted finally to answer him
back: "It is the evil that fathers visit on their daughters and sons."

But I also could name another source of evil that lay within my heart. It had to do with my little brother, Jimmy.

Mark Twain knew this source as well—at least he knew about the general topic of brothers and sin and everlasting guilt. As a young man, Sam Clemens blamed himself for the death, by steamboat explosion, of his younger brother Henry. Sam had arranged a job for Henry on the doomed boat, the *Pennsylvania*, in 1858. Twain was able to disguise this guilt—to rewrite the screenplay—in some of his books. Millions of readers know Henry only as Sid, the winsome younger brother of Tom Sawyer in Twain's eerily serene resurrecting.

In my case, the sin and guilt had a somewhat different aspect. I didn't like my little brother. Never had. I'd known this roughly since Jimmy had been born. I wasn't sure why, but it had something to do with his intrusion into my sacred place, my turf, my Hannibal. And every time I felt a surge of dislike for him, a sin grew in me.

Jimmy. I must push my memory to recall my first awareness of my brother. It would have been the summer of 1945, the summer that World War II ended and the world I knew began to vanish, although its vanishing would not be apparent to me for many years—not until a bullet shattered the skull of a man in Dallas on November 22, 1963, a date I have never forgotten.

It probably was in August when I first sensed Jimmy, about the time the United States was dropping atomic bombs on Hiroshima and Nagasaki. I was not yet four. I have a hazy recollection of my mother taking my hand and placing it on the warm swelling beneath what seems to be a blue flower-print dress. Ronnie, come put your hand on Mommy's tummy. There's a baby inside there. Put your hand on Mommy's tummy and feel him kick. Ronnie Mommy tummy Jimmy.

I never could feel him kick. But the mystery of what was inside that swelling both thrilled me and set me on edge.

He was born on November 22 of that year, four days after my fourth birthday. His full name was James Paul Powers.

I turn to photographs in old scrapbooks to this day, trying to recover an intimate sense of my brother Jimmy, and to this day find only a stranger. A rather endearing-looking thin-legged child caught squinting at Mom's box camera in the late 1940s: Jimmy in a striped pullover, hands jauntily thrust halfway into his pockets, standing with his feet pressed tight together amid dry leaves outside the white-glaring house in October 1949. Jimmy later that same year, posing warily beside a perfectly ancient tricycle, looking half devoured by his zipped-up parka with its fleecy collar and matching cap with the earflaps firmly fastened under his chin.

And this aching image, captured one day in late summer or early fall that same year. The picture frame is flooded with light. Jimmy is standing beside the driver's door of our father's Nash—a "stream-lined" model whose straight fender line conceals the top half of the front tires. He's turned out like a movie star, and he seems to know it. He's grinning at the camera from a quarter turn to his right. He has on a two-toned jacket (light vest, dark sleeves) with a spread collar, matching dark slacks and, peeking out from one cuff, a two-toned shoe. Atop Jimmy's high translucent forehead is a rakish beret, or what Mom would have called a "beanie." He is small and fair and happy and doomed.

I don't recall him as an infant, don't recall seeing Mom nurse him, change his diaper, anything like that. He starts to swim into focus for me as a toddler. He was probably around two when Mom let me cuddle with him in my bed before she put him to sleep at night. I remember the warmth of him beneath the covers, and I have an impression of enormous, dark, deciphering eyes, focused straight on me. Him on his back, his face turned to me, those eyes. The eyes of the child at the edge of heavy traffic, awaiting the Patrol Boy's enabling grace.

How did sins accumulate? Where did they accumulate? I puzzled over this in the midst of my guilt. When I was six or seven, I was baptized at the First Christian Church. The minister, the capacious Reverend Kenneth Kuntz, tilted me over backward in a font and got my hair wet. He told the congregation that thanks to the divine mercy of Our Lord Jesus Christ Everlasting, all my sins had been washed away.

From this experience I reasoned that sins accumulated on one's scalp, like grains of sand after a day at the Moose Lodge's open-air swimming pool. Sins were probably tiny and round, like microscopic ball bearings. I figured that if baptism was one way of getting rid of your sins, a far more convenient way would be a vigorous shampooing.

To this day, I shampoo every morning of my life.

I learned something else at the First Christian Church, a lesson known to all the world's guilty, I guess. I learned that snakes were the carriers of evil. The story of the serpent in the Garden of Eden really struck home with me, and I developed a phobia of snakes. Especially the one that lay coiled in my own heart.

One summer day I sat on my tricycle on Helen Street, watching Norbert Raykamp and his brother Delbert work on their jalopy, a genuine Model T Ford, its headlights cross-eyed from hard knocks. Helen was a small dead-end street a block behind our house, the last street before a plunging ravine. At the basin of the ravine wound the creek—the crick, we called it—with its skipping rocks and its host of half-glimpsed slithering life.

I admired the Raykamp brothers, who were teenage, chubby, and serious behind their thick glasses. The Raykamps were always opening up the Model T's engine by niftily lifting the pleated black aprons on either side and probing at it with wrenches, oilcans, and their greasy fingers. On the rare days when they could get it to "turn over," they would plop me in the backseat and take me along as the relic chugged up and down the neighborhood.

On this day, Norbert Raykamp withdrew his head from the engine's depths, looked over at me speculatively, wiped a dipstick on his pocket bandanna, farted, adjusted his glasses, and said: "Watch it, Ronnie, there's a snake behind you."

Those were his exact words. I remember them as specifically as I remember the sentence, some fourteen or fifteen years later, "The Pres'dent's been shot."

It lay stretched across the hot sidewalk almost under the small rear wheels of my tricycle. I got one glimpse of it over my shoulder: a small but hideous black length, a *presence*, not moving but not still, like something frying in a skillet, and then I started shrieking. I shrieked at a pitch that tore my throat, great convulsing shock waves of shriek. I kept it up, kept shrieking, couldn't stop. I shrieked and went blind, the Raykamp brothers disappeared, the neighborhood, everything was red, and I was plunging through the redness at a terrible velocity but not getting anywhere, as in a dream, and the thing undulating at my heels. And then somehow I was in the garage of my house, and my mother was there to receive me. I couldn't stop. I shrieked and shook for the better part of an hour and could not make my head turn to look behind me.

Watch it, Ronnie, there's a snake behind you. It was probably a garter snake. But I can never forget the exact phrasing and sound of that sentence, the awful precision and economy of it, or the slanting shaft of revelation it opened up to me.

That night I did dream, not about snakes, not that first night, but about insects, great thick floating bug universes, insects in deep three-dimension like flakes of falling wet snow, or like images in a kaleidoscope, microscopically detailed in all their veined wings and pincers and grasping mandibles.

And then after that, and at intervals through the rest of my life, I was visited—am visited—by the snake.

"What evil lurks in the hearts of men?" The Shadow knew. And I did too. There were others in my paradise of a town who carried snakes in their hearts. A service organization—the Moose or Kiwanis—held an old-fashioned minstrel show, with blackface and banjos and straw hats, in the Mark Twain School auditorium one night during my grade-school years. Minstrel shows had been a staple of entertainment in Hannibal since Twain's boyhood in the 1840s; he had yearned to be a joke-telling "end man" after he saw the first show ever to visit the town.

One of the blackface end men that night was the chief of police, and he was hilarious, as advertised. I remember the guffaws from the wooden seats as he rolled his eyes at some pretended scandalation, grasped the kitchen chair on which he was sitting and comically jerked it a few feet away from his interlocutor. A week later at his home the chief took a shotgun and pointed it at his head and jerked the trigger. I don't think it was due to anything as pleasant as racial remorse.

This was my introduction to suicide. I was twelve. Jimmy would have been eight. The event shocked me. The concept of someone willingly doing anything that grotesque and final to himself—to say nothing of someone I had actually *seen*—wrenched me into a fitful awareness of a parallel world, unseen but now felt, that spun out dark vapors of action and motive.

I don't know what effect the chief's death had on my brother. He'd been at the minstrel show and laughed a lot at the chief's antics. We talked about the news for two or three days in the family. But Jimmy didn't have all that much to say.

What was my brother like? I turn again to the photographs. The photographs are another kind of movie screen that I cannot penetrate. The movie being depicted in these photographs is headed for a bad ending, and I cannot get back inside the photographs and change the plot.

In those shots in which we're both in the picture, I notice a consistent difference between Jimmy's attitude and my own. While my brother is content to merely hold still for the snapshot, I am invariably Making a Statement of some sort: some costume, some prop, some screwy pose, some way of drawing all the energy in the scene into myself.

A photo from Easter Sunday, 1955. Jimmy, Dad, and I are lined up, sitting, on the rim of the concrete driveway of our house on Sunnyside Drive. The inevitable car stands behind us. It's just before church, I assume—Dad has on his best T-shirt. We look like some weird midwestern do-wop trio, each of us with his knees drawn up, forearms resting on knees, hands clasped, hair combed. But guess who is displaying his individuality by dangling an outfielder's glove?

Another group shot. Guess who is in full Cub Scout regalia, sternly saluting? Another shot. Jimmy and I are in our winter parkas and flapped caps. I'm the one packing heat: the toy six-guns in their holster. Those white-handled guns show up a lot. It's amazing how much of my childhood I spent in costume, armed with fantasy weapons.

Photographs never tell the whole story, of course. But as I flip the pages I see the beguiling little boy—Jimmy—starting to turn, rather quickly, into the Jim I remember as fixed, unchanging until he disappeared.

His eyes were weak, and he needed glasses while he was still in grade school. The ones my parents bought him were heavy dark horn-rims, and they emphasized a certain severity in his face while obscuring its more delicate beauty. Jimmy's eyes seemed to have been set a little closer together than was typical in the family; the dark horn-rims around them gave them a staring quality. He had a high forehead, which was exaggerated early on by the close, spiky flattop haircuts he got. So his features appeared to be pulled down toward the lower half of his face, toward the weak Powers chin.

And here is a bad memory, one of the worst. It's the end of noon-time recess at Mark Twain School, a hot day, probably in the early fall. I'm in sixth grade; Jimmy's in second. All the various classes are lined up at the playground exit, standing in the ankle-deep dust, waiting for the teacher's whistle so they can troop single file up the steps to the sidewalk and then to the school building.

For some reason Jimmy's class is standing next to mine. Jimmy is practically parallel to me. I'm hating it. Everybody is hot and fidgety. Jimmy is wearing a cap on his head, a Civil War campaign cap. For some reason they were popular that year; you could get them in either blue or gray at Catlett's clothing store—that flattened crown, pushed forward, and the crossed muskets pinned above the bill. With the gray ones you got a Confederate flag decal stuck to the inside of the crown. All the kids peeled the decal off and rubbed it onto the outside. I was crazy about those caps. They looked at once wonderfully authentic and deadly; they had the forward thrust of combat itself. There was no mistaking the intention of anyone wearing a Civil War campaign cap.

Somehow it annoyed the hell out of me that Jimmy was wearing a Civil War cap. It annoyed me even though I had one of my own. It annoyed me *because* I had one of my own. Everything I did, Jimmy had to do.

We all stood in the dust in the hot sun and waited for the teacher's whistle. Some older boys—older than Jimmy; my age or maybe a year younger—began to tease him. Moving his cap around a little. He looked at me. Let me be specific: he looked *up* at me.

I looked away.

Then one of the older boys lifted the cap off Jimmy's head. Reached inside the crown and unpinned the crossed muskets. For the record, I believe it was a Union blue cap that Jimmy had chosen. The kid unpinned the crossed muskets and kept them. Then he gave the cap back to Jimmy.

But he didn't just give it back. He put it back on Jimmy's head. But he didn't just put it back on Jimmy's head. He gripped the bill and gave it a yank, so that the cap was forced all the way down to

Jimmy's ears. The bill of the cap nearly covered Jimmy's eyes, but not quite. His eyes met mine again. I want to say they had tears in them, and I think that is true, but even to write those words out is at once sentimental and just plain nearly unbearable. I know this: through the whole episode, Jimmy never made a sound. And neither did I. Not to him. Not to the boys who were tormenting him. Not a sound.

The din of that soundlessness has haunted me throughout my life. It is the clangorous silence of all the fear and anger and shame and guilt that comprise the evil side of life in Eden. It is the silence of imperfection, of deliberate, conscious but unavoidable sin.

I turned off the switch in my head and flipped the car radio back on. Marian was saying, "You can participate in the process. You can be one of us who can walk and listen with a clear mind and a clear conscience."

I was sorry that I didn't have a telephone in the car. The prospect sounded attractive to me.

· 12 ·

TOWN BOY

If Hannibal could claim a real-life counterpart to Sid Sawyer, it would be Henry Sweets. Henry was a town boy who had dedicated his life to exalting the works of Mark Twain and, even more than the works, the author's boyhood years in the town. He had served as curator to the Mark Twain Museum for the many years its artifacts were crammed into a small stone building adjacent to the Boyhood Home on Hill Street; and now, at fifty, he had realized a lifelong dream: he'd conceived, designed, organized support, and raised $2 million for a graceful enlargement of the museum. The new facility was housed in a handsomely restored nineteenth-century storefront on North Main—the authentic steamboat pilot wheel on the mezzanine actually gave onto a view of the Mississippi River. In contrast to its competing attractions—the tired Twain-theme restaurants and T-shirt shops, the sandlot-sized amusement parks under blinding orange and yellow logos, hawking their Too-Too Twain kiddie rides—Henry's new Mark Twain Museum was the town's Smithsonian.

I liked visiting Henry for another reason: He knew Hannibal as acutely as anyone who had ever lived there. Nothing escaped him. He'd been born in one of its honeysuckle neighborhoods—North Sixth and Center—and had lived in the same comfortable old family house until the day he married his childhood sweetheart, save for his college years. His father had been a legendary pathologist who ran labs at both the town's hospitals—St. Elizabeth's, on Broadway, and

Levering, where I was born, on the "downtown" end of Market Street, just a couple of blocks from Jesse Toalson's Dan-Dee Bakery. Henry had grown up responsible and connected. Boy Scout, newspaper delivery boy, reader of adventure stories. Now he was a town father, a prince of committees—school board, historical commission, you name it. Owlish and alert behind his black-rimmed spectacles, well-upholstered about the middle, a shortsleeved-white-shirt-with-ballpoint-pens-and-a-necktie sort of fellow, Henry represented a figure both valuable and increasingly rare in American town life, a figure that a less tainted generation might have thought of as classically Republican: the dependable custodian of continuity, the gatherer of local stories and local values. The irreducible civilized core.

"I don't know if you remember Bessie Brown," he was saying as he sat behind the desk of his second-floor office, shaking and sipping the ice cubes in a soft-drink cup. "She taught Latin. She taught at Central School first and then went out and taught Latin at the middle school, and so on. And she told me once—she said that she could tell very easily, and had a defining point, as to when she started having discipline problems in her classes. I said, 'What was that, Miss Brown?' She said, 'When the boys started coming to school with smooth hands.' When the boys were working at home, they didn't get in trouble at school. When they reached a point where they had clean hands, the smooth hands, they weren't working. And this is when she started having discipline problems in class."

The topic, needless to say, was adolescent kids, past and present.

"You had different sorts of behavior models back then that were being looked at by the children," Henry was saying. "I can remember having to write an essay on the topic of, 'Who Do You Admire?' So that sort of thought process was being encouraged among the children. Albert Schweitzer was the person I wrote on. I found one of those kinda pulpylike picture books about his work in Africa. Just looking through there I was amazed that somebody could have that dedication. In my mind, that sort of dedication was something that would be a nice quality to have. Another time I wrote on Walt Disney. And what he had done, literally, for the world."

I could not help recall, just at that moment, that on the wall of a lecture hall not too far from where we sat were fifteen of the sixteen famous illustrations of Tom and Huck executed by Norman Rockwell in 1935. Henry had located these canvases and acquired them as permanent exhibits. As of course he would.

But just now, in his office, our talk had turned to the sorts of boys who had supplanted Norman Rockwell's visions of life in Mark Twain's town, boys with names like Robie and Zach. And to where, metaphysically speaking, these boys had come from.

"So many of the children in this town seem to just be, um—they just happen," Henry said. "They're not in a caring situation at all. They're left to their own devices. And where does one turn? Well, of course the TV has become one form of baby-sitter. Add a VCR and you've got a better one. Add a computer and now you're into the computer games . . ." He paused and thought a moment. And then he leaned forward, seized with a memory.

"When I was growing up here in town, unless it was a downpour or freezing snow, we were out playing all the time. We were creating our own entertainment. The hours that I spent playing ball on the playgrounds . . . three kids, you could have a ball game. The number of times I got a very cold meal because I was late coming back from playing ball, and so on, and my mother being mad—" He beamed widely. "It sticks in my mind."

The boy in him came brimming to the surface. "I can remember as a student at Central School, which would have been in the fifties, playing ball up there, stopping to go up on the wall up toward Rockcliffe to get the ball after somebody got a good hit that stuck in one of the bushes on the side of the hill."

I was with him. I remembered Central. Central had been my junior high school and had reappeared in my dreams at intervals ever since. It was an amazing relic, a spooky old redbrick castle suspended halfway up the side of the great residential ridge above Broadway. It had been wedged there since 1882, the year Mark Twain resumed work on *Adventures of Huckleberry Finn* in Hartford, the year Jesse James was shot in the back in St. Joseph, Missouri. Its unwindowed back side was planted just across the street from the foot of a sheer cliff, atop which brooded the sprawling old Rockcliffe Mansion, formerly the Cruikshank House, where Twain spoke from the great parlor staircase to three hundred members of Hannibal society on his last visit to the town in 1902. The school's Gothic front end, gabled and stern above a vertigo-inspiring concrete staircase, glared down over the ridge's descending treetops and rooftops. As a kid there I always thought I had about as much chance of meeting Dracula in the dark industrial corridors as of encountering the principal, "Moose" Turner, whose resemblance to Bela Lugosi was more than faint. But far from feeling horrified or depressed by its heavy environs, I recall a sense of almost illicit enchantment. It was like being educated in a haunted house, and the effect was oddly enveloping.

Clearly, Central had worked its charms on Henry as well. "One of the things that I remember about playing up there—and I'm not sure how I had the guts to do it—involved that playground right beside the building, you know, it was all closed in by chain-link fencing. On weekends, a group of kids would show up; we'd just materialize, and somehow we'd choose up teams and have a ball game. Sometimes there'd be a big age difference from the youngest to the oldest kid. Well, one day I was up there and there was a much bigger kid, and when we went out onto the field, I said, 'I'd like to pitch.' And he said, 'No, I'm going to.' Well, the way things like this get solved was usually by a contest. So he threw three and I threw three and I did better than he did on the three, and I ended up being the pitcher. And he was at least five years older than I was, which was a major affront to him. But just in the way the kids worked it out. You know, you did things like that."

He didn't have to explain it to me. I'd caught a fly ball one time, on the south side.

Henry was gazing through his office window at the still-life townscape outside. "When I was growing up, Ron, the downtown was so populated that you had two elementary schools, Central and Pettibone, that were what, about six blocks apart. And both had two sections of every grade through sixth grade, and it was all walk-in. When I started school, nobody was being bused into those two buildings. The first bused students that I saw were in fifth grade. They came in from the country, because Central was the school that had room to accommodate them."

He shook his head. "The downtown was so dense that they drew the district line, the one dividing Central and Pettibone, *between our house and the next one up the hill.* It didn't go down between the center of the street; it went between houses. I went to Central, and the kid next door went to Pettibone. And, you know, that was the

Jim Powers, senior-year high school yearbook photograph, 1963

Jimmy beside the family Nash, about 1949

My father, Paul
Powers (right), with
fishing buddy,
mid-1950s

(from left) Jim, my
father, sister Joyce
(behind him), and me,
mid-1950s. Note the
ball-glove prop on
my left hand.

Me, armed with toy
gun, standing beside
Jim in his toy car

Jim

Me during
high school

Paul Powers

Zachary Wilson in
junior high school
(Courtesy of Kyle Wilson)

Robie Wilson at a
high school dance
*(Courtesy of Kyle
Wilson)*

Kirk Wilson,
Zachary's stepfather
*(Courtesy of the
Hannibal Courier-Post)*

Jim and Virginia Walker in 1993 *(Courtesy of Virginia Walker Begley)*

The Water Hole on Market Street *(Hal Smith*, Hannibal Courier-Post*)*

Jill Whitaker
(Courtesy of Jill Whitaker)

Henry Sweets *(Courtesy of Henry Sweets)*

way it was. You didn't really question it. That's how dense the population was. Now Central and Pettibone for the most part have three of each grade, and sixty percent of the kids are bused in. So there are fewer students and it's all bused."

He glanced out the window again. "The downtown. When you walk through it, it just doesn't have kids. My mother died about six years ago, and the last few years that she was living there on North Sixth, nobody ever came to sell a chili supper ticket, or to sell books, or whatever a school group was doing. I mean there were *no kids around.*

"I remember my paper boy route. I had a route on Center Street, that went from Fifth to Tenth, and I had the one hundred block and the two hundred block of Sixth, and one hundred block of Seventh, so it was a pretty compact route. I delivered over ninety papers on that route. What I remember on that route was the nice, older people that I had. Sitting on their porches. And there were families who had kids my age, and we could always get up a ball game right there in the neighborhood, because there were that many kids around. Today, there aren't that many houses. The ones that are left have been allowed to deteriorate. Now when you drive that section of Center Street, and look at the dilapidated buildings, the number of holes where houses have been torn down, the number that need to be torn down—well, the neighborhood has just deteriorated immeasurably."

After a moment or two of distinctly uncomfortable silence, I ventured: Your family house?

"Yeah. It's gone. The space where it used to be is now part of the parking lot for the employment office that was built next door while we lived there."

He pulled out a sheet of scrap paper, took a pen from his shirt pocket, and began to sketch a diagram of all the loss. "The Presbyterian church is on this corner of Center and Sixth. There used to be a house on the corner here. It was torn down. There's an office building there now. It's been a number of things, but it's an office building."

He sketched some more. "The corner house here was torn down and the employment office was built there. Then my mother's house was here, there was another house here. Gone. Over here is the big old Robard house. At least that one's being fixed up. But our house and the one uphill are now the parking for the employment office on the corner." He sketched on. "Across the street there was an old house on this corner, then there was an apartment house. Miss Brown's house was right here, Bessie Brown. The Thomases were here, then there was another one, and then a big mansion-style house on the corner. Going this direction there were three this way. This one here, this one, this one, this one, this one, this one are all gone. And that one is parking for the Presbyterian church.

"So when I go back there, the neighborhood isn't there. It's literally gone. Oh, the Blacklers still live up here, but their four children, who were there when we were, are all married and gone. You have a couple of families still living in this apartment here. The lady that lives in here has a couple of tenants. There are two families in this duplex here. And that's what's left of what was a very populated neighborhood."

I asked Henry why it had happened.

"Look at Hannibal's growth," he replied. "It's been outward. Subdivision after subdivision. Out and away, to the west." I thought of that wall of franchise fast-food shops facing the old high school, and the land behind it, woods and farmland in my boyhood, and I knew what he meant. "They're all new houses. I think people have had an idea that success means a new house. So instead of fixing up these older houses downtown, they build. And so the downtown area has had a problem for years. A lot of those large homes were turned into group homes—care facilities, where the social-services people would bring in troubled adults to use them. I could stand in front of vacant homes and show you where some of those were, where the people they brought in destroyed the house, then were moved into another house—all this before regulations were in place for the standards of group homes.

"We were recruiting these patients from around the state. It was a lucrative business, and you had landlords who were willing to rent or sell a residential building for those purposes, and so they did. That was slowed when the state enacted some true regulations for group homes, and that business dried up, but for a while this was one of the magnets to bring people into Hannibal. And these people were not exactly productive, contributing, organic citizens to bring in, you know."

I sensed that Henry was being discreet here, treading lightly on a bit of recent Hannibal history that involved decisions by people whose animosities, given the town's small and interconnected civic structure, he was not eager to court.

But by now I'd heard the same thing, in more explicit ways, from other people around town. A common perception was that the town had somehow gotten itself into the "recruiting business" of stocking its abandoned downtown living spaces with what one person snarlingly called "the dregs" of the state's dispossessed. A lot of anger had been directed at the Hannibal Housing Authority, which in the opinion of some had been overly aggressive in obtaining grants for housing on the fringes of town.

"There comes a point," this citizen had maintained, "that you have to ask, who are you building the housing for? Who's living in this housing? Out there in the area that's referred to as our 'projects' area, you have all these apartments in there, and who's living in those? We're bringing in people from across the state to fill up this housing: single parents are coming in with kids, people that are moving out of St. Louis to get away from the crime problems there and bringing their own problems with them."

Closely allied with this complaint was the resentment against a state-operated drug and alcohol rehabilitation project that had been established in the town several years earlier. Many of the transients who occupied the old residential buildings of Henry Sweets's boyhood had been drawn into town by this project—placing the town in the "recruiting mode" that, in general thinking, had contributed much to the town's decay.

That decay, several local people believed, included the shadowy presence of urban-style youth gangs.

"I've heard some examples of kids that have come here from gangs in other cities," one businessman had told me. "Their parents, or more usually their mommas, had wanted to get them out of that, so they brought them here. Well, whether these kids really got a divorce from their gang or not is anybody's conjecture. But if you go through these public housing projects out there, just ask the question: Who is it that's being brought in to live in it? It's not solving Hannibal's problems, it's a whole problem of its own. And yet, you've got a situation that if you were to get up on a soap box and say something against it, you'd probably be crucified."

Henry Sweets wasn't willing to be quite this caustic, but he didn't back away from the topic, either. "Hannibal has had a number of landlords," he said, "who were willing to rent to just anyone, let a house be used up, then just discard it. Rather than keeping it up and keeping it repaired. As a consequence, when you drive through the downtown, there are blights everywhere. Nancy and I wanted to move back into the downtown area, and we spent a long time looking, but every time we found a house, next to it or across the street or somewhere close was a blight that you didn't want to be next to. That sort of decay has been a long-term problem in the downtown. There's some areas that are beginning to pull away from that, and you've seen some turning around."

Henry, his wife, and young daughter Amy (Henry Jr. had not yet been born) eventually settled in a tidy neighborhood off Harrison, not far from the golf course. It was here that the Sweetses first grew aware of Hannibal's creeping suburbanization.

"After we moved, it hit us that here we have a young girl, and there wasn't anybody within ten years of her age within two blocks of where we moved in. We hadn't gone knocking on doors, asking, 'Do you have any young kids?' We hadn't scouted out the territory. I'd forgotten that those types of experiences that we were talking about, growing up and always having kids around the neighborhood, isn't there anymore.

"It's almost as though we're engineering ourselves away from community. Our zoning laws have changed here in town. Now you have to have a certain distance between houses. And when you get out into these new subdivisions, the houses have quite a lot of space between them. Well, if you're a little kid, suddenly it's two blocks down there to your friend, instead of two houses down. It's a whole different aspect. And because of all the fears we now have of abduction and so on, the parents aren't as free to let younger children out the door to go play. It's like, 'Where're you going? Where *are* you going? How far are you going? How do I find you?' I think the mind-set has changed. The protectiveness has replaced just letting the kids have fun. The congregation of kids that we remember isn't possible the way our society is shifted today."

Henry Sweets thought about that for a moment, and his thoughts returned to his sunny exploits as a softball pitcher on the Central School playground.

"That is gone," he said. "You drive by the playgrounds in the summer and you don't see one kid doing anything. But what are they doing if they're not there? They're not doing group activities in the neighborhood. They're doing individual things. Many of them are just left to do something on their own. So what are they doing on their own? Why do the stores sell so many Nintendo sets? Why do they sell so many videos?"

Why do they? I asked Henry.

"You know, when you talk about the breakdown of families . . ." he began by way of reply and then stopped himself for a few moments. When he resumed, looking fixedly out his office window at the town he'd once thought he had known, Henry had muted his surge of anger under a series of anecdotes.

"Within a couple weeks of starting first grade, our daughter Amy started getting phone calls from her classmates. They just wanted to talk. We weren't allowing Amy to talk on the phone like that, so it took a while for us to convince these other kids that we really weren't going to let her talk to them. But then I got curious about all these calls every day. I did some checking, and I started finding out that these were kids who were going home, getting off the bus, and going into their homes all alone. They were in their own homes, but all by themselves. Had free run of the house, nothing to do. So they'd get on the phone. Mainly, they were lonely. I think that in picking up the telephone they were literally calling out for help."

He tapped his finger on the desk and told another one. "One of our schools here in town," he said, "has a situation where there are three children in attendance, the children of three sisters. Every one of these children has the same father. He isn't married to any of the women."

After a moment he told another: "The class that Henry was in last year, *his* first-grade class, the teacher had a picnic for all the kids. They had hot dogs and hamburgers out at her place, and she phoned a friend of ours—who also had a son in the class—and asked him if he could go pick up a particular boy who didn't have a way to get there. He drove out to get the boy, pulled up to the house, and saw five fellows stoned out of their minds, just sitting there on the porch. He went up and said, 'Is Jimmy here?' and somebody called inside, and this boy came out, and our friend glimpsed some more people inside the house, just all on drugs. The boy got in the car, and on the way to the picnic, he started talking about how the night before, he and his fourth-grade cousin were arrested for breaking into somebody's house. And our friend was sitting there behind the wheel thinking, *What's the future of this kid?* His models are people who come home and get on drugs and lie around in a stupor and let the kids play all around them. Just ignore the kids."

Henry had a final story to tell: "Our daughter Amy is a very perceptive child. Nancy and I went down to her school not long ago, for a math fair or something, and on the way home, out of the blue, Amy said, 'Thank you,' to Nancy. Nancy asked, 'For what?' And Amy said, 'I'm not sure but what you two are the only two parents who aren't divorced in my class.' "

As he escorted me out of the museum, Henry paused and gestured toward an empty space in the center of the main floor. He had big plans for that space. "One of the goals of our advisory panel here is to expose visitors to Mark Twain's writings," he said as we studied the expanse of shining floor. "The theme we're working to have in place for this summer is Huckleberry Finn. Here in the very center of this room we're going to construct a fourteen by twenty-two foot raft. Our visitors will be able to step up onto it. It will have a little motion to it; it won't be just a still platform. It will be surrounded by trees at one end, as if it were tied up at a riverbank. The other end will be painted as water, so you'll feel you are looking out over the Mississippi.

"Once the people are on the raft, they'll be able to hear the voices of Huck and Jim talking, through a speaker. We're going to expose them to eight to ten episodes from the book. One episode I particularly like is the one where Jim and Huck are debating the stars, as to whether they 'happened' or were made. Well, we'll dim the lights, and some constellations and stars will appear overhead, and this dialogue will take place. That is what will be in place this summer . . ."

I well knew the passage in *Huckleberry Finn* that Henry was referring to; nearly anyone vaguely familiar with the novel could paraphrase a line or two from it: the famous "raft" chapter, Chapter 19, one of the most beautiful flights of sustained lyricism found anywhere in Mark Twain (the critic Harold Bloom felt its opening lines to be "the most beautiful prose paragraph yet written by any American").

The section Henry had in mind, about halfway through the chapter, reads: "Sometimes we'd have that whole river all to ourselves for the longest time. Yonder was the banks and the islands, across the water; and maybe a spark—which was a candle in a cabin window—and sometimes on the water you could see a spark or two—on a raft or a scow, you know; and maybe you could hear a fiddle or a song coming over from one of them rafts. It's lovely to live on a raft. We had the sky, up there, all speckled with stars, and we used to lay on our backs and look up at them, and discuss about whether they was made, or only just happened—Jim he allowed they was made, but I allowed they happened; I judged it would have took too long to *make* so many. Jim said the moon could a *laid* them; well, that looked kind of reasonable, so I didn't say nothing against it, because I've seen a frog lay most as many, so of course it could be done. We used to watch the stars that fell, too, and see them streak down. Jim allowed they'd got spoiled and was hove out of the nest."

A transformingly gentle stream of prose writing and sly in its allusions to adolescent innocence edged by budding sexual savvy and to the Fall. Twain in his paradise mode, all thoughts of evil banished. Exactly the sort of passage that a town boy of Henry Sweets's era, or mine, might choose as emblematic of the great author who once lived in America's Home Town.

But Robie and Zachary, I wondered as I stepped out onto the hard pavement of North Main Street: Had either of them ever been in touch with that sweet music? Or did it belong to a place as far removed from them as the moon?

KYLE WILSON

M y kids come first. If I didn't have any children I'd be in Aus-
tralia on a beach."

Kyle Wilson and I were meeting at last.

We sat on opposite sides of a short-legged coffee table in his worn
bungalow on Grace Street. Grace ran parallel to residential Broadway
for several blocks to the west of downtown Hannibal, but on such a
steep grade that it seemed almost stacked on top of the longer thoroughfare. As a kid, I'd never known anyone who lived up in that line
of dusty white frame houses with their rounded twenties-era cement
front steps. I'd ventured up there only with my father in his Nash to
help him distribute Fuller Brush catalogs, and the neighborhood had
seemed remote, if not alien, even back then. It was a silent, watchful
place where dogs lurked, big, hard-eyed dogs that could round a corner and tear a strip from your calf with their fangs without so much
as a warning growl.

Forty years later it didn't seem that the neighborhood had changed
all that much.

Kyle Wilson and I were more or less circling one another. This
would be the first of several cautious meetings, near meetings, and
canceled meetings between us over several months. A lot of it would
be jockeying for footholds. Most of Kyle's relatives and ex-relatives
thought he shouldn't be having anything to do with me, a damn
money-grubbing writer looking for sensationalism. As for me—an ex-

newspaperman who got out of the business partly because I hated calling up relatives of the freshly and violently deceased and asking for interesting details—I about half agreed with them, as my father might have put it.

But here we were. And it was probably true that something besides the need to talk and the desire to listen had drawn us to this meeting. Whatever grown-up roles we might be playing, we were essentially two ex-kids from different neighborhoods in Hannibal. The childhood versions of ourselves might have fought instead of talked. We wanted to see, now, exactly what the other was made of.

The Wilson clan was hardscrabble—south-siders, a label that carried a lot of information in Hannibal culture. Kyle was a true son of the line. Lean and fighter hard at forty-seven, the skin on his face stretched tight over the bones, level-eyed behind his flashing glasses, chin high, as if inviting a left-hand lead. In truth he had boxed for years. But in certain ways, Kyle was as much a town father as Henry Sweets. He was a city councilman, a parks commissioner, an EMT dispatcher, a member of the Police Board. As a letter carrier for the post office, he was as familiar a presence in town as my Fuller Brush Man father had been. He'd become even more familiar now that the youngest of his four sons was incarcerated in a St. Louis detention center, awaiting trial on charges of involuntary manslaughter, hindering prosecution, tampering with evidence, and concealing an offense.

He was the father of five children in all; Annie, the tiny daughter, scampered about the house as we talked. But no mother was present. Kyle's marriage to Nita—now Nita Beilsmith—had been turbulent, and the divorce had left bitter feelings on both sides. (The same, I would soon discover, held true with Kirk Wilson, Zachary's stepfather, and his ex-wife Lana). My brief phone gambits to Nita and her own mother left no illusions about family unity.

It would have been easy to follow my inclinations and simply leave these people alone, at least until some of the misery wore off. But the inescapable fact was that I wanted to know about Robie. And Zachary. They weren't just two more American kids who had killed. They were kids from my place. They were emissaries from the dark side of Mark Twain's reminiscences. Though I didn't push the thought too far, they may have been extreme versions of me. Yet unless someone asked some questions, whoever they were, or might otherwise have been, would remain submerged inside the generalities that close over most adolescents who stumble into criminal trouble: the vapors of statistic, trend, case history. The likelihood that they would become their rap sheets.

Not that this first conversation was going to pierce through any of those generalities. It had turned out that the lawyer Kyle had hired to defend his son had clamped a gag on anything Kyle might have to say about Robie or the case.

So much for breaking the ice.

I asked Kyle if he would just talk to me a little about what life in Hannibal had been like for him. He clasped his hands behind his head.

Graduated high school in sixty-nine. Northeast Missouri State for a year. Played baseball there. Got tired of school. Got tired of his eight o'clock class is what he really got tired of. English. A year later, he was in the mil'tary, and eight o'clock class was mandatory.

Vietnam. Navy. Guided missile destroyer. Lot of good guys on the ship. But Kyle was a horse's patoot was a good way of puttin' it. Did a little engineering. There's some other things he did, but he won't talk about 'em. Repercussions.

"I just don't like to dwell on it or delve into it."

Kyle's train of thought was interrupted by Annie, a small, pretty, and very young girl who had entered the living room like a ghost. Now she stood beside him and thrust out her hand, which was covered by a grayish bandage. The ends of it had come loose.

"Dog bit her two weeks ago," Kyle said matter-of-factly as he re-knotted the strips. I learned later that he and Robie kept an Akita at the house. "You could see the leaders and the tendons. It's deep. I didn't want her to lose her hand. She was playin' hide-and-seek. I stopped by her and her mother's. Her mother needed a ride to the gas station to get cigarettes or something, so I took her down there." His train of thought skittered. "Her mother—we were married and divorced but she's still a friend. She needed a ride and she doesn't have a vehicle so I ran her down there, gone maybe five minutes. This happened while we were gone."

Annie ran off, and Kyle resumed his story.

Came back seventy-three.

A pause, now, at the edge of some private abyss. I asked Kyle again what he remembered about being a boy in Hannibal. I thought this might open up some clues to his understanding of Robie. Kyle launched in again, and his thoughts ricocheted from one half-formed idea to another. But no thought was far from the issue of trouble.

"What I remember about Hannibal is the same thing you remember as far as being a child or a teenager," he said. "There's not a lot to do here. And I really don't think it's any different than any other community. I tell my kids, I say, geography won't change your life. And they didn't want to admit it. I told 'em, I said, well, if you have problems and you're old enough, I don't care if you're junior high or high school, geography won't change it. It's a mind-set."

He fell silent again, brooding into the space between his splayed knees.

"We didn't have a lot to do when we were kids," he said almost under his breath. "But we did things differently."

How so, I asked him.

He was ready with an answer. "If we had a problem with somebody and wanted to fight, we did it out on a country road." He jerked his chin upward and shot me a look that came from deep inside a Hannibal I'd never known, a long way from my Patrol Boy corner. "You did the same thing," he said, in a tone that might have been ironic. "You know, you didn't do it in town. You don't want the police involved. If you get in a fight, you get in a fight. When it's done, it's done."

The number of fights I'd had as a kid in Hannibal could have been counted on the knuckles of one hand, and I sensed that Kyle knew this. But now he was deep in his own reveries of fists-up confrontation.

"I remember one time I got in trouble and they marched me down to the p'lice station, and the chief looked at me and said, 'I just don't know whether to call your dad or not.' I said, 'Don't call my dad,' you know . . ."

Annie had rematerialized in the room and listened as Kyle mentioned his dad.

"My grandpa's mean," she remarked quietly. And in that instant, Pap joined us.

Kyle broke the silence that had developed with an edgy chuckle.

"I always tell my kids, when I grew up, child abuse was legal," he said. "But it wasn't too bad. I've got a little phrase that I made up—" He glanced at Annie, who had started to walk away. "Wait a minute! Whoa, come here for a second. *Hey!*" A nod in my direction. " 'Scuse me. Come here, please. I wanna see your hands." He took the child's bandaged hand in his. "Let's see. I wanna look at it and see if it's wrapped okay." He examined the grayish cloth. "Don't get it dirty. Now, I'm gonna tell you something," he told her in a casual, confiding tone. "If you get dirty, I'm gonna beat ya. Okay?"

Kyle took a breath, and let it out, and dealt with the other presence who had entered the room.

"My Dad—John—was an engineer on the railroad. So we lived over on the south side, on the bottom part of Union Street they call Adams. Half a block from the Roundhouse. Easy for him to go to work. I knew everybody, I played a lot of sports. Not that I was any great athlete or anything like that. Played baseball, played a little football in high school and found out I *wasn't* quite good enough to play."

Abruptly he changed the subject by thrusting his forearm at me. "Excuse the dirt. You know what that is?"

I didn't.

"Okay, it's a scar."

He told what had caused it. "I was ten years old. Kirk had gone in through the kitchen of the house on Adams. Gone into the kitchen. Well, I followed him. He got something out of the refrigerator. I wasn't paying attention. He left the kitchen and walked out the breezeway and didn't shut the door. My old man comes in there, sees me standing there, doesn't see Kirk leave, sees me, and the refrigerator door is open. Grabs me and slams me into the kitchen counter.

"Those old restaurant glasses, they were round and then bigger than regular glasses. Heavy. They had little bubbles on the bottom. You remember them?" I said I did.

"My hand went right into one of those glasses and a sliver went in right like that, almost cut that tendon. See how close it is. Went in like that, the point was sticking right through here. Almost severed that tendon and that vein. 'Little son of a bitch! Leave that damn refrigerator door open! Bet you don't do it again!'

"I didn't cry. I knew if I cried . . . I went to show my mom, and the sliver is sticking out this far."

Who got you to the hospital? I asked him. The question seemed to tickle his funny bone.

"No, no, no," he said. "You don't go to the hospital, not in my family. My mom pulled that out just like . . . *this*."

You didn't go to the hospital, I repeated stupidly. It was a really St. Mary's Avenue thing to say, a Mark Twain School thing to say. But it was the only thing I could think to say.

Kyle did not dignify the question with an answer. When he spoke again there was a defiant edge in his voice.

"Anyway, my childhood wasn't any different than anybody else's. I had a lot of friends."

He frowned in concentration. Something needed emphasizing.

"*I had a normal childhood,*" he said, his eyes invisible behind the glare of his glasses. "Just like you did. Just like anybody else in town."

He worked his lean, lined jaw. "The way I am, and you'll probably find this out through a lot of people, is . . ." he seemed to reach for words that he normally had no need to summon. "I try to help as many people as I can. I'm community oriented. I'm not on the city council because of the money. I try to participate. Just like you. You know, I'm not pattin' myself on the back. There's a lot of people do this."

He ticked off his public service: Park Board member, eventually elected president of the board. In 1989, he ran for a city council seat and was elected. He had served as vice chairman of the Police Board, chairman of the Fire Board, and on three taxing commissions.

I tried once more to draw Kyle Wilson's focus toward the subculture of adolescents in town, asking him to draw on his expertise as a public servant. When a kid drops out in Hannibal, I prodded him, what does he drop into? Abruptly Kyle became expansive. And for a moment it seemed as though Pap had evaporated from the room.

"One thing I've noticed," he said, "from council, Police Board, as a parent, and as a concerned citizen. People are worried about gang-related activities. Local gangs, not 'name' gangs. The kids around here will talk, and they'll do the signs, like the Crips and all that, but they don't have any connotation like that. It's still basically a small town. You've got some people that come in from St. Louis, but it's not as drastic as it was."

Pap slipped back in.

"The funny thing is, they say my boys . . . they say my boys are in a gang called the Crew. *My boys.* Gang called the Crew. I'd laugh about it. And they'd say, 'Whaddayou laughin' about?' "

Kyle leaned forward over the coffee table. "Lemme show you what the Crew stands for. Watch this, now. Okay?"

He held a pencil over a scrap of paper. "This is how you spell Crew: 'C,' that's for Chris. 'R,' that's for Robie. 'E' is for Eddie. And 'W' is for Wilson. Chris, Robie, and Eddie Wilson. That's my sons."

For the first time, Kyle Wilson grew agitated as he talked. "I try to explain this. I say, this is for my sons. I mean—the Crew are my sons! I mean it's not a gang, it's my sons! And I'm on the Police Board. I say, Come on, guys, gimme a break. I say, Crew? I say, you're talking about my sons!" The words were tumbling out now. "They came up with the word—they heard the word 'crew.' Okay? You know what the Crew is? It's my sons! It's not a—I mean, it's . . . I don't think I'm gettin' the point across to you here. It's—that's how my boys *refer to each other.* We're part of the *crew.* Kyle's boys! Chris, Eddie, and Robie. Okay? *That's my crew.* That's—that's what it was for."

Kyle looked at me expectantly for a long moment through his rimless glasses.

Do they get it? I asked finally.

"The p'lice?"

Yeah. Though I hadn't understood we were talking about the police.

"No. Psssh"—he sliced his palm through the air—"over their heads."

Another moment of silence passed between us. But Kyle seemed to have relaxed a little. The act of denying gang activity among his sons had reminded him of something that gave him a great deal of fatherly pride, which was the fact that his sons were extremely tough.

"They're all a bunch of good kids, my sons," he said. "They all get a little wild hair in their butts. My oldest son, Chris, got wild hair in his butt for ages. He used to be very timid. Big kid who didn't want to hurt anybody. I told him, I said, one of these days, you know, you're gonna flip. And I said, you have to be careful, 'cause you *will* hurt somebody. 'Cause he's massive. I mean, you look at him, you say, he's big. Then you say, he's *big*. He's *real* big, you know? And he's not tall, he's not super-heavy and not fat, but he's thick. He's got arms this big around."

The theme of family largeness pulled Kyle into another preoccupation. "My oldest brother's six three," he said, "and my next brother's six one. My sister's taller than me."

He brooded a moment.

"My old man used to get mad at me," he mused, " 'cause I was always askin' him—I sez, some of it run down your leg?"

Kyle returned to the matter of Chris. "Chris was down on Broadway, oh, three or four years ago. Standing at the corner by old Doc Soltzman's office. Right across from the park." Annie had approached him again. "Don't interrupt me!" Kyle told her. "This guy, he was 'bout thirty-five years old, he walked up to Chris and nailed him. He was about half drunk. He hit Chris, and Chris turned around and looked at him and says, 'That the best you got?' I heard about this from two cops. 'Cause they broke it up when Chris started stickin' this guy in this mailbox there. Or I guess it was a collection box. I guess Chris just beat him 'bout half down. So people don't mess with Chris no more. They don't mess with Eddie."

Annie was looking at the "Crew" sketch her father had drawn. "Who did this?" she asked. "I did," Kyle replied. "I was showin' him something. You're interrupting."

We talked for a while longer, mostly about the ins and outs of his duties on the Police Board and the Park Board, and then I shook Kyle Wilson's hand and left his house. I drove away mulling the jagged conversation we'd had and also the deeper conversation we'd been unable to have but that hovered about us like the fog on Huck's Mississippi: the past itself, just out of reach, and yet always bearing in. Pap Finn sat somewhere nearby, staring at us, at the Home Town, at its host society, his chair tilted back, one ankle resting on t'other knee; daring all the world-awakening young striders of the future to escape the undertow of the past.

· 14 ·

RIDING SHOTGUN

Robie Wilson, Will Hill, Zachary Wilson, and I had all attended the same high school. For that matter, Jim and Virginia Walker had attended it too. We had all been sixteen there once. Differing eras, to be sure. But we'd walked on the same marble tiles, rattled the same lockers, eaten in the same cafeteria, maybe sat in the same wooden chairs, and gazed absently out at the same concrete and brick. What else did we have in common? How different could it have been for any of us?

Cars. We sure had cars in common.

I entered Hannibal High School in the fall of 1956. I came in worried sick about "getting initiated" by the seniors, about being made to wear my Levi's inside out, or rolled up to the knee, or whatever depraved tortures the junior-high rumor mill was circulating at the time. I was a sophomore—a "dam' *south*-more," as the bowlegged tight-jeanned upper-class jocks sneeringly mispronounced it—and I trod carefully.

I had an aircraft-carrier flattop and my ears stuck out. My eyebrows made me look as though I was always frowning. I had acne on my neck. I'd given up any hope of ever being good-looking. On the compensating side, I could draw cartoon likenesses of my classmates that made them laugh. That was my weapon, like Wild Bill Elliott's twirling six-guns. And I was best friends with Duly Winkler, the town rich kid and football star. Duly was a kind of golden boy. When he turned sixteen his parents gave him a dream car, a sexy cream-white Chevy convertible. Duly wore tight shirts and combed his thick blond hair up and back, like Elvis's. He had cool to burn, and I helped him burn it. I was his sidekick. He drove. I rode shotgun.

We were the first true rock and roll class to enter Hannibal High. Bill Haley and his Comets had electrified the nation the previous year with "Rock Around the Clock," but nobody, at least in Hannibal, quite knew what to do with those tingling waves. None of us was going to get caught reacting to *that*. It might not be permissible.

It wasn't permissible, but in 1956 the context was forming, and the momentum that would render "permissible" forever irrelevant. Elvis brought out "Hound Dog" that year, and that dirty wail, that beat, those rattling drumrolls got inside my skin, down below my beltline, and made me want to mash my foot down on some accelerator and peel out forever. And down in St. Louis a glistening black man was duckwalking across the stage with his electric guitar and wailing about a girl named Maybelline in a Coup deVille. No more handsome cowboy in the Jesus-white hat. Roll over, Beethoven. We were rocking in two by two.

Cars, God yes, we rode around in cars. A new layer of Hannibal opened up to me: cars, at night, driven not by parents but by kids my age. Cars and carhops at the A&W, the Checkered Flag. Cars and carhops and the Sky-Hi Drive-In. Making out. Or the rumor of making out.

Hannibal that year turned nocturnal, neon, vaguely dangerous and sexual as I sprawled in Duly's Chevy, my knees splayed, the chrome cool under my elbow. We moved under the stars, the top down, rock and roll on the dashboard radio, Duly and I, headed purposely— somewhere. Anywhere. Out of his driveway to Euclid Avenue, Euclid to Pleasant Street, then veering left into the secluded, curving street called Shepherd Place, hurrying along its tree-lined downhill contours until its terminus at St. Mary's Avenue. There we'd turn left again and take off along the central spine of Hannibal. Maybe at some point, we'd turn right off that spine—now Broadway—and plunge the Chevy down toward Market Street and Hope. Or more likely we'd stay on Broadway past the honky-tonk Wedge and straight toward the Mississippi River, making the big loop at the levee, then out northwest along Mark Twain Avenue toward Harrison Hill and Riverview Park, where we'd prowl the labyrinthine loops, looking for other cars. Maybe we did a little lights-out trick driving—clandestine tailgating, laughing and finger-giving, Elvis on the radio. Then we were on to the A&W to look for girls.

Cars were suddenly everywhere in town, it seemed, that year. Parking meters had come in. They weren't enough. The town fathers started tearing down buildings to make room for parking lots. One of the buildings on North Main near the river had contained the shop where the twelve-year-old Sam Clemens, grieving over his father's death, had learned to set type.

In the world beyond the Mark Twain Bridge that President Roosevelt had dedicated, President Eisenhower was about to get reelected. The blue flicker of television grew daily more normative. And somewhere in a far galaxy, Jack Kerouac was typing away at *On the Road,* a book that, more than *MAD* magazine or even the army paratroopers that would soon file into Little Rock, would help foreclose my world as I understood it—replacing stasis with velocity. "We returned to the apartment to go back to sleep," Kerouac's girlfriend wrote of the night before the appearance of the *New York Times*'s transforming review in September of my junior year. "Jack lay down obscure for the last time in his life. The ringing phone woke him the next morning and he was famous."

. . .

WHAT I REMEMBER about high school—I mean "high school" here to represent an entire epoch, not just the building or the act of attending classes—is virtually every moment of it. Because every moment mattered. Everything that happened was important. Every sidelong glance in the hallways, every passed note in study hall, every manufactured belch in Miss Crawford's history class.

Every person I knew had global significance, every grief was insurmountable, every cause for laughter was the funniest thing that ever got said or sung or pratfallen since Alley Oop was the king of the jungle jive.

Ki-yi-ki-yikus, nobody like us; we were the Pirates of Hannibal High.

What I remember about high school is that I was never serious for a minute, and always so serious it hurt. To cover an unspoken horror at the person I secretly knew myself to be—a self-conscious, envious, rigid, and fairly prissy kid who didn't like the way he looked in the mirror—I cultivated a reputation as a debonair wiseacre.

This was not easy. Being a wiseacre depended on having an irreducible *point of view* that differed somehow from the orthodoxy. I was as orthodox as it was possible to be and still remain gentile. I didn't even have a clue as to what alternative views were out there. Cheese, to me, came in yellow squares and was called American. Bread was white. "Spaghetti" was the first name of a dish the last name of which was " 'n' meatballs." God was a Christian. Good guys didn't smoke. You were supposed to leave your Thing alone; God would spot you if you grabbed it. And on and on.

I studied other kids who were funny and learned their rhythms. I studied Bob Hope, especially in *The Lemon Drop Kid,* though I had no idea what a racetrack tout was. I listened to "novelty" records on the radio, especially Stan Freberg's parodies of *Dragnet* and the ones where a fake reporter asked questions of people on the street, and the answers were snippets of rock and roll songs.

Duly had a tape recorder, a cumbersome reel-to-reel Wollensak, but possibly the only tape recorder in town. He and I began to splice together our own "novelty" recordings, using in-jokes from school and Duly's supply of 45-rpm records. We spent hours on weekends putting these together and then played them at the parties Duly's parents let him throw at Rose Hill.

Our friends shrieked with laughter. I watched them laugh, watched them very, very seriously.

What I remember finally about high school is sex, or the chimera of sex—always imminent but just beyond reach, elusive and elsewhere-moving as the Mississippi at night. Important as sex felt as a fantasy and an urge, it was almost incidental, beside the point, in my actual first crushes. I remember idealizing a new girl named Jean who moved into a house across the street from my old Patrol Boy corner. She was quiet and serene, a minister's daughter who wore lacy Peter Pan collars and a silver cross around her neck. I loved her so much I felt suffocated in her presence. I invited her to a party at Duly's and ached so ardently every time another boy spoke to her that my pain finally penetrated her serenity and she recoiled when I approached her, looking wide-eyed at me over her Coke glass in affable confusion and fear.

I remember a Pirate home football game. The cheerleaders doing a twirl in their pleated skirts that finishes abruptly, every girl half crouched in a statue-freeze. Donna Maupin's hemline doesn't quite make it. There came a coincidental sudden pause in the crowd sound like the hush of surf, then, at that very moment, a Eureka-like cry from the reedy voice of Bobby Jones, the smallest kid in school: *"A bare kneeee!"* No one even dares to titter; the mortification is as universal as the plague.

I could not help wonder whether Robie Wilson or Will Hill had formed memories remotely like these. Or, if they had, whether those memories would survive the other memory that had formed.

· · ·

THERE WAS ONE other memory I retained from my high school years. In one sense it had nothing to do with the worlds of Robie and Will, at least to the extent that I knew. In another sense it had a lot to do with them. This was a memory of a courageous gesture a group of my friends and I tried to make one time, or almost made, because in the end we could not bring ourselves to make it. The seeds of that little failure took root and may help explain some of the distances between Hannibal people nearly two generations later.

If Hannibal was socially segregated in the late nineties, it was even more segregated racially in the fifties. *Brown* v. *Board of Education of Topeka* had come down two years before I entered high school, and everybody was still getting used to having "colored" students in the halls. There were no big confrontations then, no fights. I suppose there didn't need to be.

But I did witness a racial incident. It involved a classmate of mine, a black athlete named Gerald Perkins. It happened in a pool hall in Sedalia, Missouri, a town about one hundred miles southwest of Hannibal, before our team was to play a basketball game there in 1958, a year before I graduated. I can't think of it to this day without shutting my eyes in mortification and regret.

The Hannibal team bus had arrived in Sedalia late in the afternoon.

I was the team "manager," meaning that I got to hand out towels in the locker room and sit on the team bench with a clipboard, looking important, during the games. There were still a couple hours to kill before tipoff, so a bunch of us went out looking for some way to pass the time. We were kids looking for something to do, a breakthrough in the blankness. After a while we found a pool hall on Main Street.

Sedalia was a town about the size of Hannibal. Like Hannibal, it was a railroad center. Its claim to fame was as the site of the annual Missouri State Fair.

Sedalia's Main Street had a greater claim to fame, although in those days you wouldn't find it in any of the state's official guidebooks. Along East Main, in the late 1890s, had stretched the "sporting belt"—the whorehouses and pool halls and taverns that attracted the black jazzmen then roving along the rivers and the railroad tracks of the Mississippi Valley. One day in 1896 a young pianist named Scott Joplin got off the train at Sedalia, gravitated to an ornate Victorian sporting house on East Main known as the Maple Leaf Club, and hung around for several years, inventing ragtime. His masterpiece of the genre, called "Maple Leaf Rag," was published in Sedalia.

The Maple Leaf Club was long gone by the day our team bus pulled into town. We didn't know anything about it, or about any Scott Joplin; we may never have heard of any ragtime. We just wanted to shoot a little pool till the ball game started.

We'd been in the place less than five minutes when we heard a voice say, "He's got to go."

The speaker turned out to be the owner, a white guy in a white crewcut. We all turned and looked at him blankly; we had no idea what he was talking about. The owner pointed to Gerald Perkins. "He's got to go. The rest of you can stay."

Gerald Perkins was "a Negro of medium height; dark, plain and neat in dress and serious in expression"—a description of Scott Joplin. He had a temperament probably characteristic of a lone black athlete in a mostly white high school in the southern Midwest in the 1950s: he was aloof, a little ironic, a lot hard to know. He was also incisively witty—though he did not make a big deal of that—and intelligent and composed. It should go without saying that he was gifted in football, basketball, and track; if he were merely ordinary, he could have forgotten about interscholastic sports. Our high school was not in the bidniss of futha-ring any civil rights agenda.

For these reasons—personal as well as athletic—the rest of us on and around the team had about forgotten that Gerald Perkins was a colored boy, as the term of art then had it. It had just slipped our minds. Although we were all capable enough of noting the negritude of other boys our age.

I remember that Gerald Perkins was holding a cue stick at the moment when it dawned on everybody that the owner was telling us that this pool hall discriminated against Negroes. Probably about half of us were holding cue sticks. I have this vision still of Gerald just then: he had on his red-and-black Hannibal Pirate letter jacket and a pair of tight faded Levi's, and he was standing slightly bowlegged in the way that fast runners stand slightly bowlegged. He had the faintest suggestion of a mustache on his upper lip. A very cool unknowable customer.

I can see him sort of throwing his head back and looking sidewise at the owner, as if he were waiting for the man to cut the horseshit and have a good laugh.

"Get out of here," the owner told him.

The half minute following that command was the most paralytic half minute I can remember in my life. Nobody spoke. Nothing moved. There was not one other pool player in the place clicking a bank shot. No jukebox, no ringing telephone, no traffic on the street. It was the utter, sudden awareness of being a long way from home.

The first person to break the paralysis was Gerald. He studied the cue stick in his hand. Then he gave a shrug and turned, still with his head back and cocked to one side, and put the cue stick down and sauntered out the door.

The rest of us remained in our places for a while, looking with intense fascination at the floor. None of us made eye contact. I have this absurd leftover image of everybody else's blue jeans; that's as far as my eyes could get. We just stood there, thinking the whole thing over.

I know the thought that every one of us shared as if it were a common force field: We wanted to follow Gerald Perkins out that door. I am convinced of that impulse. We were just waiting for somebody to make the first move.

I wanted to do it. I was about to. Just about to. In one more second I would have. In one more second we all would have. If only one of us. If only I'd had on my BadgeandBelt.

Then the moment passed when it would have been possible to make a gesture like that, and whatever each of us was feeling collapsed into a kind of planetary weight of embarrassment, and we silently shot a little pool, paid the bastard, and walked out of that place—walked out of 1896 and into the 1960s, headed for the nineties.

. . .

I THINK I know the reason why I loved my high school years so much, even the bad stuff, loved it almost moment-to-moment. It was this: I knew it was about to end, not just high school, all of it. I wished to God it didn't have to end: high school, Hannibal, the movies, the secrets, the rock and roll on Duly's dashboard radio, the new scent of perfume on a girl's wrist, the ache of awkward love, the feuds and forgivenesses over nothing, the foot-long chili hot dogs at the Checkered Flag, the great cathedrals of night and the things that happened in the night, the neon Schlitz loneliness of South Main Street near the old train yards and the river. The intense compacted civilization that all this represented to me, this stranded universe enfolded within itself and just now spinning off into history, never to be duplicated, was inexpressible and precious and lost.

In the spring of 1959, my graduation year, I kissed a girl. I kissed her standing on her porch on one of the steep-slanting streets above Broadway after a party at Duly's. The truth of it is that she kissed me; I'd just stood there staring at her for such a long time that the moment had almost passed for making such a gesture, and she probably decided the hell with it, it was late and her feet hurt, and she reached up on tiptoe and planted one on me. She was the smartest kid in our class. She was wearing one of those crinoline skirts that rustled when she moved, like branches. The last sound I ever heard before being ushered into the time of kissing was that soft rustle. We kissed for a long time, and I took her back down the steps to my father's car that I'd parked on a diagonal on the hill. I turned on the radio and we sat in there under the trees and kissed while the Kingston Trio sang "Hang Down Your Head, Tom Dooley" from the orange-glowing dial. Never mind high school, I didn't want that *night* ever to end.

But it did end, all of it, night, high school, Hannibal, in that awakening spring.

"WHO IS ROBIE WILSON?"

I returned to Hannibal in February 1999 for Robie Wilson's murder trial.

Whatever Robie's degree of complicity in James Walker's killing might have been, the greater burden of punishment had clearly fallen on him. Will Hill, the owner and driver of the Bronco that struck the jogger, and by all accounts the one who had imported the notion of "dooring" from his Iowa schoolmates to Robie Wilson's consciousness, had originally faced a crushing array of felony charges: involuntary manslaughter, hindering prosecution, tampering with evidence, concealing an offense, and leaving the scene of an accident. Preparatory to these charges, the newly turned seventeen-year-old had been certified to stand trial as an adult. But three days before Christmas 1997—a little more than a month after the collision—the Marion County prosecuting attorney, Tom Redington, had seized a chance to strike a deal with Hill.

Despite what appeared to be overwhelming forensic evidence marking the Bronco as the vehicle that had struck Walker, supplemented by a deposition confirming the boys' conversations about "dooring," Redington, a trim and somewhat professorial man who wore rimless glasses and a neatly barbered dark mustache, opted to shore up against any possibility of losing his case to a trial jury. He sowed the seeds of an opportunity to play one boy against the other, then exploited that chance when it bloomed.

On a cue from Hill's lawyer, a man named Charles Stine, Redington constructed a plea bargain. He would drop all charges against Hill save the last one—leaving the scene—in return for Hill's agreeing to testify against his friend. Redington further offered to reduce the felony status of the final charge so that Hill could be prosecuted as a juvenile, but Hill declined, saying that he wanted to avoid juvenile detention. Hill was granted a change of venue to another county for his trial on his one remaining charge. He posted bail on a bond of $25,000 and was released from custody. As the day of Robie's trial approached, Hill—from his new residence in a small town in Illinois, where he lived with his grandfather—awaited his sentencing by Judge Ronald Belt in nearby Shelby County. Judge Belt, in the opinion of many local courtroom observers, was far more lenient in his sentencing than was the judge in Robie's case, the Honorable Fred Rush.

Redington was not exactly a passive recipient of this testimonial windfall. "I had actually talked with both attorneys, Hill's and Wilson's," the prosecutor acknowledged to me later. "And said, 'I'm gonna charge both of 'em and let the chips fall where they may. Unless one of you wants to talk.' Hill's lawyer immediately said, 'Yeah, we'll testify.' "

In that agreement the aims and agenda of the Marion County criminal-justice system shifted, with profound implications for each of the adolescent boys under its dominion. They shifted from the purely public—a disinterested prosecution of two defendants under roughly equal degrees of suspicion toward the goal of discovering truth and apportioning justice—and toward the tactical: the goal of achieving victory.

Assured of his relative immunity, Will Hill appeared in the Marion County Circuit Courthouse in Hannibal on February 23, 1998, as the sole witness against Robie Wilson at Robie's preliminary hearing.

In his testimony, Hill acknowledged that he and Robie had driven past Walker that November afternoon with the intention to "door" him, which Hill defined as an attempt to scare the victim by opening the car door at close proximity to him. He maintained that on their first pass, the door of the Bronco remained shut, although he had steered the car close enough to Walker that he would have been struck had it opened.

Then Will Hill made the key assertions that according to Redington's strategy, at least, would place the criminal liability for the death of James Walker solely on Robie Wilson's shoulders. He testified that Robie, having failed to get the door open, remarked, "I missed him," and asked, "Do you want to go back and try again?" and that he, Hill, responded, "Okay." A few moments later Hill testified that on the return trip, he did not know that Robie intended to kick the door open when the Bronco swerved close to the jogger.

During this same testimony, Will Hill offered a number of other statements that seem to shed a peculiar light on his privileged status as the state's star witness.

He acknowledged that he had never heard Robie use the word "dooring" before he himself returned to Hannibal from his family's brief residence there, and also that "dooring" was a commonplace term among his Iowa high school friends.

He repeated under oath two questionable statements he had made earlier to investigating police officers. Cross-examined by Robie Wilson's lawyer, Hill stuck to his story that the pavement was rough on Pleasant Street near the site of the impact, and that the passenger door of his Bronco did not shut properly. "We looked at the scene and found brand-new asphalt, so there was no rough road," Redington told me some months later. "And we had an expert look at the door to see if there was anything wrong with the mechanism. He found absolutely nothing wrong with the door."

And Hill confirmed that Robie did not collaborate in the story Hill concocted at the Water Hole in the immediate aftermath of the collision, a story that Hill himself admitted was an "insurance plan" to shield the two of them from blame.

As to his own complicity in the death of James Walker, the youthful state's witness maintained to his questioners that it was all "supposed to be a joke."

On March 2, 1998, Robie Wilson was arraigned and charged with second-degree murder. He pleaded not guilty and was released in his father's custody. And everyone waited for whatever was to happen next.

Missouri in early February had edged into a desultory brown-greenness, not quite winter, not yet spring. The fields and tree lines had a noncommittal look about them, a vague expectancy of plow, or bulldozer, or the giant machines that were slowly, inexorably lay-ing down the parallel tongue of pavement to the remaining single-lane stretches of U.S. 61—the long-awaited fast lane out of town to distant jobs and back again.

America's Home Town had not enjoyed a great year. A plan to expand the in-town Wal-Mart had fallen through, and rumor was circulating that the company would soon construct a giant outlet just outside town, further draining locally owned businesses. The Ramada Inn had lost its franchise. The Golden Corral, a franchise eatery, had closed down, abruptly locking its doors at the end of a work shift. The Miller Country Bar announced its intention to shut down at the end of the year. The city's development director quit.

Individual behavior had mirrored the civic trend. A man set his house on fire in what police later called a suicide attempt. A fifteen-year-old was sentenced to ten years with the Missouri Department of Corrections for armed robbery of a pizzeria. A friend whose daughter attended the high school had written to me that the youth's fellow black basketball players wept on the team bus after his arrest. One of the players observed bitterly that ten of his former friends were either addicted to crack or in prison.

The stepfather of a young boy walked into the newsroom of the *Hannibal Courier-Post*, sought out a cluster of reporters and editors, burst into tears, and spilled out a story of household hell paved with good intentions. (Many middle-class Hannibal families, particularly churchgoing families, volunteer as step- and foster parents; their efforts in recent years have been increasingly marked by futility.)

Signs of trouble began early. The husband and wife began to observe the boy coaxing his small stepsister toward the edge of a staircase. When one of them admonished him, "Don't you know she could get hurt?" he would calmly answer, "Yes," and keep coaxing her. The boy's aggression intensified as he grew older; there were some signs of sexual molestation by him and he began to set fires around the house. Eventually the man and his wife separated so that the children would be apart. Then they divorced. Not long afterward they reconciled, but the mother's son remained impervious to discipline or compassion. The couple decided to cede their parental rights to the boy so the state would pay for therapeutic help they could not afford. He was taken to a group home and subjected to weekly counseling. His mother and stepfather lost contact with him. Because he remained a danger to his stepsister, his supervisors refused to allow him to return home.

Two weeks prior to the man's *Courier-Post* visit, the boy violently shoved a teacher and another student at his middle school. He was incarcerated in a juvenile detention center.

"The guy was hoping we would somehow jump in and save the boy," a reporter recalled to me later. "Of course that won't happen. It can't happen."

The boy was, by some local standards, a late bloomer in his anti-social rages. In nearby Quincy, Illinois, at about the same time, a disruptive student was kicked out of kindergarten.

Beyond these disturbances, another eruption of lethal pathology had struck at the Hannibal area in the months since the two Wilson episodes.

On Christmas Eve 1998, a fifty-one-year-old bail bondsman's older wife discovered him slashed to death in the recreation room of their house a few miles south of Hannibal. The man's body had been criss-crossed with knife wounds. "They went for his right shoulder first, to immobilize his arm," a woman familiar with the autopsy report told me. "Then they went to work on his stomach. His liver. They really carved him up." Police found no signs of forced entry. The sheriff of Ralls County, which borders Marion County to the south, remarked that it was the first case of homicide in the county since he had taken office.

The victim was widely believed to have been a homosexual who formed relationships with young boys he'd invited to share his hot tub. More than a year after the murder, no suspects had been arrested. But the commonly accepted theory was that he had been killed by one or more of his young consorts.

People who lived in the area processed the atrocity with the emerging fatalism that was becoming a hallmark of the area. "Well, at least the neighborhood's safer now," remarked one resident.

. . .

AT A LITTLE before noon on Monday, February 8, I pulled into a diagonal parking space at the Pike County Courthouse at 115 West Main Street in Bowling Green, Missouri, where Robie Wilson's trial had been scheduled on a change of venue from Marion County. Bowling Green, about twenty miles south of Hannibal, was a town of around three thousand people that belonged to a vanquished time; it was a remnant of the old family-farm/farm-town era. The upright courthouse, two stories of Bedford stone and Georgia granite, eighty-five feet square, had been completed in 1917, clearly at the center of town. (The previous courthouse had burned down in 1915; the one before that had burned during the Civil War.)

The town center had since shifted, or dissipated into the obligatory (and sparsely developed) franchise strip on U.S. Highway 54, several blocks north; the courthouse now commanded a gray, dazed-looking neighborhood of struggling storefront shops, peeling bungalows with wire-fenced boundaries, and cars mounted on blocks. Pike County had lost nearly 40 percent of its population since the courthouse was built; the figure stood at a little over sixteen thousand. Annual farm incomes were less than 6 percent of the total—a stunning figure for a county of fields and woods that revealed virtually no other readily visible source of income whatever. Of the forty-five hundred children in Pike County, nearly a quarter lived in poverty. Almost one in ten adolescents had violated the law between 1994 and 1997.

No other edifice, public or private, with remotely the compacted elegance of the Pike County Courthouse stood between it and the horizon. The venue for Robie Wilson's trial was thus a kind of mausoleum to a society that once, but no longer, had given function to young men of his age.

· · ·

BOTH THE FIRST and second floors of the courthouse were chockablock with people when I entered. They milled in the corridors, tried to keep a distance from the steaming radiators, leaned against the balustrade on the staircase. Men with ball caps sat on a wooden bench with their arms folded over prominent bellies, squeezed next to women in brightly colored knit pantsuits, their purses on their laps and their gray hair tightly permed. A black man in a leather jacket scowled at a crossword puzzle he had wedged against a wall. There must have been sixty or seventy of them, all wearing white name stickers. Jury selection was going on, and these were the people from the pool—I could hear lawyerly phrases scrawking through a microphone in the courtroom upstairs. A courthouse clerk in a pink blazer threaded among the jury candidates like a hostess, handing out pieces of wrapped hard candy: "Sump'n for y'all to munch on."

Old rural Missouri was in assembly here, mustered to deal as best it could with whatever afflictions the new Missouri had to offer.

By early afternoon the selection was complete. A bailiff called the names of the jurors; everyone else exited the courthouse with as much speed as decorum would allow, tearing their white name patches off as they hustled without running, an adult fire drill. The twelve selectees moved in a single file into the courtroom, a little glassy-eyed in their unapproachable new dignity.

Robie Wilson sat at the defense table as the courtroom doors opened, hunched over, writing something on a notepad. This was my first glimpse of him. It was hard to recall what I had expected. What I saw was a slim boy, pale, his brown hair freshly barbered and parted on the left side. He had on a green-and-white plaid pullover with a green collar, short-sleeved, and a gold wristwatch. At his side in a brown suit was his lawyer, Branson L. Wood III, a severe-looking man with a high hairline and a small bristly mustache. Robie lifted his head to watch the spectators and then the jury file into the courtroom. He squinted a little; otherwise his expression remained blank. The jury members took their seats in the box at the left side of the room as one faced the bench. The few spectators arranged themselves in clusters along the eight rows of wooden pews. Above them were several chandeliers. Two old-fashioned oscillating fans were mounted above the doors flanking the judge's bench.

I looked around for Virginia Walker and members of Robie's family. None of these were inside the courtroom. I did, however, catch a fleeting glimpse of Kyle's face, goateed now, through the window of the closed entrance door, as he paced outside.

Tom Redington rose first to make the prosecution's opening statements. Robie, who had slumped forward and rested his chin on his fists, studied him from behind, his mouth unconsciously open a little.

Redington uncapped a red Magic Marker and scrawled a phrase in large, slashing characters on a flip chart, then stepped back dramatically. "These words—'Do you want to "door" him?'—killed James Walker on November 11, 1997," he declared to the jury. "Let me tell you how that happened." The prosecutor identified James Walker and described his jogging habits, he placed Will and Robie in the Bronco on Pleasant Street the night of the collision, and then he returned to Robie's "strange sentence" regarding "dooring." He stipulated where the concept had originated, as a practical joke among high school students in Iowa, where Hill had lived for several months until July 1996. "William Hill will tell you he never heard of anybody getting injured doing that," Redington said. "It was just a little prank that they did.

"Well, on the evening of November eleventh, Robie Wilson wanted to 'door' Mr. Walker. I'll tell you now that William Hill said okay, and his testimony will be that he drove, that he swerved over a little bit to get closer to Mr. Walker." Redington recounted how the door did not open the first time, how Robie said, "I missed him," and urged Hill to make another pass. "William will tell you he said, 'Oh, well,' but Robie said, 'No! Go back! Go around again!' And William Hill will tell you that he did . . . he made a U-turn and came back again, driving towards Mr. Walker as he jogged up Pleasant Street. The testimony will be that at that point William Hill again scooted closer as Mr. Walker ran up the left side of the roadway . . ."

Having established for the jury that Hill brought the concept of "dooring" to Hannibal, that Hill was at the wheel of the Bronco on both its first and second passes at Walker, and that Hill deliberately steered the vehicle alongside the jogging man, Redington now sought to implant the point of view that Hill could not have been more astonished at what ensued—that Robie Wilson was masterminding the scheme the whole way.

"The testimony will then be," Redington continued, "that without any knowledge by Mr. Hill—Mr. Hill didn't know what was going to happen—this defendant turned in his seat, put his foot on the door and smashed it into Mr. Walker's face, and it killed him. We will show you pictures of what that door did to Mr. Walker. Then Robie Wilson said, 'Go! Go! Go!,' because he was the one that was going to get in trouble since he opened the door. And in fact that is what they did . . ."

Redington recounted—and, in doing so, subtly lent partisan color to—the boys' flight from the impact scene to the Water Hole. "The evidence will be that they did not stop, that Robie Wilson did not call nine one one. . . . The evidence will be that William Hill is charged with leaving the scene of an accident, and he'll tell you that he is in fact guilty of that crime."

Robie Wilson alone was responsible for not calling for help, although Will Hill was incontestably guilty for leaving an accident scene. "Leaving an accident scene" was admittedly an offense worthy of criminal penalty. And yet it became, by implication, somehow less onerous and more abstracted than—somehow crucially *different* from—a failure to report the event: especially when the term "accident" was embedded in the official terminology.

Thus the narrative in the trial for the killing of James Walker, in its opening moments, had already begun to slip away from strict exposition and into two competing versions of conjectural narrative. As it slipped, Robie himself seemed to grow less consequential, less tangible even, until all that seemed left of him as he sat unnoticed at the defense table was his rapt, provisional, unconsciously parted mouth.

Redington hinted at the forensic evidence the police had gathered: "On the side of that vehicle Officer Dean found and preserved as evidence some orange fibers [fibers from Walker's fluorescent hat]. We'll present to you parts of the glass which was seized as evidence which indicates that it was from a Ford product."

He permitted himself a dash of dark rhetorical irony: "We will present to you the testimony, you know, on the street at that time of night. We could, if he were here, we could ask Mr. Walker what happened, *but of course we can't.*"

And he gave the jury an advance glimpse of his assembled manpower. "Let me tell you that there will be about fifteen or sixteen witnesses," he warned the panel, "so it may be a long few days." He had reviewed all the police reports, Redington allowed, "and I have tried to cull down the number of witnesses that we need to present so there are a lot of witnesses that we will not present to you that were there as this case developed." Once again, the prosecutor alluded to the many photographs taken at the scene: "We'll show you the pictures of Mr. Walker and the damage that was done to him that caused his death. And at the conclusion of this case I intend to ask you to convict the defendant in this matter."

Now it was Branson Wood's turn. Looking somewhat less authoritative than the trim, dapper Redington—looking, in fact, somewhat less like a courtroom mandarin than like a slightly sleep-deprived assistant junior-high principal—Wood arose, buttoned his suit coat, and launched himself into a rambling peroration that made, in its lucid moments, the plausible point that Will Hill brought to the episode the know-how and the transportation necessary to see it through: "The evidence is gonna be that when Will Hill moved back he brought an idea with him, an idea that he thought was a prank. It was called dooring." But then a moment later, Wood seemed to undercut his own implied argument that Hill had been Robie's Svengali: "Tragically, as it bore out, Will Hill didn't really have a very good idea what it was he was talking about when he brought this idea of a prank from his hometown in Iowa back to Hannibal."

Then Wood moved to a description of the stretch of roadway where Walker was struck, drawing attention to the dim streetlighting and to a road-repair zone that somewhat narrowed the traffic in both the east- and westbound lanes: "On the right-hand side of the road as the Bronco was headed down the hill, on the jogger's left, there was a construction area where there was a hole. There was a mound of dirt and there was a fairly steep grassy area. There's no sidewalk. There's no shoulder." But now Wood's syntax grew a little jumbled, and whatever exculpatory point he had been driving at seemed to dissipate into vagueness: "There was nowhere for the jogger to go, and as a result of nobody knowing what they were doing on this dooring thing and the circumstance that Mr."—he paused and appeared to grope for the victim's name—"the jogger would not be able to see and would not be able to get out of the way there was a collision which killed him." It was as if this narrowness had limited the maneuverability of Will Hill, reducing his volition, and as if James Walker might have danced out of the opened door's path had he only had a little landing space on the side.

Now Branson Wood embarked on a description of the impact itself and its effects on the two boys. Again, his line of argument sounded, however unintentionally, more like an apologia for Hill than a defense of Robie.

The collision, Wood averred, produced "an explosion of glass from the passenger side door all over Robie, all over the driver, all over the car." And then: "You guys who know teenagers know that the most prized possession of any teenager is the car. There was certainly no intention that anything happen that might damage that car. That was a complete surprise. Maybe they should have known, but it was a shock and a surprise to them that that happened." Plausible enough. But Hill, not Robie, owned the Bronco. By Wood's own logic, then, it was Hill, and not his companion in the passenger seat, who was most likely to lack motive for the violent contact with Walker.

Shifting emphasis abruptly, Branson Wood now seemed on the verge, at last, of painting a character portrait of his young client that would establish him as unlikely to engage in potentially lethal mischief. "Who is Robie?" he asked with dramatic emphasis.

But in his very next utterance, the attorney managed to suggest that as far as he was concerned, that was a pretty damn good question: "Robie was born on—" Wood groped. He frowned and looked down for a prompt at the boy seated beside him. "February eleventh of eighty-one?" "Yes," came the defendant's audible reply.

"He was sixteen years old back at the time this happened," Wood revealed. "He's seventeen now. He lived with his mom, Nita . . ."

Wood's revelation of "who" Robie Wilson was lurched even deeper into what had begun to sound a little like compulsive lampooning—"He had struggled over the years some in school and as a result of that in 1997 he had gone out of the regular education classes, had registered and had begun taking what was described as alternate classes, alternative classes . . . they were easier . . . The evidence will be that, uh, Robie was not an experienced driver. . . . He was someone who had gotten his learner's permit, [which] is mandatory for most young people, as soon as he turned fifteen and a half . . . by the end of March he'd lost his privilege of driving a car . . . he couldn't live up to the conditions that his parents had imposed . . ." I shifted my attention to Robie himself.

He had developed a nosebleed—unsurprisingly, perhaps, in light of the performance taking place at his side. He was hunched again over the surface of the defense table, dabbing at his nose with a white pocket handkerchief and then studying the bright splotches on it, then refolding the handkerchief and dabbing again. He seemed to be trying to keep the flow from spreading onto his obviously new plaid pullover. No one in the courtroom appeared to take notice of his plight; no one moved to help him. Just in that moment, and in full consideration of the horrible and irreversible thing he had done, Robie Wilson struck me as the most isolated human being I could ever remember seeing.

. . .

IT WAS ONLY in the final moments of his opening statement that Branson Wood managed to get down to some brass tacks regarding the weight of responsibility and the imbalance of punishment already meted out.

He drew attention to an obvious but crucial point: that the prosecutor, Redington, had in his opening remarks relied heavily on Will Hill's version of the events—"the version that [Will] told after he made a deal that was going to protect him from prosecution"—and promised that in the defendant's forthcoming testimony, "Robie will tell you that what Will has said is not right . . . when Will turned back down Pleasant Street, he turned to Robie and said, 'Open the door. Door him.' " Wood promised testimony to the effect that Robie was "taken aback" by this command. "Will Hill repeated, 'Open the door, scare him,' and Robbie started to push the door open. Will Hill swerved, swerved to the right to get close, and he later told a girl-friend when he wasn't trying to make a deal that they were trying to scare him and that he swerved too far and they hit him. They got too close."

Wood pointed out that it was Hill who'd made the decision to flee to the Water Hole, Hill who concocted the lie that the Bronco had been vandalized, Hill who placed his billfold on the seat of the car to suggest a motive for vandals and a rock in the rear to suggest a cause of the shattered window. "And even Will Hill will tell you that Robie didn't make that story up and Robie didn't offer to support it and told him he wouldn't support the story. Will Hill calmly got in the police car with Officer Darren Smith and made a report of vandalism. Robie wasn't even in the car when the report was made."

And yet, Wood reminded the jury, "Will Hill will never be charged with second-degree murder. Will Hill will never be charged with involuntary manslaughter." Nor, Wood went on, with evidence tampering or concealing an offense or making a false report. The one charge he accepted—leaving the scene of an accident, a Class D felony—allowed him an even "better deal" than Redington's offer to have his case handled as a juvenile offense, which would include some time in a detention center. Better, because even though the maximum incarceration time for such a felony is five years, "it was agreed that his case would be transferred to a county where there was a judge that his lawyer thought was favorable." Thus Hill would have a good chance at probation or a suspended imposition of a jail sentence, "where he would have no conviction and may do no time."

The upshot was that in the months before the trial now underway, Robie Wilson had already spent 119 days behind bars, and then was released on condition of house arrest, while Hill, "the author" of all the deceit following the collision, had been released on bail back into the community.

This line of argument cut to the core of the deep and obvious inequities already built, virtually as a matter of expedient routine, into the state's pursuit of justice in the matter of Jim Walker's death. Wood's emphasis on the radical differences in accountability facing each young defendant—differences that had nothing to do with degree of probable guilt, and certainly not with any verdict rendered by a jury of their "peers"—raised the possibility that Robie Wilson's prospects might take a turn for the better as the trial progressed.

But at what cost, and what benefit? If Robie Wilson were to be acquitted, or given a suspended sentence out of consideration for his unlucky status as the fall guy in the plea-bargaining sweepstakes, how would this satisfy Walker's grieving widow and son in their wish for retribution? For that matter, if he were to be found guilty as charged and sentenced to prison, while his companion escaped such a fate, what meaning would "retribution" have for the Walkers, or for the community at large? What lessons would either outcome hold for other adolescents looking to "the lessons" of the criminal-justice system as a regulator of their behavior?

The rest of the afternoon was given over to the parade of Redington's witnesses: the driver, returning home from a visit to his mother, who discovered Walker lying crumbled on Pleasant Street and called 911. (As an enlarged photograph of Walker's body made its way from juror to juror, Robie Wilson coughed, then covered his mouth with both hands.) The examining coroner, who testified that Walker's death was indeed due to massive brain trauma caused by blunt-force trauma to the head. A pathologist, who caused some members of the jury to shift in their seats and clench their fists as he described in unsparing detail exactly what the autopsy consisted of. As the pathologist dwelt evocatively on the precise nature of the damage to Walker's brain, Robie's nosebleed returned. He extracted a fresh white tissue and dabbed at it, folding and refolding, and when he had it under control he clasped his hands in front of his face, one thumb stroking the flesh below his eye.

There followed a few more professional witnesses, and then a bailiff led Virginia Walker into the courtroom, past Robie and onto the witness stand.

Dressed in a beige jersey and a fluffy cardigan sweater, she seemed to have willed herself into a mild trance in an effort to hold herself together. Her time on the stand was short. Yes, she responded to a Redington query, her husband was "an avid jogger." The prosecutor placed a photograph, numbered Exhibit Number 43, into her hands. Was it her husband? The photograph was kept carefully turned from the observers in the pews, and judging from Virginia's reaction to it, that was probably a good thing. After a long interval, she whispered, "Yes." A few minutes later she was excused from the stand. She took a seat beside a small man on the front row, whom I had not noticed before—her son Michael, it turned out—removed her glasses, wept briefly, and put her glasses back on.

Virginia was the last witness of the day. The proceedings were adjourned until the following morning, when the state's witnesses would continue.

There was a little light left in the afternoon as I drove back to Hannibal, and on a whim, I thought to check in at the Children's Station to see how things were going there. I told myself that after a day watching an adolescent boy stand trial for manslaughter, I could stand to spend a few minutes in the glow of an enclave dedicated to the cheerful nurture of young children and babies. But somewhere in my thoughts lurked the memory of my last image upon leaving the premises the previous fall: the director Jill Whitaker talking into her cell phone, and the distinct feeling I had that her conversation was not about happy things.

Never had a hunch of mine been more on target, nor my timing been more eerily perfect.

As I walked toward the glass-door entrance of the day-care center at the end of the industrial gravel road, I spotted Whitaker inside, exactly as I had encountered her on my first visit. She still had the cell phone pressed to her ear, as if she had not stopped talking into it since the previous October. Near her stood the familiar warning sign: "Only Positive Attitudes Allowed Beyond This Point." But as I neared the door I could see that in fact everything had changed. Her eyes were red, and she dabbed at them with a pink tissue.

"We're closing," she said to me as she opened the door. "We got our eviction notice the first day of this month. We just couldn't meet the expenses."

Inside, in what had been her office, as members of what had been her staff bustled around taking down decorations and putting things in boxes, Whitaker found a few moments to explain why her dream had failed.

"Basically, from the day we moved in we were in debt," she admitted. "We had kinda strung it out month-to-month, hoping that things would get better somehow. We'd borrow Peter to pay Paul, one month to the other. We leased-to-own this building from the company that built it for us. We paid them thirty-four hundred dollars a month rent. Then we had to meet a payroll of sixteen to eighteen employees. That was our main expenditure. Then we spent another twenty-five hundred dollars a month in food, utilities, and supplies for our kids. We needed about twenty-five thousand dollars a month in income just to cover everything. And we were averaging seventeen or eighteen thousand dollars. Eighty-five dollars a week for infant-toddler care, sixty-five dollars for full-time school and preschool, sixty dollars for part-time. Some other rates for before and after school."

She put away her tissue and drew a deep breath, making her voice matter-of-fact. "We didn't have the funds to begin with, we should have never moved out here, it was a wonderful concept but it was not well planned," she said in a brisk, agenda-clearing sort of way.

When did you start to understand you weren't going to make it? I asked her.

Jill Whitaker considered her answer for a moment. "What got us in real trouble," she replied quietly, "was, we got behind on the Social Security taxes and payroll taxes."

I played another hunch. Are you by any chance personally liable for those? I asked her. She paused, then nodded. How much? I prodded. Jill Whitaker flashed me her best Positive Attitude grin. "I'm negotiatin' with 'em. But it's to the tune of about forty-five to fifty grand. I'm gettin' so I know every one of those IRS people by name. They're being pretty reasonable. And I kept thinkin' I could pull it out. It's just such a wonderful place for these kids."

Not so wonderful, though, apparently, that the Hannibal business or charitable community was willing to subsidize it—although many of its young charges were the sons and daughters of Hannibal professional people.

Forty-five to fifty grand.

I thought of Marshall Kreuter of Health 2000 and his diagnostic visit to Hannibal a year earlier in search of "social capital." I thought of the qualities Kreuter had listed as comprising social capital—trust, cooperation, civic engagement, reciprocity. I thought about what Don Nicholson had told me regarding Kreuter's analysis of the data he'd collected—with that sense of fatalism, the feeling of, "Well, whattaya going to do?"

I asked Jill Whitaker what she thought she was going to do next. She told me she thought she had a job lined up in downtown Hannibal, in the Mark Twain Historic District, working behind the counter of a store that sold souvenirs and knickknacks—the sort of stuff I had seen being hawked at the Folklife Festival.

· · ·

SOMETHING WAS UP the following morning inside the courthouse at Bowling Green. A freighted absence was apparent as soon as I walked in. The courtroom was vacant and remained that way as reconvening time came and went, save for the scattering of spectators. No judge, no jury, no lawyers, no defendant. Most of an hour passed. Clearly, the action had shifted to the judge's chambers. No one in the pews spoke to anyone else; everyone sat alone with his or her thoughts. I spotted Robie's mother Nita for the first time, in a gray jacket, her chin in her hand and a tissue between her fingers; I saw Kyle, several pews away, wearing a navy pinstripe suit; I saw the mute Walkers, mother and son. Everyone, I suspected, was thinking the same thought: Robie Wilson's trial was over. His fate and accountability had been taken out of the hands of the jury. It was being negotiated, as the fate and accountability of Will Hill had been negotiated, by professionals with a view to their own professional needs and cal-culations.

Confirmation came at a little before ten A.M. The bailiff swept in and declared the proceedings in session. On his heels were the dra-matis personae, including Judge Rush, who announced that amended information had been filed: Robie would be given the chance to plead to a reduced felony charge, from second-degree murder to involuntary manslaughter. The prosecutor would recommend five years in prison.

Robie took the witness stand, wearing a white shirt with window-pane stripes and white chinos. As the judge turned to face him and began to stipulate the implications of such a plea, and Robie's op-tions, the boy rolled his head from side to side a little, as if trying to relax his muscles.

When asked whether he accepted the plea, Robie Wilson mur-mured yes. Asked whether he wished to make a statement, he re-peated what he had said earlier: that it had all been just a prank, that he and Will had not meant to hurt anybody. It was just a joke that went wrong.

Then he placed a tissue to his eyes, pitched his shoulders forward, and sobbed.

· · ·

AS I LEFT the courthouse and hit the road back to Hannibal, the day washed over me. The fields edged toward green, a typical early Mis-souri spring, but the trees were still several weeks from showing buds. The late-morning sky burned a hard blue through thin sheets of scat-tered grayish clouds. The air already left a warm touch on the skin.

I was unexpectedly taken by an odd, boyish sense of truancy as I drove. I remembered early-spring days like this from forty years ago, how they tantalized me from the other side of a schoolroom window. I'd longed to be out in them then, free at midday. Just exploring, touching the land. There was a quality about the land in those days before deep spring, hard to explain or recover from distant memory but having to do with a solitary intimacy. The land was not quite yet ready to yield up textured experience—the frogs and snakes and tur-tles still asleep in the ground, no living vines or berries yet, the streams icy-cold when you slipped into one, soaking shoe and sock—but all the more personal for that barrenness, a promise of things soon to come. I thought of the way days would lengthen out now in this time of year—a promise of woods, the prospect of stuff to do outdoors after dinner. A special scent that soon would be overpowered by the more obvious musk of spring.

For Robie Wilson, such concepts as "land" and "spring" were about to become distant abstractions. His defense lawyer having handed him over to a prosecutor who privately doubted his own ability to convict, Robie—an abstraction himself by now, in a certain way of looking at it—awaited the pleasures of the adults who had brokered his destiny.

. . .

ON MAY 17, Judge Rush handed down the sentence that Redington had asked for and that most observers expected: Robie Wilson would spend five years behind bars with the Missouri Department of Corrections.

About a month later, on June 10, Circuit Judge Ronald Belt in Shelbyville, Missouri, announced William Hill's punishment. Again, it met the expectations of those familiar with Judge Belt's tendencies. Hill would serve no prison time; Redington's request of five years was turned aside, as many had predicted. He would spend sixty days in the county jail; after that, he would undergo five years of supervised probation, would pay $8,466 in "restitution" to Virginia Walker, and would have a drug and alcohol evaluation.

Hill's attorney, Charles Stine, told the court that Hill would like to express his extreme remorse. He understood the seriousness of his actions, the lawyer said.

Hill, speaking next, verified this. "I'm sorry for what I did," he said. "It was a stupid mistake. I'm sorry for the family of Mr. Walker."

In his own statement, prosecutor Redington said, "The only good thing I have to say in William Hill's defense is he agreed to cooperate. I will tell the court Mr. Walker was a man that the entire town of Hannibal loved. He was an avid jogger and was out jogging the night the two defendants hit him."

He added, "I will say that without his [Hill's] testimony, we would not have been able to file any charges against either defendant."

In a way, Robie Wilson and Will Hill had intersected with the cutting edge of life in their host state, and nation. Incarceration was among the hottest trends in Missouri that year. "Prisons are a booming business in Missouri, a seemingly recession-proof industry," the *St. Louis Post-Dispatch* had only recently reported. "The Corrections Department is teeming with new hires, 3300 since Gov. Mel Carnahan took office six years ago, bringing the work force to 9419. The Governor proposes hiring 657 more employees by summer of 1999."

Northeastern Missouri—the Hannibal area—was at the forefront of the boom. The 1,460-bed Women's Eastern Reception, Diagnostic and Correctional Center at Vandalia, forty-three miles southwest of the town, had opened in December 1997, creating jobs for five hundred people and unfurling a payroll of $9.6 million. Vandalia, with a population of twenty-seven hundred, had since been graced with two new subdivisions and a fifty-thousand-square-foot shopping center.

At Bowling Green, where Robie would likely spend the next five years of his life, the new men's prison (it opened in February 1998) had gestated a satellite economy that already included a new hotel, a bank, and a fast-food franchise. An Italian restaurant was in the planning stages. Farmland prices had tripled in some parts of the area.

"The pace is staggering," the *Post-Dispatch* article reported. "The Corrections Department takes in a net statewide increase of five prisoners each day, and its caseload jumps by 20 probations a day. Currently, 24,919 felons are locked up in Missouri's 20 facilities. The Department also supervises 51,000 probations and 10,000 parolees."

The Missouri figures, of course, reflected national trends. By February 2000, the prison population in America reached two million, a doubling over a decade. The United States, which accounted for one-twentieth of the world's population, harbored one-fourth of its prisoners, at a cost to taxpayers of more than $41 billion a year.

As one commentator noted, "This doubling of the prison population has come about during the greatest period of economic expansion in memory. That is noteworthy because historically it has been the other way around." He added that to keep pace with this, one of the "most extraordinary publicly financed growth industries ever," the United States would have to build the equivalent of a new one-thousand-bed prison facility every week.

"Who is Robie Wilson?" Branson Wood had asked. His question, forgotten virtually the moment it was asked, had, in a sense, answered itself: There was no such person as Robie Wilson, certainly not as defined by the acutely abstracted public universe that governed the lives of American adolescents, even adolescents in venues that imagined themselves to be "traditional" or "heartland" or "hometown" communities. Within this rubric, the personal identity of a given young person was an irrelevance, an inconvenient variable best subsumed into the ever-escalating aggregate.

Thus Robie Wilson, child of a broken home that had known violence, pigeonholed as "incorrigible" by a public-school system that had little interest or prowess in exciting his intellectual curiosity, inheritor of the blankness known as "not much to do," agent of bad judgment and hideous fate, commodity in the self-serving power transactions of attorneys in a criminal-justice system designed for velocity rather than the reclamation of an emerging human persona—thus Robie Wilson braced for a life under the identity that had been dealt him: inmate.

・ 16 ・

POSTMORTEMS

A few days after Robie Wilson's fate was decided, I visited the
prosecuting attorney, Tom Redington, in his Hannibal law office.

Seated in a thoughtful posture behind his desk, Redington elaborated on the uncertainties the Wilson-Hill case had presented him,
uncertainties that led to his series of tactical maneuvers that pre-
empted a trial for either boy.

"Frankly, we sort of suspected all along that it was more a case of
manslaughter than of murder," he said. "Reckless, unintended death.
But when faced with one of the principals who says, 'Here's what
happened'—and now he's a state's witness who I don't totally believe.
I recognize the fact that he may try to push it off on Wilson more
than might be exactly true—well, now I'm faced with his statement
versus, 'I dunno, I didn't have anything to do with it, it was a bumpy
road and a defective door.'

"Faced with that evidence, I filed murder in the second degree.
There are a number of different forms of that charge. The form that
we filed was, Wilson purposely acted to cause serious physical injury
and it caused the death of Mr. Walker."

As Redington ticked off his tactical maneuvers, I was struck once
again by the sense of surreality that had surrounded this brief trial.
Its prosecutor had just told me quite calmly that he had never been
convinced that his case was about murder, then, just as calmly, had

recited the reasons why he had filed for murder in the second degree anyway.

Perhaps I just didn't get out to enough criminal trials. Or perhaps I was not yet inured to the machinations faced by American adolescents who stumble into the criminal-justice system.

Redington was continuing ahead. "Even back when the defense attorney started jury selection, I could tell that he was not going to maintain with the rattling-door explanation, that he was probably gonna put Wilson on the stand to say, yes, he did open the door, that it was a prank, it was supposed to be just to scare [Walker], but they didn't intend or ever talked about injuring him or killing him, it was more of a reckless thing."

This was in fact about how everyone had come to view the event, I thought.

Redington moved on to describe the moment of his decision to reduce the charge. "Some of the things I heard the defense attorney saying [on the trial's first day] really fit better with what I think really happened than what William Hill was saying. So I talked to the widow and her family. I said, here's what we really think: Manslaughter probably fits better. And there's always a risk when you have one defendant testifying against the other. The jury might disbelieve everything. So there is some risk here, and if we continue on, they might find him not guilty at all." Redington paused and reflected for a moment. "And that would be something that I felt would really be unsatisfactory."

I brought up the matter of Will Hill as a state's witness. Why had Redington allowed him this chance?

Redington's answer was conspicuously at odds with his stern courtroom promises of sixteen witnesses and damning forensic evidence. "In a situation like this, you really don't have much of a choice," the prosecutor replied. "There were only three people there, and one of 'em's dead, and the other two are both defendants. I felt we had to have one of them [testifying] to get beyond a reasonable doubt.

"As to the forensic evidence—frankly, none of the forensic evidence really makes much difference unless we can explain exactly what happened. It was certainly possible, when we started into this, that Mr. Walker could have tripped on a rock and fallen in front of the car. To be able to explain what happened, we really needed some explanation from somebody that was there, and that ends up being either Wilson or Hill. Because there were no other eyewitnesses at all."

Which defendant would you have preferred to turn state's evidence? I asked.

Once again, Redington portrayed himself as a man without a choice. "Only one of them came forward and made that offer. It's a difficult decision, really, to decide even when only one of them comes forward. Do we want to do that? Do we want to give somebody a better deal even though they were one of the bad actors in the crime? But in a situation like this you don't really have much choice. In fact, the first time I talked about this kind of thing with Mrs. Walker, she became kind of angry. 'Why are you treating one of them worse than you are the other? Why'd you give a deal to one of them?' And I said, 'We don't really have any choice. It's one of them or maybe none, that we're going to try to convict.' "

Given that each boy will go before a separate judge for sentencing, I asked Redington, and that one judge may be of a different temperament from the other, what is the likelihood of the two receiving comparable sentences?

"I'm going to recommend the same sentence to each judge," he said. "The defense is going to argue probably for the same thing to each judge. And we'll have to just see how it goes. The conventional wisdom is that Judge Belt is much more lenient than Judge Rush. But Belt can be very strict, and frankly in cases like this, where there is a death, and such a senseless death, I wouldn't be at all confident if I was the defense attorney that probation or something was a lock."

Not quite the case, as things turned out.

There seemed only one question left to ask the prosecutor: Who wins in a trial such as this one?

For once, his answer was direct and unqualified. "Nobody wins," he said.

. . .

THE FOLLOWING DAY I sought out another viewpoint for some of these questions. (Branson Wood had chosen to remain aloof from discussing the case.) I looked up a respected public defender in Hannibal, Raymond Legg.

Finding Legg's office was hardly a routine matter. (Finding public defenders' offices is rarely a routine matter, I had noticed.) The telephone directory had him in the old county courthouse building at Tenth and Broadway; the directory there had him on the basement floor. (Public defenders' offices usually are on basement floors, I'd found.) But on descending the stairs into a level that stank of mold and bad air, I discovered—thanks to a computer-printout sign on the office door—that his quarters had been transferred. As it turned out, they had been transferred to H-Roc, the semioccupied old hospital building that provided learning space for Hannibal's feral children.

"I know hardly anything about Robie as a person," stipulated Legg, a rawboned Missourian with an air of proletarian combativeness, when I had finally made it to his quarters. "But from what I did see, from my distance, I thought the driver of the car got far better treatment than Robie did. And without knowing more, it raises the question in my mind of why. Why did the driver get offered such a better deal? Right out of the box, and Robie had to push it all the way into the second day of the trial.

"I've seen that happen in some of my cases. My client's mistake is nothing more than coming in after the other guy. Some codefendant who, in my opinion, is equally culpable but is offered some sweetheart deal that basically absolves him.

"I've never had a client treated that well. I mean I've worked out good deals for clients, but nothing on that order." Legg paused and thought for a minute. "I guess there are probably a few things we can learn from this case. One is that when a criminal charge is filed, you can do a better job of prosecuting if you pull the decision makers away from public sentiment.

"You've got what is often called the criminal-justice pyramid or funnel. You start with the cop on the scene. He's the first decision maker. Then it funnels to his supervisors, then it funnels to the prosecutor, then the judge and the jury. I think sometimes there's people in that funnel, when they're making the decisions, it's hard in a small community like this not to consider public sentiment. I think for the most part most judges and prosecutors do a good job of that. But there are always cases where decisions were made not so much on the facts, the evidence, but out of political considerations. And I think, you know, with Robie Wilson, they thought, *somebody has to pay.* And then you do anything you can do to get somebody to pay."

Our talk turned from the prosecution of the case to the defense. Legg did not choose to comment directly on how Robie's defense was handled but offered a novel perspective on dealing with a prosecutor who had "turned" one of the suspects.

"I have defended cases when they turned the wrong person," he said. "In fact, I love it when they pick the wrong guy. Because it gives me ammunition to cross-examine. When that happens, I don't even have to talk about the facts of the case." He smiled a hard little smile. "I just get into cross about your past.

"But it usually makes the prosecutor's job easier," he acknowledged. "So they're at least willing to entertain an offer to turn. Their evidence gathering has not necessarily been the best. The cops don't know everything that's going on in a given case. In some ways I probably have a better idea about what's happening in Hannibal with the criminals than they do. So they're always looking for ways to open doors that they didn't even know existed.

"And the more high profile a case gets, there's more of a tendency for some prosecutors to just look for that final nail that they can drive in."

I asked Legg a version of the question I'd asked Redington: What difference does it make, getting that final nail? Who wins? Who wins when a sixteen-year-old kid does a horrible, stupid, lethal thing, without meaning to, and gets incarcerated? What changes? Who is served? Is it a deterrent, for example? Is it a matter of getting rehabilitated?

Legg smiled again and looked away. "The last place on earth a person is gonna be rehabilitated," he said after a minute, "is in prison. They've got a couple programs in the Department of Corrections that seem to be making some difference in rehabilitating kids. But then I can think of kids, sixteen, seventeen, eighteen years old, good kids, kids from good families, who go out and do something stupid, I mean just inherently *stupid*, and they end up getting charged with a felony. If you can't get the state to back off, they walk out with some type of felony conviction. And now you've just put an eighteen-year-old kid who's never been in any trouble in jail, or on a felony probation, and taken away from him a lot of meaningful little opportunities to invest in his life. And nobody is served by that.

"You don't get many breaks in this system, not even if you're a kid. Missouri ranks with Texas as the toughest criminal-justice state in the United States. They're as conservative, they're as harsh, they're very come down hard and with stiff penalties. I've talked to public defenders in other states about what the end results are. They're amazed at how harshly our clients get treated.

"But really, it's the whole country. Prisons are the growth industry of the nineties. We incarcerate more people than South Africa. As a country we have always been real retribution oriented. Now we are even more so. Retribution, revenge, punishment are the bywords. It's couched in sanctimonious language, but when you get right down to it, that's all it is, in my opinion. We don't like what you're doing, and we're going to put you away just as long as we can.

"So what it comes down to in this case is that nobody's going to win. You hate to see the suffering of family of the victim—I mean, it's a horrible thing to have happen to you. It destroys families to have that happen. But what does the victim's family get? Five years from now, what has the family gotten by sending Robie Wilson to prison? Nothing. Maybe we can't give 'em anything. But what did Robie get out of that? A five-year prison record where the only thing he'll learn is how to be tougher than the guy that wants to have sex with him.

"If Robie goes to prison, I would not be surprised to see him come through this system again. Because that's what he's gonna learn. If he doesn't go to prison, people like me will never see him again. And I think that's the end result you want. When people like me never see a client more than once."

If you could devise an appropriate punishment, I asked Legg, what would it be?

He stretched out a hand, palm up. He shrugged. He thought it over. "Some people," he acknowledged, "the only way you can reach 'em is to lock 'em up. And even then sometimes it doesn't reach 'em. I don't want to sound like, oh, we shouldn't punish people. I think we should punish people. People deserve to be punished for what they do wrong. But sending an adolescent kid to prison for a crime he did not commit on purpose is not a punishment that fits the crime."

What sort of punishment does fit the crime? I pressed. Legg thought it over some more. The quick self-assurance with which he had responded up until this point had given way to a pained hesitancy. It was becoming clear to me that he was struggling to find a persuasive way of making a suggestion that most of his fellow lawyers, most of his townsmen, most Americans, would find fundamentally unacceptable: that for all but the most willful acts of antisocial aggression and violence, "punishment," as society has come to understand it in relation to its errant children, is utterly beside the point.

"On a broad plane," Legg said at length, choosing his words meticulously, "I'm concerned on a larger scale with this. We take kids at a relatively young age in America and we write 'em off. We demonize our kids. Our children are bad unless they prove themselves otherwise.

"Now, I've represented bad kids, and I know they're out there. But I truly believe that for the most part, our focus with children should not be so much on punishment as on building hope and structure into their lives at an early age, before they go out and do these bad stupid things. We should focus on groups whose stated purpose is to take children and help them develop as good people. I mean groups like Four-H, Boy and Girl Scouts. Maybe that sounds corny, out of the past. But these groups are still operating, and they all have the same basic goal: to instill in kids personal value systems they can draw upon later in life.

"I'm active in scouting. I'm an assistant scoutmaster and a cubmaster. And I love it. And I'll tell you this: It would work—it would work a lot better than it is—if parents would get more involved. We have parents sending their children to our program, but that's just it. They *send* them. They want to *dump* their kids into the program but not be involved in program itself. It's difficult to find adults to volunteer. And if we don't get that wide volunteer support, we're always going to remain stuck cleaning up the mess. Talking about punishment."

There it was again. In Raymond Legg's frustration were the echoes of Jill Whitaker's defeat—the living rebukes to minimal civic dignity known as "feral children" who took refuge in this same discarded hospital building, the phantom ingredients of Marshall Kreuter's "social capital"—trust, cooperation, civic engagement, reciprocity. There lay the remnants of Market Street and all the Market Streets of the nation. There lay the voice of stunted brotherhood that could declare a neighborhood "safer" by virtue of the butchering of one of its residents.

I thought back, months later, to Raymond Legg's pained hesitancy at giving voice to a proposition that should be ringingly self-evident. These were the boom months in the nation's great economic surge. My train of association did not, for once, run automatically to Twain. It ran instead to Steinbeck, describing the destruction of the oranges in California by the "men of knowledge," rather than share the bounty with the dispossessed: "There is a crime here that goes beyond denunciation. There is a sorrow here that weeping cannot symbolize. There is a failure here that topples all our successes."

· · ·

THERE WAS NO celebrating going on at Virginia Walker's house when I stopped by before leaving town. The Walkers' son Michael, who had driven up from St. Louis for the trial, greeted me at the door and welcomed me with a solemn gesture into the familiar darkened living room. Virginia sat in a chair near the drape drawn across the picture window giving on to the front lawn.

"I tell you, I was very disappointed," Virginia told me in a voice hardly above a whisper. "This morning, I was just in turmoil. So I guess maybe . . ." her voice trailed away.

But didn't you get to approve the prosecutor's decision? I asked her.

Her voice was steadier now, but still wan. "Well, I did have that choice. He would have done, you know, what I wanted. The way it looked, it was this or nothing. I mean, you don't know what the jury's going to do. If he had went with the murder charge, and the jury didn't take all that evidence into account, then he would have got off scot-free. This way . . ." her voice trailed again.

I asked Michael how he felt about it all. He was a small, thin man of about forty who wore his soft longish hair parted in the middle and sported an outsized walrus mustache. His back showed an extreme curvature. He had on a vintage pair of bell-bottomed denim trousers over black cowboy boots with sharply pointed toes. All of this, combined with his sad, expressive eyes, gave him the aura of a forlorn Wild Bill Hickock.

"Well, like Mom said, I'm disappointed," Michael replied in a low, husky voice, "but he has to be punished somehow, and this was the only viable way of going about it basically. Otherwise, like Mom said, he might have gotten off, maybe. It was a gamble."

Could you tell me a little bit about your father? What kind of man he was? Your boyhood memories of him? I asked.

"Give me a second," the son murmured and pressed his fingers to his eyelids.

After a bit, he said, "He was a very loving man. I learned a lot from him. I loved him dearly. There wasn't anything he wouldn't do for me. We had a lot of fun times together. We did a lot of things together. Railroading was a major hobby with us." Michael was crying now. "I remember when I was like four or five years old, and Dad, Mom, and I would go down to the train station and watch the trains coming in at night. The big roundhouse that they didn't tear down till 1984. And my interests just blossomed from there in railroading. His dad, my granddad, was a railroader. Dad had the chance to go into it, but we kinda talked him out of it."

Why'd you do that? I asked.

"Kinda afraid of change," Michael answered, a little cryptically. "Didn't want to move."

But you and your dad went down there to watch the trains?

"Yes, we watched just about every aspect of the railroad. Train dispatching, locomotive repair. We made friends with a lot of the railroaders down there. I had hands-on experience operating a lot of the locomotives. I made friends with the locomotive engineer who ran one of the switch engines down there. Every once in a while he would let me run the switch engine in the yards. I was maybe twelve, thirteen, fourteen. Something like that. It was almost like a college education in the railroad. I learned a lot about railroading.

"My dad's dad worked for the Wabash for nearly fifty years. And I think on both sides of the family that railroaders go back years, back to the beginning, more or less. I've always thought that it's been in my blood, and I've always had an interest in it."

I recalled—silently—that Kyle and Kirk Wilson's father had been a railroading man.

Is railroading what you went into? I asked Michael.

"No. I had a bad back. For that type of job that I had to have perfect health, so I didn't go into it."

He had become a draftsman for Southwestern Bell. He drew outside plant records, cable networks, terminals, phone poles. All computerized. He did a little database management. It was all pretty fun, he said. He was unmarried.

I moved to the hard part. What it was like when you heard about it? I asked Michael.

The silence in the living room came back for a little while. Virginia Walker sat immobile, staring at her son. I had the feeling that she herself had not yet heard the answer to this question.

"I was in my apartment in St. Louis," Michael said finally. "I was watching a Clint Eastwood movie. I can't remember which one. I remember that's what I was doing. Next thing, I heard that Dad was in an accident. And I put the phone down and I was on the road, posthaste. I didn't have any idea of what kind of shape he was in, how bad he was. I was praying he was okay. And when I got here . . ." He stopped.

What has it been like since then? I asked him.

"I don't know. While planning his funeral I got extremely angry." He fell silent for so long that I began to think he had finished talking altogether.

"I haven't liked to talk about it, unless I'm with Mom, or with some of our really close friends. I just don't talk about. I don't express any emotions about it. I just keep it all locked in." He wept a little, his head down. "It's been rough." His voice broke.

What would you say to Robie, to Will Hill, I asked him, if you had the chance? And then, stupidly, awkwardly, I added, Do you see them as human beings?

Michael Walker raised his head and shot me a long, measuring, sidelong look. Our eyes held for a few moments. "Yeah, they're human beings," he said. "The other day I remember thinking that if this was the 1870s, in the Wild West, if that kind of mentality was around, I would have done something about it. I think you know what I mean. But there's nothing I can do. So I just sit and ride it out."

Leaving the Walker house, I became aware again of an enormous absence. I'd vaguely noticed the same sensation as I'd walked up the small sidewalk to the door an hour or so earlier, but I had been too preoccupied to pin it down. Now I realized what was missing: the enormous blue spruce, which Virginia and Jim had planted as a $2.98 grocery-store shrub when they bought the house.

What happened to it? I asked her as she stood in her doorway. A yardworker she'd hired had cut it down a few months ago, she told me. It had been an accident.

LEAVING HANNIBAL

I could never have anticipated it as the time drew near to leave Hannibal, but what I would cherish most about the town in my memories were the very qualities that later generations of its children found unendurable: its silence and isolation.

We were isolated. We all knew that. The movies, the cars, the new TV shows, the nighttime neon, the rock and roll, the Fall Festival, even the chimera of sex—all these quickenings—did not, finally, seem to us a part of Hannibal's essence. They were interesting artifacts from some other galaxy, a meteor shower that moved and excited us and made us want to accelerate and dance fast, but they weren't part of us; they did not come from the local water or the local soil.

Hollywood supplied most of these quickenings, or the clues for how to use them. Hollywood was still a long way off then; it had not yet expanded, metastasized, colonized towns like ours, coated every square inch of America's surface, drifted like a vapor onto the consciousness of every living being as a constant enforcer of scale and true significance. Hollywood may have been connected to us by concrete—Highway 36, cracked and tar-caulked, shot off due west in its direction—but the distance and obstacles were satisfyingly daunting.

One would have to drive through a string of Missouri settlements far tinier and more inscrutable than ours—through Monroe City and Hunnewell and Shelbina and Clarence and Macon and on through St. Joseph some two hundred miles to the west on the Kansas border,

U.S. 36 running along the old Hannibal–St. Joseph Railroad line. The highway ran all the way out to Colorado, ending at Denver, unthinkably far, and yet only half the distance between us and Hollywood, where Lana Turner lived in her sunglasses and capri pants.

Hannibal was isolated from that vastness, all right. It hardly seemed possible to think of connective matter at all, to imagine that any of us could start heading west on U.S. 36 someday and, without leaving the planet, actually contrive to fetch up in Hollywood some weeks later, provided we didn't screw up and get lost in the desert.

We all knew how isolated we were. But I don't recall that we cared.

"Madroad driving men ahead," wrote Jack Kerouac, this new beatnik voice, "—the mad road, lonely, leading around the bend into the opening of space towards the horizon of Wasatch snows promised us in the vision of the West, spine heights at the world's end."

That was fine for him to say. But I don't remember that people in Hannibal were all that avid to get onto the madroad, or to see any of those spine heights at the world's end.

I think we felt a grandeur in the distances between Hannibal and everyplace else, an exalted mystery that only distance can confer. We liked the separateness and the wondrous breadth of American culture. We liked it that cities were far away and a little frightening, and that getting to one and coming home again was a real and singular achievement.

We liked it that driving sixty or seventy miles to a basketball game at another high school was an occasion that thrust us into a distinctly different, outer world. We liked the sense of making that journey, but also the sense of its specialness, of out of the routine. We liked tooling along toward Jefferson City an hour after school, the winter sun already setting behind silhouetted barns and tree lines, our car caravan of players and cheerleaders and me, the team manager: all of us listening to the McGuire Sisters singing, "Sugar in the Morning, Sugar in the Evening, Sugar at Suppertime." And it being suppertime. We liked it that the host team's gym smelled different from ours, that the crowd's echoes were different off the walls, and that the script on the other team's jerseys was different. This was about as exotic as we needed things to be.

We liked what Thomas Wolfe (whom none of us had read) called "A bracelet of a few, hard lights along the river, a gem-like incan-

descence . . . so poignantly lost and lonely in enormous darkness."
We liked the illusion of deep lethargy that many visitors to our town
perceived, and we knew the key to entering the richer life that the
illusion concealed. We knew that everything depended on what lay
on the other side of that lethargy and paralysis, at the end of the
enormous darkness.

I knew that. And as I later discovered, my brother Jim knew that
too. One of us made it through to that other side, and one of us did
not. I am not absolutely certain which of us made it and which of us
didn't.

Here is what I mean by this knowledge of what lay on the other
side, the secret side, of our apparent lethargy, our presumed loss and
loneliness in the enormous darkness. This is from a letter I received,
typewritten and single-spaced, from a classmate of mine in May of
1973, when I was working for a newspaper in Chicago. She was small
and dark-haired, quiet, and shy, and wrote quiet little poems for the
Hannibal High School paper, the *Black and Red,* about the rain coming in on little cat feet. We had all thought she was pretty good, to
be making that kind of stuff up.

This letter arrived just after I had gotten an article published in
Playboy magazine and was feeling pretty much the man of the world.
This letter pulled me back to where I belonged, into the quietude. I
have never stopped reading it.

> . . . I have tried to keep track of everyone in our class and except
> for a few I have something on just about everyone. You were one
> of the ones that I had wondered about. Where you were? Were you
> married? Had you fulfilled your cartoon and newspaper dreams?
> Now I have a couple of newspaper clippings of you to put in my
> yearbook.
>
> When I read in the Hannibal paper that there was going to be
> an article written by you in PLAYBOY, I asked the store here that
> carries it "when" it would be out. A few days before it was due, I
> called down to be sure I had the correct date and when I asked
> about the "June issue of PLAYBOY" my 11 year old daughter
> about died. "Well MOM"!
>
> I consider myself an "Average American" . . . I watch the news
> on TV and read most of the paper (Courier-Post) on the happenings
> in government, the Vietnam War, etc. But, I really don't know

"What" is going on and "Who" to believe. Rather, who NOT to believe. News articles scratch the surface as do TV and a lot of times unless you're very well versed in all of this and read every word in different papers, you cannot grasp it all or at least I don't. Your article seemed to put a lot of things neatly in place for me.

It occurred to me as I was reading the article that 14 years ago this month we were both graduating from the same High School. I'm married, live 20 miles away [from Hannibal]. My world evolves around my husband and six children. Your world is one well in-volved in the world. You travel. You meet people that I hear about or see on TV.

While the questions you ask are full of knowledge and on a world scale concerning the affairs of the world . . . mine are the questions of importance to the woman who is a wife and mother: Will the garden I planted come up or will there be too much rain now and not enough later? Will my children go thru the summer with no serious accidents or illnesses? What will I fix for dinner tonight that will please my family and which is within the budget?

. . . In High School we all felt that you would go places with your cartoons. (I'm proud to say I have one or two that was on the hall bulletin board) but I never dreamed HOW far.

I imagine you have heard from other of our classmates . . . Do you ever see any of them? I'm sitting here thumbing through our senior yearbook and a lot of kids are still close by. Wonder where Margaret Ellis is now? Ward Smith? Baylis Glascock, I heard, is in Hollywood or thereabouts and he is a producer (or something) isn't he? My info about him came from Johnny Burger one night about 2-3 years ago when he tried to sell me a vacuum sweeper. I wasn't interested at the time and we sat for over an hour and talked about the 10 year class reunion that I missed . . .

Well, I meant to drop you a short letter and I've rattled on and on. It is so quiet around here this time of night that I can type on and on without realizing how late or how much I'm typing. It's only 1 am May 28. My husband is on the Midnight shift these next 2 weeks and all 6 sound asleep . . . except for one who is talking in his sleep . . . I thoroughly enjoy these late hours at night . . .

I wish you continued success in whatever you do . . .

That letter is from the great quiet-beating heart of the Hannibal that always will have been. Part of the Hannibal that, I thought then, would always be there, intact.

But it wasn't. High school ended, and I was out of Hannibal for good, heading west, almost before I knew it. The silence and isolation were over. The life prefigured by the silence and isolation was about to begin.

In the summer of 1959, just after I'd graduated high school, my father was assigned a new Fuller Brush territory. Jefferson City was in the middle of Missouri, the state capital. I guess we'd put our house up for sale—we were living on Pleasant Street by this time, next to a family named Paradise—and I suppose somebody bought it. I don't remember any of those details. I just remember that the day came when we had to leave forever.

We packed up everything into a big white moving van. I was seventeen and an exile. My grief at leaving Hannibal was muted slightly by the size of that van—it seemed to confer a substance on us that I hadn't known till then that we'd had—and by the fact that I would be allowed to drive one of our two cars out of town to our new life. My father had switched from Nashes by then; we owned two used Studebakers. Cut-rate. I got to drive the two-toned green one with the tail fins. We left Hannibal in the glare of a summer morning, and I drove with one elbow resting on the open window jamb, my mother and brother Jim, in his T-shirt and glasses, in there with me. I kept my eyes away from the rearview mirror, and I did not mark the moment when we crossed the town line.

I prepared to go off to college in the fall, the first member of my family line since Adam to do so. The University of Missouri at Columbia had a school of journalism. In those days, it was still possible to imagine newspapering as a romantic way of life.

Jefferson City drew our edgy family closer together for a while. I remember driving somewhere in the new town with thirteen-year-old Jim beside me in the front seat. A guy in a Volkswagen cut us off, honked, and gave us the finger. "What was that?" I asked my brother. "A *hornet?*" A comradely wisecrack. How novel it sounded. It may have been the high-water mark of our relationship.

My father built up new Fuller Brush routes. He had decided to keep on selling door-to-door until he "got the hang" of his "field manager" responsibilities. He never got the hang and essentially kept selling door-to-door until the summer he died. But he did locate a good bowling alley and soon was in a league, one of the crewcut beer sippers, wearing a yellow team shirt with his name stitched on the back.

I put a dent in our cut-rate Studebaker one day. It was the other driver's fault; he cruised through a stop sign at a four-way intersection and put a soft crease in the passenger door. When he got home my father ripped his belt off and lashed me a few samples anyway, just for old times' sake, maybe. I was practically a college freshman. Maybe that explained it. Putting on airs. Not to the liking of Pap.

Jefferson City probably improved my brother's life. He'd been a loner in Hannibal, to the extent that I was interested in observing such aspects about him, but here, like my father, he slipped into a circle of regular guys. His new pals spent time in one another's basements, touching electrical wires together and nailing and shellacking things. They gave Jim a nickname: "Pro." That was fine with me; it meant he was no longer even nominally my responsibility.

Joyce, at nine, blossomed as a star of the city's parks department tennis instruction program, run by a woman who looked like a deeply tanned Queen Elizabeth. We all went to her Saturday matches and sat on hard wooden benches on the sidelines, clapping as politely as the best country club people when she won a point. It was the first time in family history that any of us had gone to see another one of us do anything without somebody dropping a soda pop on the floor or nearly falling off an auditorium stage.

At the university I encountered a new kind of human being. These creatures bore some resemblance to teenage kids like me: unwrinkled skin, full supply of hair and teeth. But beneath this surface, they radiated *adultness*. The boys displayed baffling prowess with sport jackets, cologne, political opinion, business, prophylactics, gin, avant-garde jazz. The girls knew how to sit on a sofa while maintaining perfect posture; they knew how to cross their ankles and tuck their legs slantwise; they knew French (*"C'est la vie!"*).

I was fascinated. Here were a bunch of grown-ups walking around the campus inside the skins of kids my age. I'd never seen teenagers do adult behavior so well. Where I came from, I'd rarely seen *adults* do adult behavior so well.

What I was watching, I guess, was the last remnant of the Silent Generation—those dutiful postwar children of the small-town mercantile gentry, of whom Clark Kerr, chancellor of the University of

California, was just at that time predicting, "The employers will love this generation. They aren't going to press many grievances. They are going to be easy to handle. There aren't going to be any riots."

Wrong.

The university became my new hive, replacing if not supplanting the hive that was Hannibal.

It took a little time; it took the first autumn and winter. Far more compact than my hometown, the campus seemed nonetheless out of scale with any environment I'd known. It seemed bigger, taller, denser, impervious, disinterested, *up to something* that probably did not include me.

The residence halls had fire drills in the fall of my freshman year, loud buzzers that got everybody up and out, and I took them seriously, just as I had the drills in grade school. One morning I half awoke and stumbled into the shower room across the hall. As I peeled down to get into my stall, another student entered the room, out of my sight, and plugged in his electric razor. The loud buzzing caught my attention. In my Fruit Of The Looms I staged a one-man evacuation of the building, down three flights of stairs and out into the morning sunlit campus, nearly naked, entirely safe from flames.

It proved one of the last gestures of my boyhood. In November 1960, I sat in the parlor of my girlfriend's sorority house and watched several of her Alpha Phi sisters weep, actually weep out loud into their handkerchiefs, because John F. Kennedy had defeated Richard Nixon for the presidency, and their fathers had explained to them that the country was about to go to hell.

Two years later, in the fall of 1962, it appeared that the fathers had called it right. American spy planes, flying over the island of Cuba that Fidel Castro had taken over during my senior year of high school, had returned home with photographs of Russian-made nuclear-missile bases on the island. In October, President Kennedy ordered his famous naval blockade of the island. Russian leaders rumbled about war. Suddenly we all divided our thoughts between homework and the prospect of a close-range nuclear attack.

For eight days students walked around glassy-eyed. There were prayer vigils, lighted candles at night outside the Greek houses.

Finally Nikita Khrushchev "backed down," as the newspapers put it, and dismantled the bases. The crisis was over and everybody went back to doing the twist and wondering why Marilyn Monroe had committed suicide.

The sorority girls' fathers were right, though, about the world being about to go to hell. They just weren't right for the reasons they had given.

I drew cartoons for the campus weekly and for the campus humor magazine. Entering journalism school my junior year, I drew for its daily paper, *The Missourian*. A right-wing anti-Commie cold warrior by osmosis, I drew stern editorial cartoons chiding Khrushchev as the neighborhood bully, strutting along the top of a picket fence and juggling nuclear missiles as if they were oranges. Let that be a lesson to him. I also wrote for the sports page and drew sports cartoons.

Meanwhile, back at home in Jefferson City, my brother Jim was making his own reputation. The student newspaper at his high school, the *Red and Black*, ran a profile and photograph of him, all horn-rims, jeans, and a genial grin, as a "budding mechanic." "I like to mess around with anything that isn't working right," he's quoted as saying. In the photo with him is one of his contraptions, a homemade phonograph. The article reports that, "With only a small number of tools, Jim has repaired broken radios, fans, and clocks." Its snappy sign-off: "Antiquated articles will always be rejuvenated if they are deposited in the workshop of Jim Powers."

I was never aware that Jim knew how to make a phonograph.

His growing prowess with things that weren't working right didn't extend to the tensions between us. One of our last big fights, before we both left the family home for good, came on the Christmas morning of my senior year in college and his in high school. I can't remember what started it, only that it was raging before we were fully awake, and it lasted a while. We fought and cursed and wept throughout the day. Pap looked on with his salesman's grin.

If my last act of boyhood was my nearly naked flight from the electric shaver in the residence dorm, my first experience as an adult involved the incident at the Student-Faculty Supper Club.

A few of the adults-under-boys'-skins had organized this club in the spring of 1963, just before my graduation. The idea, probably borrowed from the fabled sherry soirees at Yale and Oxford, was to bring "student leaders" and professors together in a social setting—minus the sherry. My credentials as a "student leader"—to the extent

I had any—must have devolved from my column in the campus weekly paper.

Our inaugural supper was held in a "country inn," converted from a farmhouse a few miles outside town. I put on a tie and my new bleeding madras sport coat and rode out there on a bus with my fellow student leaders—fraternity guys, beefy business majors from the midwest gentry. We were in a horsing-around mood on the bus, but as we trooped into the darkened dining hall we stopped our snickering and fell silent. Each of us must have felt the weight of true adulthood descending with its rites of passage and subtle pressures. We were learning the first lesson of being men: how important it is not to screw up under scrutiny.

A little ritual had been planned and explained to us. The students were to line up on one side of a long row of candlelit tables. Lining up on the opposite side would be men of the faculty. Each student was to introduce himself to the professor directly opposite.

I tried not to stare at the professor across from me. I took in an impression of sandy hair, rimless glasses glinting in the candlelight, no facial expression whatsoever, and tweed. I noticed that he stood not facing me square on but with his right shoulder turned slightly toward me. That should have been warning enough. But I read it only as an interesting way to stand.

The murmurs of mutual introduction rippled along the table toward me and my partner. When my moment came I cleared my throat and then added a little something to my greeting. I performed the one basic gesture of etiquette that my mother had taught me back in Hannibal: as I said my name, I stuck out my right hand, for a shake.

The professor studied my hand and did not move. Not a twitch. His right arm, armored in tweed, remained at his side. Time slowed down. I sensed silence in the dining room. My hand hung out over that candlelit table, fingers splayed. It hung and it hung. Waiting to be taken across the threshold.

It is hanging there still. Shy by inches of inclusion within a world beyond the world I grew up in.

And that, I decided later, long after the shock and humiliation of that moment wore away, was the way it should be.

What that professor—that smug betweeded twerp—had done was to liberate me from who I was. At that exact moment of my transition into adult society he relieved me from a lifetime of pretense. He gave me back the grandeur beneath the surface of my Missouri isolation. He gave me freedom from the covetous longing for entitlement that was my father's special burden.

If that professor had taken my hand he might have pulled me across a line that would forever separate me from my authentic social class, my origins, my true instincts, my mother and father, flawed and crazy as they, I, might be.

It's not that I forgave the son of a bitch. I never forgave him. But I'm grateful to him for what he handed me. He handed me the freedom to say, as Mark Twain had handed Huck the freedom to say, "All right, then, I'll go to hell."

· 18 ·

"DIANE DID IT"

The murder trial of Zachary Wilson was set to begin on Wednesday, April 21, 1999. But a day earlier, a fresh national horror dwarfed its significance even among the people of northeast Missouri.

I heard the first radio bulletins of the student massacre at Columbine High School in Littleton, Colorado, in the early Tuesday afternoon as I drove north on U.S. 61 toward Hannibal from the St. Louis airport. The news reverberated in my head. Braced for several days of testimony regarding the emotionally detached shotgunning of a defenseless victim by an adolescent, I was now hearing a version of the same event multiplied almost beyond imagination. The first reports estimated that there were three young shooters, armed with semiautomatic weapons, perhaps with the support of a larger circle of plotters, and a death toll of up to twenty-five, nearly as many wounded.

The world seemed to have gone unhinged. Its statues had crumbled. Obscene children with guns stalked the landscape. Wild Bill Elliott was dead, and the Patrol Boys had all taken cover.

As if in keeping with the surreality of it all, the trial of Zachary Wilson would be defined by a stunning reversal in his story. He had not murdered J. D. Poage after all, Zachary now claimed. By implication, Diane had done it.

His assertion of innocence had taken shape with eerie timing, in eerie circumstances: from his cell in the Marion County jail, in the predawn hours of June 4, 1998. In a three-page letter, written in pencil, addressed to the prosecuting attorney and dated two-thirty A.M., Zachary asserted: "Everything I have stated to any police officer has been false. The verbal statements I made were made to protect Diane. I did not kill James D. Poage or have any knowledge of the killing until after the fact. I feared for Diane's safety and tried to cover for her."

Later that same day, in what may or may not have been a spectacular coincidence, Diane Myers pleaded guilty in the Monroe County Courthouse to a charge of second-degree murder for her role in the slaughter of J. D. Poage. She entered this plea—which was not accompanied by a specific admission of the act itself—and received a relatively light sentence (twenty years in prison) in exchange for her agreement to testify against Zachary in his trial.

My first thought on hearing about Zachary's confession as a noble lie was perhaps an unworthy one: I wondered seriously, for the first time, whether he had ever made his way through a copy of Mark Twain's greatest work.

I've already suggested that the parallels between Huck's escape from St. Petersburg and Zachary's flight from Hannibal were circumstantial, if diverting. The noble deception to save the skin of the traveling companion opened up a new resonance between the two stories. "I felt good and all washed clean of sin for the first time I had ever felt so in my life," Huck tells us after writing a note to Miss Watson, from inside his wigwam on the raft far down the Mississippi, disclosing the whereabouts of Jim. The runaway slave is being held captive on a farm in Arkansas, and Huck can reap a $200 reward for turning him in to his owner—the moral thing to do in that time and place. In fact, in that time and place, "people that acts as I'd been acting about that nigger goes to ever-lasting fire."

But "I see Jim before me, all the time, in the day, and in the nighttime, sometimes moonlight, sometimes storms, and we a floating along, talking, and singing, and laughing. . . . Somehow I couldn't seem to strike no places to harden myself up against him," Huck continues, "but only the other kind. I'd see him standing my watch on top of his'n, sted of calling me, so I could go on sleeping; and see him how glad he was when I come back out of the fog . . . and how good he was . . ." And so, Huck says to himself, " 'All right, then, I'll *go* to hell'—and tore it up."

Had Zachary Wilson's confession been a deception to spare his girlfriend, even if it meant that he would face a life sentence, or even death, for a murder he did not commit? Was he recanting now only after having gotten word of Diane's plea to a lesser charge, secure in the knowledge that she could not be tried twice for the same crime?

It seemed . . . farfetched. And the recanting of the confession seemed the desperate scheme of a clever boy who had perhaps read a bit more literature than he hoped the prosecutor had read.

Still, there had been that cry of "I'll go to hell!" in this real-life parallel to Twain. And it had been uttered—at least in Zachary's telling on the night of his arrest in Ohio—by Diane.

* * *

HANNIBAL'S STREETS WERE deserted—more so than usual, it seemed—upon my arrival in the late afternoon. It felt as though everyone had taken cover. If true, the hysteria had its precedent. My mother once told me that in 1933, when John Dillinger's midwestern bank-robbing rampage had made him Public Enemy Number 1, a rumor had swept through town that the dreaded outlaw was "shooting his way up Union Street Hill," and people had dived under their beds. Today, more likely, everyone was glued to a TV set. I rounded up a takeout hamburger and fries, checked into my motel near the Historic District, two blocks from the riverfront and within the line of sight of the Tom 'n' Huck statue, and flipped on my own TV. I had planned to spend the evening reviewing what I knew of Zachary Wilson's case and its likely trajectory, starting with tomorrow's trial. But I couldn't help dividing my attention between Zachary and the coverage of the Littleton shooters and their victims. And, for that matter, the ways America was processing this latest rebuke to its illusions.

Reporters and commentators by now had fixated on the imagery of black trench coats. The teenage killers, it had been learned, were wearing black trench coats during their deadly promenade. "Trench coat Mafia" entered the lexicon of reportage. "It may or may not be relevant," one correspondent intoned, "but today is the one hundred tenth birthday of Adolf Hitler."

Adolescent faces, ravaged adolescent faces, kept filling the screen. The videotapes played and replayed, aerial footage of boys and girls stumbling out of the school building in a ragged animal stream. (Only days later would I learn that Howard Stern, the god of shock-jock radio, had wondered aloud on the air why the fleeing boys didn't try to have sex with the fleeing girls.) The Columbine students had breached one confinement only to encounter another: the restraining perimeter of news media. "She kept telling him she didn't want to die and she didn't do anything to him," I heard one girl bawl into a microphone. "But—and that's all I remember hearing before the gun went off." On another channel, Larry King kept breaking into the pauses in the remarks of a thin boy, who, still dazed and trying to collect his thoughts, was not performing up to the fast-patter standards of CNN. As the evening wore on, I began to recognize half a dozen or so students' faces, this boy's included, as they were passed from network to cable system and back to still another network. Dazed, fatigued, but gamely shuffling from camera to camera, slaking the appetite, they answered the same questions, almost unwittingly refining their responses into efficient sound bites. On the killing grounds of Columbine, adults and children had finally united, for a little while, in common labor.

Children were not the only ones holding forth, of course. Adults' perspectives on the causes of the massacre grew steadily more assured as the evening wore on. I surfed, at some point, into the inevitable Reverend Jerry Falwell, who was explaining God's take on the situation to a reporter. There has been a general turning away from the Lord in this country, Falwell revealed, an "attempt" to secularize the nation. Plus, it was the media's fault: "I do believe sadly—and I hate to have to say it—that until we have a spiritual awakening and until Hollywood becomes more responsible, until we get this terrible violence off the screen, it's painting the pictures in the minds of the children. And those who are disenfranchised or who feel deserted or lonely or rejected are retaliating."

Not every channel on the spectrum was focusing on Columbine; a select few attended to the other vital concerns of the nation. On E!'s

Talk Soup, the emcee took a call from Bambi, nineteen, of Riverside, who—emboldened, perhaps, by the Reverend Mr. Falwell's omission of sex in his indictment of the media—allowed as how she needed a crooked penis to hit her spot.

By the next morning, certain ambiguities had distilled into facts. The death toll was fixed at fifteen, including a faculty member and the two shooters themselves. No other accomplice was believed to be involved. A network reporter revealed "evidence of a virtual bomb-making factory" in one suspect's home and, in car trunks near the high school, several twenty-pound propane gas tanks, pipe bombs. Inside the bloody high school, two twelve-gauge sawed-off shotguns, a nine-millimeter handgun, and a .223-caliber carbine had been found.

Into this unscrolling diorama of adolescent morbidity, my own imagination supplied one more image: Zachary Wilson standing over the purplish remains of J. D. Poage, feeling like God, like judge, jury, and executioner.

Diane Sawyer's voice followed me out of the motel room: "As we have been saying all morning, this is now the eighth such incident in thirty-nine months. . . . If you could do one thing tomorrow that you think really would stop this, what would it be?" she asked someone. I didn't stick around to hear the answer.

· · ·

MOBERLY, SITE OF the Fourteenth Circuit Court, where Zachary Wilson's trial was to be held, lay about sixty miles southwest of Hannibal. Judging by the call-in shows I could pull in from St. Louis stations as I drove there, public opinion had by now pretty well firmed up in the matter of Columbine and what it would take to "really stop this." The hosts and callers alike seemed confident in the efficacy of a few basic remedies: dress codes (the "trench coat Mafia" had seized hold of many middle-aged imaginations), parental strictness with children bordering on intimidation, and a recapturing of control over one's own young that had somehow been wrested away by the government—possibly in the form of the Department of Health and Human Services.

"Personally, I think the parent rules the roost until the child pays rent," one host was opining to his copersonality. "My daughter goes to a school where there's a strict dress code, and that's just the way it is. If you wanna go to that school, that's the way you dress. So it's the same situation. You don't know what kid is from what background based on what they're wearing and they can't wear any of that, uh, designer stuff; no names, none of that stuff with pictures all over everything. No logos. All that."

His colleague chimed in, "Well, there's also the sense that the children get—that someone is in control." She elaborated: "I'm not allowed to wear whatever I wanna wear. My hair can't be green, uh, because someone has made a rule that I have to abide by."

"Sure," said the man. "And the problem with the public-school situation is, you know, you don't have that control."

A caller named Juanita could not have agreed more. As a school bus driver of four years' experience, she fully supported the notion that "we do need dress codes. Uniforms. You do have the children that dress different. The trench coats are nothing but a fad, no different than your quote name-brand articles. I mean I had girls that got on my bus. If they were to sneeze, you'd have saw everything." Juanita then linked this sorry how-de-do to the loss of parental control. "It goes back to, they took the rights away from us parents for correction. I was corrected growing up. I had the utmost respect for my parents. I correct my kids."

Who took it away from you? The woman host wanted to know. "Well," Juanita said, "if you correct the child, the teacher tells the child, that's child abuse. A woman told me, the teacher told her child, if your parents make you take out the trash, that's considered child abuse."

"Well, if that's the case, then I suffer from spousal abuse, too!" blurted the male host and got a good professional drive-time guffaw from his partner before both of them recollected the somber tone of the day. The male host quickly regained the pose of social commentator.

"The more time goes by, I'm just a bigger and bigger believer in the pluses of kids wearing some sort of a standard dress code to school," he said. "It doesn't have to be a plaid skirt, and it doesn't have to be something silly. Even if it's just a pair of dark blue slacks and a white shirt. Whatever you want to do."

A caller named Joe then muddied the waters a bit. "This really hits home for me," he told the call-in team. "I lost my daughter about a year and a half ago because a young punk shot her." The boy, who was seventeen, as it turned out, had followed the man's daughter into her house, pointed a nine-millimeter gun at her, and pulled the trigger. He received a three-year prison sentence for manslaughter. "I don't know who to hold responsible," the man said. "It's out of control. My daughter was a fantastic kid, a cheerleader, a beautiful person. She's gone now." He paused until his breathing was under control again. "The system doesn't work very good," he concluded.

The radio hosts were not able to say how a strict dress code might have prevented this tragedy, but they agreed wholeheartedly that it was "unfortunate." The woman delivered a commercial for a video-rental center that included a deli—or perhaps it was a deli that included a video-rental center—that was offering a five-day video rental and an eight-piece bucket of oven-fresh or fried chicken for $5.49.

Scott called in to say he thought there were too many guns out there. You could almost hear the hosting team calculate the popularity of this remark vis-à-vis their core demographic.

"But that's not going to change," the male replied quickly. "The guns will always be there. And we're going to have to get around that issue."

"The guns have always been there," the woman agreed and went deep. "The difference is that you have teenagers who are willing to pull the trigger."

Her colleague pounced on this insight and probed its nuances. "Well, yeah, and you have teenagers, which is what scares me, who are willing to say—because you have to do this before you commit this kind of an act—'*I am willing to die in the commission of this. I am willing to die.*' And for a seventeen- or eighteen-year-old to say it, to just declare that he or she is ready to die, is quite . . ." Words, at last, failed him.

His partner picked up the colloquy. "Right. And something else you said this morning. This was not a spontaneous, this was not spontaneous combustion. This was planned. I mean, every single second of this crime seemed to have been planned down to the minute."

Joyce phoned up to express her strong doubt that "unless a child is emotionally ill, things like this happen. . . . The kids don't think anymore," she added. "Everything's done on a computer. They don't use their brains anymore to think out things. I think we need to get strict with the rules. Just flat get strict. We gave that away a few years back, and that's why we have problems." Shifting ground a bit, she mentioned that the movie industry "ought to get checked out."

The woman host said, "You can't have an ankle bracelet on your child. But you're the one who rules the roost. You're the one who sets down the law of the house. If you don't want your child to see a violent movie, then by God, you better make sure that your child is fearful enough not to see the violent movie for fear of dealing with you later."

Her partner broke in to say that time was running short, but "we're all in agreement that something has to change."

A "trench coat Mafia." Hitler's birthday. Refugees from a bloody massacre having sex with one another on the run. A turning away from the Lord. Hollywood. Doing something (what?) "tomorrow" that would "really stop this." Dress codes. Uniforms. Ruling the roost. Children needing to be cowed into obedience via fearfulness. A five-day video rental and an eight-piece bucket of oven-fresh or fried chicken for $5.49.

Listening to this madhouse babble of superstition, denial, wishful thinking, spleen venting, and airheaded posturing—which must have been amplified a thousandfold around the nation (within a month, the inevitable academic published the inevitable apologia for sterile suburban culs-de-sac on the op-ed page of the *New York Times*)—it seemed almost permissible, if not psychically necessary, to wonder, in the fashionable spirit of satanic humor, why it had taken so god-damn long for America's children to start shooting up their habitat. I thought immediately of the very young Diane Myers and of how she must have looked that night in her chopped and blackened hair. Of Zachary, kicking or perhaps not kicking J. D. Poage awake.

Natural-born killers.

Moberly's low-slung skyline took form on the flat agricultural horizon. It was nearly time to meet those two.

· · ·

A FREIGHT-TRAIN whistle sounded two blocks from the Randolph County Courthouse, where heavyset people in shirtsleeves, pantsuits, and sunglasses—relatives of J. D. Poage, mostly—idled in tight, insular clusters on the steps and sidewalk, waiting for the proceedings to begin. A younger, slimmer blonde woman in blinding white pants and jacket and oval shades sat on the curb munching what looked like a cheese sandwich in the shadow of her TV station's news van. A light breeze ruffled people's blown-dry hair, birds were chirping, the thick shrubbery piled against the courthouse staircase had come out a deep green, sunlight poured from a cloudless sky. It all seemed familiar, secure, eternal springtime in a timeless heartland town.

Certainly Moberly (population 12,037) had enjoyed its moments of local distinction, even of glory. Established as a railroad company town in 1866, it was the hometown of General Omar Bradley, the great World War II general whose Twelfth Army Group liberated Paris in 1944. It was home to the Sycamore, established in 1911 to serve the railroading trade as one of the premier houses of prostitution in northeast Missouri until it closed down in 1963. Its junior college was a basketball powerhouse of occasional national repute. And from 1962 through the end of the century, Moberly was home base for the rock and roll group Plato and the Philosophers (originally the Checkmates), whose late sixties single, "13 O'Clock Flight to Psychodelphia," galvanized some local attention, and who several years later recorded an album that was almost, but not quite, released.

Most of that old town texture had by now receded into dim civic memory. Moberly's surface, like that of Hannibal, like that of most of the towns I'd visited since roughly the heyday of, say, Plato and the Philosophers, was opaque and self-enclosed. The view from the courthouse revealed the usual signs of atrophy: the pawnshop with its garish red lettering on an orange field: Buy Sell Trade GUNS; the boarded-up Magic City Mini Mall; the gift shop with its Beanie Babies come-on taped to the plate-glass window; the dusty brick facades of what once might have been a downtown apartment complex for who knew?—young office clerks and salesmen, maybe, librarians, ragtime piano players. The vanished Main Street nation.

Directly across from that failed facade was the classic emblem of town decay, the abandoned movie palace—in this case, the State, which must have been snazzy in its day. Most of its embroidering red-and-cream Art Deco tile was still intact, and its curving marquee still hovered, but its box-office window was long since smashed and jagged with unremoved shards.

The second-floor courtroom was nearly filled with spectators—tense, forward-staring spectators—by the time the judge (the Honorable Channing Blaeuer) called proceedings to order. The setting was at once smaller and more up-to-date than that which had contained Robie Wilson's trial. The judge's bench, wedged diagonally into the left corner of the room opposite the jury bench, towered above the witness stand in the center. It faced three rows of spectator benches, filled to capacity now by the same shirtsleeve people I'd seen outside the entrance; the bailiff had accommodated the spillover with individual wooden chairs placed against the left wall. Sunlight filtered through thinly slatted venetian blinds on the right.

Zachary Wilson sauntered in, unshackled, escorted by a sheriff's deputy, and I was immediately aware of his absorptive effect on a room—how he drew energy his way. He was nineteen now, pale with prison pallor but built strong, bulky through the shoulders. His blond hair had been neatly barbered, and he sported a white dress shirt, a bright-patterned necktie, and tan suit pants. His hands were buried in the deep pockets of these pants, where they would remain—a gesture of careless insouciance that actually worked; you could almost hear the loose change being jiggled—whenever he was standing. A woman in a white pantsuit and tight dark curls, whom I understood at once to be his mother, arose and stepped toward him. She reached up to his face several times with her fingertips while he stood in front of her, his head cocked over a little, his upward-slanting eyebrows quizzical, suffering her touch. He might have been a college student home for a week or so before heading off to his summer job at a brokerage firm, instead of a boy about to be tried for murder.

The two prosecutors and the two public defenders assigned Zachary's case approached their tables, all rose for the judge's entrance, and the trial was underway.

The state's case would be led by Michael Wilson, the Monroe County prosecuting attorney, and assisted by Elizabeth Kohler, a prosecutor from Jefferson City. Wilson, a compact man with closely trimmed and parted gray hair, had served for twenty years as an Air Force judge advocate. His flat midwestern twang camouflaged a steely residual military hauteur. He delivered a disdainfully crisp opening statement—he walked the jury through the murder from Zachary's confessional perspective, without bothering to acknowledge the defendant's change of plea—that gave no hint of the ferocity he would later unleash in cross-examination. He seemed almost to be inviting the defense to seize the emotional initiative. One of the two Moberly-based public defenders, a youngish man named Frederick Tucker, arose, fastening the button of his thin suit coat, to take the bait.

Tucker's first words—"This case is about making a hero out of a mentally deficient person"—indicated the complexity of his task. And, perhaps, the limits of his capacity to pull it off.

If Zachary's team had a prayer of deflecting the weight of evidence and plausibility arrayed against their defendant, it lay in their ability to construct a portrait of him as a kind of addled Galahad. They would grant his erratic, violently aggressive, self-destructive childhood and youth, his lifelong manipulation of others, his clinical symptoms of attention deficit and hyperactivity, his chronic and manifold substance abuse. But, having granted this damning inventory of traits, the public defenders would try to persuade the jury that Zachary was nonetheless an innocent bystander in the murder to which he had originally confessed, a boy guided by romantic impulse who'd chosen at first to face decades of imprisonment rather than allow his girlfriend to stand accountable for her murder of a hated abuser.

"Fifteen-year-old Diane Myers needed a hero to take the blame for what she had done, and she found Zach . . ."

It was a tactic that would test the eloquence of a Johnny Cochran or an F. Lee Bailey. Tucker, it quickly grew clear, was neither.

He reviewed Zachary's catastrophic early years. "The evidence will also be that, like most kids with a hyperactive disorder, he is often perceived as very bossy, that he's easily fired up to take on the world, and that he very often feels an overwhelming sense of panic."

He reviewed for the jury how Zach and Diane had met: "They were in a detention center for behavior modification. Juvenile detention is like a jail. It's a jail for kids, only they receive some kind of treatment . . ."

Tucker summarized Zachary's release from the center a couple of months before Diane, and their loss of contact until Zach's mother moved to Hunnewell in October 1997, to the house across the street from the one where Diane lived: "For about a month and a half, they saw each other about every day. Fell in love, or in lust, or whatever teenagers do. Had sex, talked about wanting to have kids.

"She talked about having been molested by her grandfather, and by her brother, and she thought that that had changed her somehow, so that she couldn't have any kids. Now, they're talking about getting married . . .

"Well, they both have somewhat of a drug problem, and Zach, with his impulse problem, cannot get off the drugs. He thinks he needs some kind of treatment. He checks himself into the Hannibal Council on Alcohol and Drug Abuse . . ."

As I listened, I found myself focusing on the public defender's air of offhandedness toward the case he was presenting. I wondered whether the jury was picking up on it as well. The "love or lust," the "whatever," the "somewhat," the "some kind of." And the reference to juvenile detention as "a jail for kids" had a weirdly casual ring. As did, for that matter, Diane's imputed "thought" that her molestation "had changed her somehow, so that she couldn't have any kids."

These were minor quibbles set against Tucker's opening allusion to Zachary Wilson as "a mentally deficient person." If the jury had entertained doubts as to his capacity for mayhem until that point, surely those doubts were now wiped away.

My preoccupation with the defender's word choices had nothing to do with any sentiments in favor of the defendant. If anything, my discomfort with Tucker's tone warred strongly with my near-absolute certainty, at this stage of events, that Zachary Wilson was guilty as charged and needed to be sequestered from society. Still.

Tucker was reviewing Diane's visit and her disclosure to Zach that she thought she was pregnant. "And they see this as a good thing. Zach has one son already . . . A couple of days later, Diane calls or gets ahold of Zach somehow on the phone, and says, 'I've lost the baby.' Miscarriage, maybe what they call a spontaneous miscarriage."

He described Diane's visit, bringing Zach his "cheap cigarettes"; he described Zach's decision, after that visit, to leave the clinic: "And Zach just leaves. I mean, it was an impulse to check in. His parents didn't even know he did it. It was an impulse to leave. And also, he hasn't had sex in six, seven, eight days and, I mean, I think he's probably kind of horny."

Gets ahold somehow. Maybe what they call a spontaneous miscarriage. Cheap cigarettes. Probably kind of horny. Remoteness and condescension were not, I began to realize, *precisely* the terms to describe what I was hearing in the public defender's rhetoric. I was hearing something that called up early memories—the ways certain people of my boyhood spoke of certain other people. I couldn't quite make the connection. I turned my attention back to the argument.

Now Tucker was taking the jury deeply into the hours leading up to the murder, the dreamy, almost trancelike serendipity of events that gathered malevolent force in this formless American night, this night of nothing to do.

How Diane and her friends bring Zach back to Hunnewell. The layout there; Zach's house across the street from Diane's house; the house of Mitch Poage, Diane's stepbrother, just across the yard. The pair drifts to Mitch's house; Mitch at work; Mitch's girlfriend there. Amanda. Diane, Zach, and Amanda smoke some pot, get high.

How, at about five o'clock, Diane leaves the house and goes to her house and gets some food. Then goes to a friend's house. Zach follows her to the friend's house. They all wind up, eventually, back at Mitch's house, the stepbrother's house. And stay there for some time.

How, at about seven o'clock, Diane and Zach go out for a walk. They walk out by the Salt River, and Diane is crying a lot. She's upset and depressed that she lost the baby. She wants to get out of town, get away from her parents. And she wants Zach with her.

How the two return to Mitch's house after their walk and stay there for a while. They keep going into the bedroom, but Diane isn't willing to have sex with Zach because of her period. He doesn't care; she doesn't want to, though. They hang out there. At about ten o'clock, Diane goes back over to her house, to wake up her stepfather, as she did every night.

How this time she stays gone for quite a while, at least an hour. During that time Zach talks to Mitch for a while, then cuts his own hair (how he liked to keep his hair really short) and plays some Nintendo. Just hangs out.

How Diane gets back eventually. When she opens the door, she pulls her parka hood back enough that Zach can see that she's cut her hair really short and dyed it really black. She then puts her hood back down over her hair and says, "Come on."

How the two of them go out for another walk. (It's about eleven-thirty now.) Diane is talking about stealing a car now, stealing the things they need, just getting away. Zach is, like, "Whatever you need, whatever you want, I'm there for you."

How they get back to the house at around twelve-thirty. Diane says, "I need to go home and get some dinner for my little brother"— Justin, who is eight—and tells Zach to go on over to his house; she'll be there in a few minutes.

How Zach does what Diane told him to do. He goes to his house across the street, a mobile home, actually. His mom and dad aren't home. They haven't seen him since he got back. They didn't even know he'd left, actually. He lies down on the couch and falls asleep. He'd gotten up early that morning. He was in the treatment program, and in those treatment programs, you get up early. He'd gotten up early, and it had been a long day, and he lies down on that couch, and he falls asleep.

How the next thing he knows, there're some headlights shining into the room, waking him up; it's late, he doesn't know how late. He jumps up and looks out the window and there's a pickup in his driveway. He sees Diane get out. He goes outside, and she says, "Come on, let's go!" He jumps into the driver's seat, and they take off.

How it's quiet, and they're driving toward Hannibal, and it's quiet because it's exciting that they're on this kind of adventure thing. Diane is crying a little bit, but they make it to Hannibal, and they cross the Mississippi River at the Mark Twain Bridge, and Diane says, "Pull over there." She's pointing to this little park at the base of the bridge.

How Zach pulls over, thinking, "We're out of this state, maybe I'm going to get some sex." He pulls over. She's crying, and then she's just sobbing more and more and rocking and crying. He's asking, "What's the problem?" And she says three things, and she says them over and over.

She says, "My God, I'm going to hell. I've killed my grandpa. My dad's going to kill me. My God, I'm going to hell. I killed my grandpa. My dad's going to kill me." How she says these things over and over.

Tucker reviewed the disposal of the shotgun—his version had Diane heaving it onto the ice of the Mississippi River—and the couple's wayward zigzag in the 4×4 through Chicago, Indiana, and then into western Ohio. In the process, he managed once again to portray his client in terms that would not have troubled the strategic aims of a prosecutor: "As they leave Chicago, they see a sign that says Indiana, and an arrow, and they think, 'We're going to go to Indiana.' They get on the road to Indiana, and Diane settles down a little bit. And Zach, he starts asking her questions. I mean, he's really curious. He's been, in Zach's words, 'juiced' since he found out about this. He's really pumped up. He's just—it's all he can think about. He's just living just on the surface of his skin. He's just completely absorbed with it."

At Rensselaer ("I think that's the name of the town"), Zachary pawns the second shotgun for $100 cash. ("I don't know if it's a pawnshop, or a gun shop, or what kind of store it is"). Zachary guilelessly supplies the proprietor with his correct name, address, and Social Security number. The two drive to a mall in Indianapolis. ("And I think they go into a music store and grab a tape or something. I don't know if it's a CD or a tape; I don't know what the truck had, but they got some music to listen to.")

Then Tucker explained the matter of the missing license plate. Zach pulled into a hospital parking lot with the intention of removing the dealer's plate from the back of the truck and replacing it with a stolen one. He accomplished the first task and had unscrewed a substitute from a parked truck, but before he could attach that plate to the 4×4, he heard people approaching from the hospital. He gunned the truck out of the lot and drove to a gas station. "Too many lights, too many people," explained Tucker. "Can't get that plate on the truck. They just get out of town."

Their next stop was on Interstate 70 in Preble County, Ohio, courtesy of State Trooper Richard Noll.

"I don't think they see each other anymore after that," said Tucker, building to his conclusion. "Zach is saying everything he can to be believable. He's going through all the facts. He's trying to be believed, shocking people. He's trying to tell people that he did it.

"And at some point, decides, realizes, it soaks in, what the heck's going on. And he realizes that he needs to deal with the truth." Tucker summarized—paraphrased—Zachary's letter of June 4 to the prosecutor: " 'I was so scared. I was scared for her. Everything I said was a lie, to protect her. It was a horrible thing that I did, but I did not kill Mr. Poage. I didn't do any of that stuff.'

"That's it." And Tucker sat down.

The trial accelerated smoothly after that. Mike Wilson, the prosecutor, shuttled his witnesses on and off the stand, establishing the key evidence—testimony, expert opinion, photographic and material exhibits—with clinical efficiency.

He called on the Ohio troopers to attest to Zachary's taped confession and to reaffirm the boy's conspicuous aplomb in handling himself: his capacity, for instance, to recite his own Miranda rights almost word for word as written on the troopers' prompting cards; his meticulous recall of how he'd stolen the twelve-gauge shotgun from Ronnie Poage's house; how he and Diane had walked the four miles down Route V, the dirt road, from Ronnie's house to J. D.'s house in the dark; how Zach had forced his way into Poage's house from the downstairs after breaking the basement window; how he'd switched on all the lights in the house and ripped the telephone wires from the wall; how he'd made his way into Poage's bedroom and found the farmer in his bed, asleep and "bare-ass naked"; how he had first placed the shotgun against Poage's head, then decided the results would be "too messy" and so backed off a couple of steps; how he'd then kicked the bed so that the victim would know who was going to send him to his maker. How he had fired the first blast, then moved coolly to Poage's pants pockets to rummage for keys and money; how he'd been distracted by Poage's "snoring and gurgling" and so slipped another shell into the chamber and fired again, putting an end to these annoying sounds: "I went pop in the side of his head. And the motherfucker was still moving and snoring and shit, and so I popped him again."

Wilson drew from the troopers their memory of how insouciantly Zachary described Poage's purple brains and the neat crescent his first shotgun blast had cut into the victim's shoulder. And of how certain the boy seemed of his appropriate punishment. "Basically," Trooper Noll told the court, "he stated several times that he wanted the death penalty. He wanted the lethal injection. He asked us if Missouri had a death penalty, because he wanted—he used the 'm-f' word again—the m-f'n lethal injection. And he stated that several times, to both myself and my partner."

I found myself studying Zachary more intently than any of the witnesses. Given the implausibility of his revised account—would a fifteen-year-old girl have ripped the phone wires out of the walls? fired once at close range into the head of a sleeping man, much less reloaded and fired again?—his demeanor showed no trace of anxiety. There were no nosebleeds from this young defendant, no tears, no bowed head. He sat with knees apart at the defense table, interested in the proceedings in an amiably detached sort of way. Frequently he would bend his head for a whispered exchange with one of his lawyers, straightening up again with a half smile, as though the two had enjoyed a little joke. During recesses, when the spectators' benches emptied out, he liked to stand up, stretch, shove his hands into his pockets, and sidle up to a bailiff for a little chitchat. I became aware of a tall, serious-looking mustached man who sometimes joined Zachary in these interludes, always when the mother was not present. This, I realized, was the stepfather, Kirk. It was in these moments, with one or another of his parents, when Zachary Wilson came the closest to dropping his mask, when he seemed the least calculated and the most recognizably human: a teenage boy aware of his rapidly narrowing fate. The mask never dropped very far.

Michael Wilson's last witness of the day was Ronnie Poage. Thickset, hunched uncomfortably in the stand, his body so rigid that it seemed bound around his emotions, the victim's son provided terse affirmations to the prosecutor's routine probes into his memory of that night. Then he was excused and stalked out of the courtroom, taking with him whatever deep knowledge he may have possessed about Diane's sorrows within her family. (When I approached this man outside the courthouse with questions about Diane's childhood and temperament, he turned his back without a word.) By midafternoon, court was adjourned. The heart of the trial would unfold the following day, when both Zachary and Diane Myers were to take the stand.

· · ·

I DROVE BACK to Hannibal faced with the prospect of whiling away a long late afternoon and evening—more fast food and Columbine news, almost surely—but when I reached my motel room I found a telephone message that promised some relief from the sense of nothing to do. Henry Sweets wanted to have coffee. He had something urgent on his mind, something about the town that he was almost certain I would find interesting.

"Do you know about Beanie Babies?" he demanded as we squeezed into a booth at the Mark Twain Dinette. He looked at me sternly through his heavy-rimmed glasses. "I've been observing the behavior of people who collect Beanie Babies around here. It's incredible!"

I had to confess that I didn't know as much about Beanie Babies as I probably should. No one who lived in America in the late 1990s could be totally in the dark about Beanie Babies, of course— their idiot round beaming faces and beady little eyes seemed to pop out from every gift shop bin and mall window. And maybe I'd absorbed a story or two about the nationwide mania for the four-inch plush figures, thousands of dollars paid for a discontinued character, lottery sales, auctions, fistfights among women at flea markets— but somehow it hadn't really registered. With Henry's help, it was about to.

He had made the horrible mistake, some months earlier, of stocking a few Beanie Babies in the ground-floor gift shop of his Mark Twain Museum. As he told the story now, the effect on him and his staff had been similar to that visited upon any dozing character in the last reel of *Invasion of the Body Snatchers*.

"People have become a problem," he declared with none of his usual brio. "If they know we have a new shipment, they'll flood the store. And they're getting nasty with each other. They'll grab Beanie Babies out of one another's hands. They'll make a sweep of them off the counter with their arms and sit down on the floor till everybody else goes away. They get mad at my salespeople when we're out. They want us to sell them as many as they want, and on their terms.

"We've tried to assign them numbers. But they still shove one another out of the way. I'm talking about people of all ages. Little kids. Grown women."

These nasty little scenes, as it turned out, made up only the tip of the iceberg.

"It has gotten to the point of these Beanie Baby groupies following the delivery trucks around town to see who's getting new deliveries. On delivery day, you'll see a UPS truck followed by a line of cars, twenty-five or thirty cars long."

And it wasn't just downtown Hannibal, Henry insisted. It was happening everywhere.

"The Hallmark store up in Quincy," he said. "The mall up there. Even the central warehouse. People go to the central warehouse the night before a delivery and wait there."

A watershed of sorts, Henry said, had come with the issuance the year before of a commemorative Princess Diana Beanie Baby—a white bear with purple roses across its heart. "Ty, Inc., the manufacturer, announced a limit of twelve of these for each store," he said. "We ran a silent auction for our twelve. Our total take was twenty-one hundred dollars."

We talked about it a little longer while we ate our tenderloin sandwiches. Henry recalled the woman who had barged into his gift shop, bought up an armload of Babies, and then asked Sandy, his assistant, "I was just laid off at work—you need any help?" He relayed some tales making the rounds. There were rumors of great selling frenzies out on the midwestern plain, of migratory Beanie Baby dealers traveling cross-country by van, setting up their Beanie Baby racks in the cornfields of eastern Illinois, working with headsets and computerized inventories; of dealers who could trace every Beanie Baby that had ever been issued, doling out the goods to people who came and parked their cars in long roadside rows. He was describing tableaux that must have resembled scenes from *The Grapes of Wrath*.

Henry had the good taste to leave the central irony of all this alone. In its flatulent blatancy, it hardly allowed the legitimizing dignity of speech. Here was a society that could simultaneously tolerate Beanie Babies and feral children, Beanie Babies and closed-down day-care centers, Beanie Babies and trench coat Mafia, Beanie Babies and "I blew his motherfuckin' head off."

Nor was it just Beanie Babies, of course. The inventory of fetishes in American life was unending, the waves of mass-crafted indulgences, the cartoon icons on which the emotionally cauterized inmates, young and old, of the national asylum had learned to separately discharge their unconsummated affections. I thought of pet rocks, Cabbage Patch Kids, Muppets, Barney, Barbie, G.I. Joe, the Teenage Mutant Ninja Turtles, the Mighty Morphin Power Rangers. Such a consumptive need Americans had for being caressed and protected by their toys. I thought of real babies left in Dumpsters.

I thought of the economic might invested in the great supply line, the mobilization of talent and genius and human industry necessary to keep sending those plush and plastic minions into the maw. (Ty, Inc., the privately held maker of Beanie Babies, grossed more than a quarter billion dollars a year through the late nineties.) Rosie the Riveter stitching up another Care Bear. And of the volume of wealth amassed to advertise these minions on television. (Though Beanie Babies moved strictly by word of mouth.) U.S. advertising expenditures exceeded $200 billion in 1998, nearly a 25 percent increase from the 1990 figure and a 90 percent jump from the nearly $106 billion of 1980, in figures adjusted to 1998 dollars. The ad industry spent nearly $2,000 to reach each American household. Some $2 billion a year went for advertising directed at children, more than twenty times the amount spent a decade ago. (Emotional impoverishment aside, American children by the late nineties controlled a treasury of $100 billion a year, not counting their influence on parents' spending—a figure estimated at $188 billion in 1988, with projections to $290 billion by the early 2000s.)

I thought of the enormous pressures on American families to forage incomes that would allow them to keep up with the constant pressure to consume these and other goods (and, in the act of consuming, to subsidize their vast advertising budgets). In 84 percent of intact households, both the husband and wife worked. As the Children's Station in Hannibal had demonstrated before it succumbed to underfunding, the American workplace had become a significant drain on parent-child relationships, not to mention adult-child relationships generally. A report by the Carnegie Council on Adolescent Development confirmed the trend. Noting that "kinship and neighborhood networks have eroded and divorce has become common" (as divorce surpassed death in 1974 as the leading cause of family breakup, more than half of all American children spent at least some of their time in a single-parent family), children of the nineties, the council found, spent "significantly" less time in the company of adults than a few decades ago. The council linked this fact to the growing sense of desolation in young lives, to the one-third of all adolescents who'd contemplated suicide, and to the half who were at moderate or high risk of abusing drugs, failing in school, getting pregnant, or otherwise seriously damaging their lives.

But the news proved even worse than that. The corporate American workplace was not simply a passive force in the breach between adults and children. As an article in *Fortune* magazine put it: "Families are no longer a big plus for a corporation; they are a big problem. An albatross. More and more, the business world seems to regard children not as the future generation of workers but as luxuries you're entitled to after you've won your stripes. It's fine to have kids' pictures on your desk—just don't let them cut into billable hours."

As loneliness and alienation spread through the booming consumer economy, the advertising symbols themselves, of course, had long since grown indistinguishable from the products as magnets for displaced affection. I thought of Ronald McDonald and Tony the Tiger and Michael Jordan rolling his eyes at Bugs Bunny.

And of Joe Camel. No icon better symbolized the marketing world's perceptions of children's hunger for connection, and its corruption of cartoon imagery to harvest it, than this captivating death's-head with its three-veined snout.

Joe Camel arrived on the scene in 1988, at a time of crisis in the tobacco industry: the nadir of a generation-long decline in teen smoking, thanks in part to tireless grass-roots efforts to educate the young about the severe health hazards of tobacco. Clad variously in a motorcycle jacket, a tuxedo, or jeans, and shown shooting a rack of pool or lounging at a neon-saturated nightclub, he disarmed adolescents' anxieties about the dangers of smoking even as he beckoned them into a life of glamorous rebellion. And what child could not fail to love him? After all, he wasn't some cynical human pitchman; he was a cartoon.

His creator, the R. J. Reynolds tobacco company, insisted from the outset that he was not aimed at underage customers but rather at young adults. Market results suggested otherwise: Camel's share of the adolescent smoking market grew from .5 percent to 13 percent between 1988 and 1992. The leap in revenues from sales to teenagers was from $6 million to $476 million.

Joe Camel was ultimately banished from billboards and magazine ads, a casualty of the massive litigations against the tobacco industry organized by crusading trial lawyers and supported by state attorneys general. But he reigned for a decade, the symbolic master of an orgy that continued long after his exile under pressure in 1997. More than any other marketing icon ever created, Joe Camel was a symbol of conquest: proof that American commerce had succeeded in converting inexhaustible avarice into a self-justifying moral system, a system utterly indifferent to the minds and souls of American children.

This moral system—unrestrained, virtually unregulated corporate capitalism—had asserted itself with historic force in the early 1980s, with the election of Ronald Reagan. Its rapid ascendancy in international market competition produced a great victory—the dissolution of the Soviet Union and American triumph in the Cold War. But it also produced a victory of more ambiguous value within American society, a victory of commodities over community, of dollar value as the measure of moral value. The Reagan era's "commodification of everything" was seen by many social critics to have left a double-edged legacy: unprecedented material wealth, especially for those with access to wealth already, coexisting with unprecedented social nihilism, alienation, and the atrophy of spiritual idealism. The deregulation of the broadcasting industry, to cite one example, opened up the nation's airwaves and cable circuits to exactly the excesses of market-driven coarseness and cynicism that outraged defenders of "family values." It enabled the shock-jock revolution that exalted Howard Stern and such imitators as Don and Mike—whose nationally syndicated radio slimefest, carried for a while in America's Home Town and a favorite of adolescent boys, featured such segments as the sounds, picked up by an open telephone receiver, of a couple having sex, and a reading of the Bill of Rights by a woman using the breathy delivery of a phone-sex provider.

Among those who noticed the paradox was James R. Pinkerton, writing in *Newsday*, in 1996: "[And] herein lies the irony of the Reagan presidency. By unleashing capitalism, Reagan accelerated not only the decline of big government, but also the dissipation of the old social order. The unrestrained profit motive that Reaganomics nurtured is what drives entrepreneurs today to buy, sell and broadcast anything that might make a buck."

Given this context, it was almost possible to view Beanie Babies not as a symptom of empathetic impulse gone haywire but as an entrepreneurial act of mercy, a kind of emergency relief for the emotionally starved women and children of America.

As for American menfolk, they apparently sought balm from other sources. An hour or so after my lunch with Henry—right around store-closing time in Hannibal—I found myself browsing the General

Nonfiction section of the paperback bookshelves in a kind of CD/ poster/Halloween mask/movie-rental outlet across the parking lot from the Wal-Mart. "If you were to go into any bookstore, you can buy six or seven guides to Beanie Babies," Henry had assured me as we left the dinette. My curiosity had drawn me to test whether it was so.

Henry Sweets rarely erred in his sense of his hometown's artifacts, but this was one time he had badly miscalculated. Not one Beanie Baby volume graced these racks. The marketing here was aimed at another distinctive niche. What I found instead were: *Rogue Warrior,* by Rich Marchinko: *The Best-Selling Autobiography of the Controversial, Death-Defying Founder of the U.S. Navy's Top Secret Counterterrorist Unit, Seal Team Six!*; *Seals: Top Secret! Steal into Hell . . . Then Fight Your Way Out*; *Death in the Jungle: Diary of a Navy Seal*; *The Teams: An Oral History of the U.S. Navy Seals*; *Seals: The Warrior Breed*; *Seals at War: The Story of U.S. Navy Special Warfare*; *The Element of Surprise: Navy Seals in Vietnam.*

This is not to say that every nonfiction book on the shelf was about Navy Seals. Far from it. I also discovered *Marine Sniper: 93 Confirmed Kills*; *Blood on the Risers: An Airborne Soldier's 35 Months in Vietnam*; *Bravo Two Zero: The Harrowing True Story of a Special Forces Patrol Behind the Lines in Iraq*; *Dear Mom: A Sniper's Vietnam*; *Top Guns: America's Fighter Aces Tell Their Most Daring and Spectacular Stories*; *One Shot, One Kill: American Combat Snipers in World War II, Korea, Vietnam and Beirut*; *First Recon—Second to None: A Marine Recon Battalion in Vietnam, 1967–68.*

Nor did this section limit itself to military themes exclusively. For variety, there was *The Hot House: Life Inside Leavenworth Prison.*

AN INNOCENT ABROAD

B efore I went to hell, at the end of my adolescence, I had to live
out the rest of my adult life.

My father chauffeured me down to that life, drove me from Jefferson City to St. Louis a few days after graduation to begin my career as a sportswriter on the *St. Louis Post-Dispatch*.

My first salary was $100 a week, and my beat (after a summer of indoctrination on the copydesk) was to be "prep" sports—the eighty or so high schools in the area. This would entail driving to a lot of high school stadium and gymnasium parking lots, taking down a lot of grubby notes with a pencil on folded paper as future furniture salesmen churned and grunted and oofed, and later asking a lot of coaches what they thought was the turning point of the game. Then I would see it all in a great metropolitan daily under my byline. I could not imagine a better life.

I started out renting a tiny room in the downtown YMCA. It made me feel wild and urban and reckless. I've never had more romantic digs. I can still smell the soot on the blackened window screen, a delicious smell, heavy and sinister. I can still hear the traffic on Olive Boulevard about twenty-three floors below me, all night, horns and brakes and sirens. It thrilled me; I was part of it. I remember waking up at dawn to orange and purple skies over the Mississippi River, my old pal from Hannibal, several blocks to the east, and to my bird's-eye view of downtown St. Louis's silhouetted rooftops. It was like being inside *Rhapsody in Blue*.

I would get dressed, usually in some hideous western-style green sport coat or gangster blazer I'd bought at Bond's Clothing with my entire previous week's paycheck, take the elevator down to the Y lobby, and set out at a brisk strut for Twelfth Street and the *Post-Dispatch*'s fifth-floor sports department copydesk. Sleepy, happy, hungry, famous inside my head, I tasted the sooty summer-morning city air in my lungs. In front of the Sheraton-Jefferson I'd pass cabbies on their knees shooting craps on the sidewalk. Great. City vice. I loved it. I was a sportswriter.

By the end of the summer I was able to risk a lease on a studio apartment in a nearby high-rise complex. I bought my first car, a blue Volkswagen. I invited my parents and sister down to visit. I wanted to show off my new city savoir faire, but it was my father who stole the show by continually getting disconnected from us on the high-rise elevator—failing to get through the sliding door, either entering or exiting, before it closed. We would all be either in or out except for Dad; we'd hear his muttered "*Aht*-dam!" just before the *slam!* and then we'd have to round him up again. This happened many times and gave the visit a kind of motif.

Not that I was a great deal more worldly than my father. I was naive, for example, about the professional athletes my sports department wrote about. I still thought the Cardinal ballplayers were exactly like what it said on the backs of the baseball gum trading cards. I thought they Hunted and Fished in the Off-Season. Swell bunch of fellows. Heroes of mine from afar, some of them from my small boyhood. Now I was meeting them up close, getting into the Redbird baseball games free and sitting in the press box not far from the legendary announcer Harry Caray himself even though I was only covering high school sports.

The older sportswriters, who spat into spittoons and kept flasks in their drawers and silently hated me because I had a college degree, sized me up. They saw a skinny baby-faced rube whose ears stuck out.

The writers liked to eat lunch at Manny's, a sports bar and grill about two blocks from the paper. It had a steam table and red vinyl booths. Manny was a tough little Greek who favored the death penalty and told everybody so, loudly, and who cozied up to the sports stars in town.

One day Ken Boyer strolled into Manny's while I was having lunch there with the writers. Boyer was the Cardinals' great third baseman, a home-run hitter and acrobatic fielder, possibly a Hall of Fame candidate. He was also the best-looking guy on the team, dark and sharp like the old movie star Tyrone Power. My dad idolized Kenny Boyer. My dad worried quite a bit whether the Cardinals were paying Boyer what he was worth, worried, in fact, whether they were paying a lot of the players what they were worth.

Kenny Boyer sauntered over and sat down at our booth. Right next to me. This may have been planned. Manny hovered. The other writers rolled their cigars around in their mouths and grinned, watching the show. I didn't know what to say. About four years earlier, as a high school kid, I'd gotten Boyer's autograph the night he hit a grand-slam home run against Milwaukee. I'd paid my way into Busch Stadium that night, or rather my dad had. Now Boyer and I were colleagues, in a weird sort of way.

So I sat there, my green western sport coat bunched up around my neck, trying to think of something cool to say to my new pal Kenny Boyer. Trying to think of *anything* to say to Kenny Boyer. The writers rolled their cigars and grinned.

A young woman walked past our booth. She was wearing a tight skirt. Kenny Boyer took a long look at the woman's retreating backside. Stockings with seams. Then he turned to look at me. "Looks like," he said in a deep confidential drawl, "two cats fightin' in a burlap bag."

I know that the shock I felt was smeared all over my face, shock and a kind of sickened feeling, as if somebody had pulled back the sheet from the face of a corpse. The writers lapped it up. Kenny Boyer was married. I knew that for a fact. To a beautiful woman. He wore red stripes on his uniform pants. Goddamn it, he *hunted and fished in the off-season*. The baseball cards said he did. I was twenty-one, a full-grown man, and I was just learning that the baseball cards lied.

I told my dad that I'd had lunch with Kenny Boyer, and he was impressed. I left out the burlap bag part.

• • •

ABOUT FOUR MONTHS after that, the whole country lost its innocence.

I awoke one Friday in November to sheets of rain outside the window. It was a day for a hat, a brimmed hat. I'd never worn a brimmed
hat through college; hats were irrevocably adult, somehow. But my
fellow sportswriters all wore them, and in weather like this it didn't
make sense to be without one. I told myself I would remember this
day; this would be the day I bought my first brimmed hat.

The editorial cartoon in the *Post-Dispatch*'s first edition, up from
the pressroom a little before noon, showed the rival factions of Congress as two gunslingers trading hot lead. The bullets were whizzing
over the head of the president, who was in the middle, ducking.

On my lunch break that Friday I did what I'd planned: I went to
a department store and tried on some brimmed hats. None of them
exactly flattered my round face, but I bought the one that pained me
the least in the mirror and jammed it on the back of my head. Then
I went to the bank with my paycheck and tried flirting with the cash-
ier. She looked at me in a stricken way. I figured it was my hat. I felt
like a big cheese head with this stupid hat. But it was raining. I kept
it on and slogged back to the newspaper office.

When I stepped off the fifth-floor elevator I heard bells ringing.
The wire room of United Press International was just off the *Post*'s
city room; it was filled with Teletype machines constantly clacking
out stories. When a story merited "bulletin" status, a bell in the machine would ring. The more important the story, the longer the bell
would ring.

When I passed the UPI room every bell on every machine was
ringing away. It sounded oddly beautiful, like wind chimes.

Every story clacking out of every machine was datelined Dallas.

I broke a date that night and sat in the *Post-Dispatch* city room
until very late, watching the editors remake the late editions and the
white-shirted reporters on the phones getting local reaction, local angles. I wanted desperately to be of help, to be a part of it somehow.
But I was just a sportswriter.

Ken Boyer had hit .285 that season, two points below his lifetime
average. The following year he would hit another grand-slam home
run, off Al Downing of the Yankees in the World Series. At the end

of the season after that, he would get traded. He would play for several teams and end up coming back to manage the Cardinals for a few years. In about 1980, Ken Boyer would contract cancer. His family would try to save his life by taking him to Mexico for a "wonder" drug called laetrile. It wouldn't work, and he would die at age fifty-one, a few years younger than I am as I write this. I've made a couple of comments about women that I'd like to take back myself, I suppose, to be honest about it.

All right, let's be specific. I made one of those comments to a buddy of mine in the men's john of a restaurant while joyously sloshed during a *Post-Dispatch* Christmas party. I made it about my date. It was not the basest comment in the history of male chauvinism, God knows, but it did connote a certain air of confidence regarding my prospects with the young woman later in the evening. The young woman happened at that moment to be in the adjoining women's john, and the walls were thin.

This was beginning to shape up as my eternal destiny with women: a series of fiascoes stretching beyond the end of time. Even when I tried to be suave and worldly I screwed up—especially then, perhaps. I murdered a promising relationship, a holdover from college, when I took the woman to a pretentious faux Gallic restaurant in her family's suburban neighborhood and instructed the waiter to bring us a bottle of the *chabliss*. (Ignorance, I had occasion to reflect later, is chabliss.) Another hopeful connection ended in agony when my extremely well-bred and Ivy League–educated blind date, nearly sobbing from boredom and the absence of any conversational common ground whatsoever, made for her front door with the desperate parting pleasantry that I had "a fun car."

The worst part was that it wasn't *even* a fun car. It was the goddamn blue Volkswagen.

But in time I blundered into acquaintanceship with a young woman of the sort who occasionally blundered into acquaintanceship with young men of my sort. She was tall, beautiful, intelligent, quiet, good-humored, softly empathetic and the product of a town in Illinois even smaller than my hometown in Missouri. What was more, she seemed genuinely to like me. I was beside myself with joy and gratitude. Here, finally, was what the songwriters called my Chance of a Lifetime. Here was my opportunity to Go All the Way.

We dated a few times and gazed into one another's eyes. She loved my sense of humor; she hung on my repartee. I discovered that she liked sports, and I impressed her by producing two free tickets to a professional ice-hockey game, courtesy of my department at the paper. We made giddy small talk at rinkside. Don't you think it adds a lot to the team spirit, I asked her, flashing my most enthusiastic Pepsodent smile, that they play all that amplified pep music between periods? Oh, I do, I really do, she enthused in reply. A lot of people might think it's corny. But give me the organ every time.

We both clammed up just then and paid intense attention to the game and concentrated on not touching that one with a ten-foot pole.

In the ensuing weeks, though, as our make-out passion increased to the point of three A.M. dementia, we both knew that a decision would soon need to be made, a threshold crossed. We didn't discuss it—sex—we were both far too lofty in our mutual regard to let things descend to that vulgar level. And yet it had got discussed, somehow. And agreed on. Affirmed. Yes.

On what proved to be the Big Night itself, as we cruised down Broadway after a movie at the Fox, Brett—as I'll call her—remarked very conversationally, as though it had just popped into her head, that science was making the most incredible advances these days. For instance there was this fascinating new product on the market, called Emko. It was a foam. A spermicide, actually. People were making the most astounding claims for it.

Really, I rejoined, attempting to toss my left elbow casually on the window jamb but finding the window closed. What will those modern science guys think of next?

A block or so later the orange light of a Rexall drugstore thrust itself deeply into our consciousness. Casually swerving across traffic into a no-parking zone near the corner, I asked Brett if she'd mind waiting just a minute; there were a couple of things I needed to pick up. She said she'd be very happy to.

The clerk inside looked to my eyes like a moonlighting Lutheran minister. He thought that Emko was the name of an oil refinery. He'd never heard of the product. What was it supposed to be good for, again? I was twisted, bent nearly double with mortification. I could not conceivably be any more embarrassed than I already was, and I could not return to the car empty-handed. I asked the son of a bitch for a package of Trojans and got the hell out of there.

Back at Brett's apartment, we feverishly cleared the decks. Brett yanked down her sofa bed while I tore open the tinfoil and held in the palm of my hand the legendary fish-brown cylinder that had enflamed and oppressed my fantasies since puberty.

Brett reached for her lamplight. In a moment the room would be in total darkness and we would be madly entwined. I placed the cylinder carefully on the nightstand adjacent to the bed. When the moment came I would know exactly where to reach for it. Just to make sure nothing could possibly go wrong, I rehearsed exactly *how* I would reach for it: In my mind's eye I saw my thumb and forefinger descending over the cylinder, working their way inside the cylinder's rim, transporting the cylinder to where it would do the most good, while stretching the mouth of the cylinder wide. Maximum efficiency, minimum distraction.

The moment did in fact approach. In the pitch darkness my right hand hovered, groped, descended. My thumb and forefinger felt the sticky circular surface of the Trojan. I worked them inside the cylinder's rim. I lifted my arm.

Twannnngggg.

I had widened my thumb and forefinger a little too quickly. I had launched the rubber off into the darkness like a projectile across a grade-school classroom. Frantically, I groped for the tinfoil package, for a backup. It was nowhere to be felt.

In the darkness, Brett's soft, empathetic voice asked me if anything was wrong.

The upshot was that we had to turn the lights on, get out of bed, and ransack the apartment for the wayward rubber. I spotted the tinfoil package on the floor, with the backups, but Brett's curiosity had got the better of her—she was dying to know just how far that sucker had traveled. It had evidently had a good deal of torque on it when it left my fingers, because we never did locate it, not that evening, not ever. Perhaps it flew through the open slit in the window and headed for outer space, gaining velocity, my childhood chastity taking wing.

Some days later we did locate an establishment that dealt in Emko, and I soon slipped safely into the sorrows of sex.

Duly came back from Vietnam one of those summers, and his parents threw a homecoming party at Rose Hill. I drove up from St. Louis alongside the Mississippi River in my Volkswagen.

He had veered a little toward the fast life after I'd left Hannibal; the totaled Chevy was just one of the early results. I gathered vaguely that he had spent his way through an inheritance, seen and done some things, and then, in a typically Duly gesture of atonement, enlisted as a sharpshooter in the marines.

His experiences had not been the best and not the worst; he was not inclined to talk much about them. He was the same golden-haired, strong-bodied Galahad of our childhoods, still carefree on the surface, but there were some pauses in his conversation. He did say that the concussive force from a rifle round, zipping near his head, had knocked him to the ground, and that a mortar shell, landing near his feet, had burst in the opposite direction.

After the party, I spent the night at Rose Hill. I slept on a cot in Duly's childhood bedroom on the second floor, the room where we'd spent hours poring over comic books and making silly tape recordings. Very little in it had changed since our senior year of high school. Even some of the magazines of that period still lay scattered around.

That night I had a dream: I was in a rowboat being tugged by the powerful currents of a river like the Mississippi. I was keeping the boat from drifting downstream by hanging on to a couple of tufts of grass on the shoreline. I awoke from that dream to find myself on my stomach on the cot, holding tight to the windowsill with both hands.

After he graduated high school my brother enrolled at the School of Mines and Metallurgy at Rolla, Missouri. He pledged a fraternity, Sigma Nu. ("Our goal is to see you initiated as one who has *become* Sigma Nu, not one who has merely joined a Fraternity," assured the standard form letter. "We want to see you through to graduation; and to have you as one of us for life.") From the few postcards and letters that survive of what he wrote to Mom and Dad, it does not seem that he had much interest in drawing them into any kind of glamorous world. His handwriting was tiny, and what it had to say was to the point:

Thursday morning

Dear Folks,

I still need the I.D. Haven't got it yet. I need to overdraw my part of the checking account by about $65–$75. My pay check should come in about the 15th. I won't come home this weekend probably. I'm not sure, though. I'm ready for a blanket now. I would like to try that football blanket of Ron's. Have to go now.

Love,
Jim

And from a later one:

Send me information on how to contact Dad. Also, I could use more spending money. In a fraternity you are expected to do things to-gether and that takes money, besides buying necessities.

Keep telling me how the Jays are doing and what Ron is doing. Is he going with anyone?

I may not see you until Thanksgiving, but maybe I won't go to Lindenwood next weekend [to visit a girlfriend] and will come. New walk-out date is Nov. 26. St. Louis again. Tell Dad not to come around and say anything.

Love,
Jim

"Walk-out date" probably refers to a fraternity activity. Dad's presence hovers at the edges of that letter: the shortage of spending money, Dad's notorious naughty-boy capacity to "come around" and cause embarrassment ("Teh-heh-heh"). But why would Jim need to know how to contact him?

There is so much I never knew about his life.

I saw him rarely. Holidays back home in Jefferson City, usually. One encounter took place in the summer of 1964. He had a summer job practically just across the river from the *Post-Dispatch*, at a steel mill in Alton, Illinois. I knew that. But I never called him.

One day Jim called me. His voice was friendly. He wanted to get together. I invited him to come along and have dinner with me and Brett. I knew a place with candlelit tables, and I knew how to pro-nounce the white wine. It was a hot summer night, but Jim showed up formal, in a heavy wool sport coat and a necktie. This was the first time I had ever seen him in the guise of a grown-up. His manners, his affect were correspondingly endearing.

I was touched. I think I was even somehow proud, to show off this version of my kid brother to my girlfriend. This might have been the moment of transformation for us, the moment when we put aside our childish rivalries and angers, as grown-up brothers do, and reestablish ourselves as friends.

Jim sat across the table from me, in the candlelight, in his jacket and his horn-rims. I recall being friendly, cordial. But I also recall not being able to take the hand that he had in effect extended toward me. One of us could not pull the other across the threshold. I did not call him again after that night.

· 20 ·

A BEAUTIFUL DAY

The second morning of Zachary Wilson's murder trial brought nning testimony and cryptic evidence. The testimony was from a prison guard, who recalled that Zachary had prated on, without prodding, about having shotgunned J. D. Poage. The cryptic evidence was contained in a series of letters to and from Zachary. One letter, handwritten by the defendant to a sometime girlfriend, contained sentences suggesting strongly (although not conclusively) that he had pulled the trigger. This day also brought the two principals to the witness stand.

Richard L. Koch, a corrections officer in the Marion County jail system, testified that in midafternoon in January 1998 he had escorted Zachary from his cell so that the boy could take a shower and make a telephone call. Zach had started talking first about how it had been a while since he'd had a shower, then, quickly, about being picked up by the state troopers in Ohio.

"He went into quite a few details about how he broke into [Poage's] house," Koch recollected. "He went upstairs, and Mr.—the older gentleman—pardon his language—he referred to him as a motherfucker—he shot him in the head. Said the old guy never heard him coming, he was the same as deaf.

"Said the old guy just laid there. He made a gurgling sound that sounded like he was snoring. He said that he knew he was dead, but he went ahead, reloaded, and shot—pardon the language—the old motherfucker again. That was basically his comments to me."

Under cross-examination by Thomas Marshall, Koch said, "This is all spontaneous utterances. Mr. Wilson was very excited. As he got more into the story, he became more animated, and more excited as he told his story."

The letter, addressed to a young Paris, Missouri, woman named Angela Kay Hinds, was written about two months after this exchange. It amounted to the first recorded evidence that Zachary planned to change his story, shifting the blame to Diane, but its wording was ambiguous enough to allow multiple interpretations of what went on that night as Poage lay naked in his bed—interpretations of whether, and how, the boy and the younger girl collaborated in the farmer's death.

Angela Hinds had known Zachary since his Hannibal days. On the witness stand, she testified that their relationship had been one of "friendship, companionship." At least by Zachary's lights, it had been tinged with romance. She had corresponded with Zachary while he awaited trial, in Marion County jail, and in mid-March 1998 had received a letter from him at her Paris home. Prosecutor Wilson read it aloud:

> Angela, what's up, Sexy? How are you and your boyfriend? Last time you said the two of you weren't doing very well. That I don't understand. First you tell me that you have a really great man in your life that is with you and Ashley, then you say, oh, well, no tears shed over this one; I wasn't that serious anyway. To me, that is sort of a contradiction.
>
> But then again, maybe it's just me. Anyway, I got to reading my old letters, and I found something back when [a mutual friend] and I talked to Aaron about that car. I thought that you didn't like me. As a matter of fact, I thought you hated me, because I was always in the basement with Aaron, getting high. Please explain . . .
>
> So I am really bored. There's nothing to do but play cards. That gets boring after a while. So tell me, what is it you do all day? I don't do shit. As far as what you said in your other letter, about waiting for me if I'm still single, I am. And you might not have to wait that long. All the evidence is pointing to Diane. Plus, I'm blaming it all on her.

I'm just going to tell the story how it happened, and just take myself out after she "killed him." Although I think everyone knows who really did it. I just hope people don't look at me different. I mean, I had a really good reason. But that's a long story. I don't remember if I told it to you, but if you want to know, just say so.

P.S. Write back soon. Love, Zach; (signed) Zachary Jeremiah Curt Wilson.

The letter—particularly its critical last two paragraphs—is striking for its string of self-canceling hints and assertions. As he writes, Zachary appears to shift his ground from sentence to sentence, even phrase to phrase. "All the evidence is pointing to Diane"—a curiously distanced remark, especially given its follow-up: "Plus, I'm blaming it all on her." In the ensuing paragraph, "I'm just going to tell the story how it happened" seems immediately undercut by the quotation marks in the phrase, she "killed him." The sentence, "Although I think everyone knows who really did it," sounds staunchly accusatory, the two following that one turn wary and defensive.

A dualistic piece of work, in short, but one that Mike Wilson would exploit quite single-mindedly in his cross-examination.

The state rested with the reading of the letter. The first witness for the defense was Zachary Wilson.

Given the raw yearning just then consuming the nation to pierce through the blankness and fathom the unfathomable nature and motives of adolescents who turn homicidal, the boy taking the oath would hardly have been a useful guide. He was in fact the enigma incarnate.

If his letter to Angela had hinted of alternate personalities in reserve, Zachary Wilson in the flesh fulfilled the promise. Nothing in his tone or attitude suggested the bragging, obscenity-spewing predator of the officers' and jailers' testimony. In place of that monster sat the generic teen, necktied and barbered, a reasonable expression on his affable face, prepared to speak in a workaday voice tinged with the received idioms of high school composition, his own questioners, the evening news.

And yet Zachary Wilson did have a story to tell.

It was familiar to me by now, deadeningly so in some ways, except for the new particulars of self-exculpation that Zachary now brought to it under direct questioning by Tucker. But as I listened yet again to that tedious itinerary, the listless and almost dreamlike meanderings of Zach and Diane on the day and night of J. D. Poage's killing, and the day and night beyond, I began to grasp its true significance. Its significance lay exactly in its blankness, its utter conditionality of thought and action from moment to moment, its sense of proceeding from no history and toward no future. Here, more than in the extinguished psyches of Eric Harris and Dylan Klebold, lay the key to the horror. The key was that there was no key and nothing to unlock. The murder of J. D. Poage had been caused, in one manner of looking at it, by a day and a night in the life of America.

Led by Tucker, Zachary recapped his turbulent childhood, his diagnosed "attention deficit hyperactivity disorder," the anger outbursts that led to fights and eventually to commitment at age ten in a treatment center north of Hannibal, his prescribed medication: Catapres, Ritalin. The medication was finally halted by his parents, Zachary said. "It was real expensive. At the time, we couldn't afford it."

He described his encounter with Diane in rehab and his reintroduction to her in Hunnewell. Asked about the nature of the relationship they developed, he leaned forward earnestly: "Just your basic teenage, high school relationship." He paused and appeared to reflect for a moment. "It was—honestly, truthfully, it was mostly sex."

"Was there any discussion of getting married?" Tucker asked.

"Sure. Yeah," Zachary replied. He went on, borrowing a phrase from Tucker's own opening remarks the previous day and managing almost to suggest a mature man looking back on the follies of his youth: "Everybody talks about that when they're young. They think they're in love, in lust."

Tucker pressed him on his motivations for entering the drug treatment program in Hannibal.

Zachary's aura of wry self-reflection persisted. "Well, at this time I'd moved to Hunnewell because I was trying to get away from problems. But my problems were just following me, so I figured it must have been me that was the problem.

"I wanted to get into the Job Corps. I'd spoke with my father about going into the Job Corps. But I was doing drugs, and I was drinking a lot. So I decided to get myself clean in the rehab center. I knew that Job Corps would get me away from where I was at, to a new place.

Maybe get a job or whatever. But I knew I had to get the drugs out of my system first. And I had to learn to live without them."

Led by Tucker, Zachary averred that he and Diane had discussed having children: "She spoke of how she would love to have children, but frequently would say she didn't believe she could."

"And did she tell you why?"

"She said that she didn't believe she could have children, and she believed it was because she had been sexually molested by her grandfather and her brother at a young age, at a very young age."

Tucker inquired whether Zachary had ever met J. D. Poage.

"As far as I can recall, I might have once. I worked for [he named an employer] there in Hunnewell, and I remember we went to Poage's farm. And I met a Poage, but I'm not exactly sure if it was J. D. or not." Zachary said he never had been to Poage's house.

He recalled the moment, at the rehab center in Hannibal, when Diane told him she thought she was pregnant by him. "I was excited, and—you know, at first, I was shocked. And then I was excited, because she had said that she believed she could not have children. So it was a mixture of excitement and shock. I didn't know what to say. I didn't know what to do. So I gave her a hug, and I gave her a kiss, and I told her that it would be all right, and that we would talk about it, and I would call her late on that night."

The following day, Diane had a late-afternoon doctor's appointment in Hannibal. In a telephone conversation after the appointment, "she was very upset, crying. She told me that she had lost the baby. She said she was having cramps in her stomach and that she was bleeding."

When Diane visited the rehab center on the day after that, Zachary awaited her with an ardency that, in his testimony, sounded genuine: "I saw them arriving. You can see, if you look down [through an upstairs window], you can see them. You can see where people pull up the road to the rehab center. And I saw them pulling up. I had already made up my mind that I was going to leave, that I was going to go home. I went into my room, grabbed my stuff, and went back outside." He called up the details of the small talk: "We talked for a moment and joked. She joked around about, 'I'm taking you home with me.' And I said, 'Okay, let's go.' And I reached in the door, grabbed my bags, and we were off."

The journey to Hunnewell took a morbid turn. The very landscape seemed to cry out to the teenagers about oblivion. Diane had fallen silent, and Zachary was coaxing her to talk. "When we got to this intersection, she started explaining how her friend Joe had passed away at this intersection, got in a car wreck. We sat there and talked about that for a moment. We crossed Thirty-six to another road, went down this road, looked at some houses, and some white crosses where people had got in car wrecks."

Then Hunnewell. Mitch Poage's house, Amanda and her daughter inside, the small talk, the getting high, the familiar routine of passing time, nothing to do. "I played a game, Playstation, or Nintendo, or something like that. Something on a video game. I played it for a while."

Diane drifts off, doesn't come right back; Zachary wanders over to her house after a while, knocks on the back door; no response; he walks up the street to Nicki's house: "I can't even remember her last name, but she lived right up the street from Diane and myself."

Diane is there. Time passes. J. D. Poage's time draws short, although at this point no one has given the idea of murdering him a thought. It's about five o'clock now. Not much to do at Nicki's house. "We just sat there. I talked with Nicki for a minute." Then Zach and Diane leave and go back to Mitch's house.

It's dark now. At around seven o'clock, Zach and Diane leave Mitch's house for their walk. It lasts about an hour. "We didn't say much at first. We got to talking about it was a beautiful night, we got to talking about the stars and things. And then all of a sudden Diane just broke down crying. And I was trying to get out of her what was wrong. Which, I knew what was wrong. She'd told me that she had lost a child. So I tried to talk to her about that."

Diane doesn't want to talk about that. Diane wants to talk about flight. "What she wanted to talk about was getting out of Missouri, was getting completely away from her family. From everyone, everywhere. Which, she talked about she didn't care how we got—see, she wanted me to go with her. She wanted it to be her and I, you know, starting over somewhere. She talked about how she didn't care how it happened, she would steal a car. If we stole a car, she would steal money for food, or for gas, or whatever. She just wanted to go."

Zachary recalled asking Diane, If we did steal a car, how would we eat? And Diane saying, Oh, well, we could rob somebody, you know. And Zachary: Okay, if we did steal a car, and we did rob somebody, and we did leave, what about the police? Diane: Oh, we'll just lay low.

They return to Mitch's house around eight. They sit around for a little while. Not much to do. They get high again. Zachary asks Amanda whether Mitch or Russell (Diane's other brother, who was living in the house at that time) had any hair clippers. " 'Cause I like to keep my hair neat." Diane argues with Zachary; "she didn't want me to cut my hair, for whatever reason."

It is in the midst of that argument that Diane suddenly asks Zachary to come with her into Amanda's bedroom. Amanda scolds them "not to be having sex back there," but sex is not what is on Diane's mind. "We got back there and she was asking me, she was like, 'So are we going to steal a car, are we going to leave, are we going to get away?' And honestly, I was all for it. You know, I had just left the rehab center. The whole point of me going to the rehab center was to get away. I was all for it. I was all for, you know, stealing a car, getting away."

But Diane has more on her mind than just getting away. "Diane said something to the effect of, she wanted to rob the bank. And I'll put it into her words. She said, 'That'd be a hell of a lick.' She said that would be a perfect opportunity, basically, to rob the Hunnewell Bank. Something about there's no good guards, it's a country town, we could get away with it, you know."

Zachary didn't take that suggestion very seriously, he recalled. He just kind of let that one go.

Diane leaves the house to go to her house and wake her stepfather up for work. It's around ten o'clock now. She is gone for a long time. "And it was strange. Because, you know, she usually—it was an everyday occurrence. We would go to Mitch and Amanda's house, she would wake her father up, and she would come right back. She would take some food from the house, because we were always getting high over there, and bring it back to her brother's house. And it was almost like never more than fifteen minutes. Never." This time she is gone for more than an hour. Zachary thought that was odd.

Finally Diane pokes her head in the door. Zachary has cut his hair by now. He sees that Diane is wearing a heavy blue starter jacket with a large drawstring hood, and when she pulls the hood back, Zachary can see that her hair has been chopped short and dyed extremely black. "I mean, it was almost purple it was so black. The whole time we'd been together, her hair had been past her shoulders. Her hair's usually almost a red color." "Are you ready?" she asks. "Come on. Let's go."

The second walk. "We walked out on the blacktop. I asked her, 'We're not going to your house?' She said, No, she wanted to clear her head, is what she said."

A half hour walking out; Diane crying: "Except for this time, she seemed more—I don't know what the word I'm looking for is—she seemed more determined to do it, like, right now, let's go." The turn-around; another half hour walking back. It's about twelve-thirty now. Diane leaves to make supper for her little brother Justin, who's alone. Zachary returns to his trailer. He enters by the back door and lies down on the couch. He turns on the TV. He is still high. He falls asleep.

How long he sleeps, he doesn't know. There are no clocks. He is awakened by the headlights. It's late; he doesn't know how late. He thought at first it was his stepfather, Kirk, bringing Zach's truck back to him, the one he'd had fixed. He hears a knock on his front door. A voice: "It's me."

Zachary asks Diane who brought her over. She says, "I did." She says, "I stole the truck. I told you I was going to steal a car. Let's go. This is our chance. Let's go. Let's get away."

Zachary drives. There's no conversation at first. They drive into Hannibal; Zachary stops at the Shell station on Broadway to get cigarettes. He spots a police officer who may know him. "I believed I had warrants in Hannibal, so I didn't really want to stay around too long." The warrants were for assault and burglary.

Diane is focused on getting out of the state as quickly as possible. That means Illinois. Across the Mark Twain Bridge, at the John Hay Recreation Area, Diane asks Zachary to pull over. "Honestly, I pulled over thinking we had gotten out of the state, so she really wasn't worrying about anything anymore, she wanted to have sex. You know, I'd been in rehab for quite some time, and I thought that she wanted to stop and have sex."

"Had you been trying to talk her into that through the day?" Tucker asked.

"All night. All night I had."

Instead, Diane starts crying again. She gets out of the truck and raises the top of her fold-up seat. "She reached behind the seat and came up with a twelve-gauge shotgun, holding it by the barrel almost like she was scared of it. Like holding it away from her body from the end of the barrel. I was asking her what was going on, what was the gun for? At the time I thought she was suicidal; she was very depressed. And the way she was holding the gun, it looked like she was almost holding it toward her face."

But instead Diane begins dragging the shotgun toward the edge of the Mississippi. "She picked it up almost like a baseball bat and just threw it. Threw it into the river. Zachary hears the gun hit the ice and slide for some time.

Diane returns to the truck and reemerges with a wallet. Sobbing, she places the wallet under a large rock near the riverbank.

At length, Zachary ushers Diane back inside the truck. "She shuts the door. She's still crying extremely loud. And the only things she's saying is, 'Oh, my God, I'm going to hell.' And I'm asking her, 'What are you going to hell for?' She says, 'I killed my grandpa.' She's saying, 'Oh, my God, I'm going to hell. I killed my grandpa. My father's going to kill me.' She said those words repetitively for, like, twenty minutes, a half hour, as we sat at the recreation center. She said it repetitively, over and over."

They hit the road. "I didn't try to think about it at all, is what I did. I decided not to think and just go. I decided to help her get away. And at that time, I quit thinking about it as 'her' and I started thinking of it as 'we.' "

They drive to Quincy, Illinois, and from there on to a series of back roads, where Diane fishes out a set of her step-grandfather's work clothes for tossing into the woods. Zachary gets rid of all the paperwork in the truck—everything behind the seat, everything in the ashtray. "Except for a twelve-gauge shotgun, which I started to get rid of. She said no, leave that in there. She said we might need it. She said, remember we were talking about if we needed money we could rob someone. We could rob a gas station in a country town in the middle of the night. So I left it in there, but not thinking about robbing. I was thinking I might be able to pawn it somewhere."

They made it to Peoria, where "we came on a sign that said Chicago," and then to Chicago, where Zachary knew a couple of people. He'd met them in DYS. "I looked them up. They said they couldn't do anything for me, they had just got in some more trouble; they were on probation." They drive around Chicago, hit some pawnshops, but Diane does not want to pawn the gun. They drive to Indiana. "I just saw a sign that said Indianapolis, and there's a lot of places I haven't been. I'm just so full of energy, and ready to go, and ready to get this show on the road that I didn't care. I just wanted to do anything and everything, all at the same time." First, a stop in Rensselaer. Jerry's Guns. Zach sells the shotgun for $100. He has no ID but lies about his age and provides his address and Social Security number.

They drive through the Indiana backwoods for a while, then the highway to Indianapolis. They stop at a mall. "Because I didn't have any good music to listen to. I wanted to get something to listen to. And plus, I was getting tired of sitting in the truck the whole time. I was getting cramped up. I wanted to get out and walk around for a minute."

They buy a cassette at Music Land. It's now around nine o'clock at night. They go to the hospital parking lot—"I believe it was the fifth level of parking"—to find new tags for the truck. The failed effort. They drive to a gas station to try the same thing—put the stolen plates on the truck—but there are too many lights. They are feeling fatigue now, so they go a motel, to try and get a room. "They needed ID. They were not coming off the fact that they needed ID." Back on the road again. "I figured if I went and found a small country town, that I could probably get a hotel room without ID."

They drive to Ohio, to Preble County near the Ohio-Indiana border on Interstate 70 and the attention of Trooper Richard Noll. A lighted cigarette: "You want to hear a confession?"

• • •

NOW TUCKER BRACED himself for the most difficult piece of evidence in his client's defense: the letter to Angela Hinds that prosecutor Wilson had read into the record. Could you explain, he asked the defendant, how in that letter you are essentially saying, "I did it but I'm going to say I'm not"?

Zachary leaned forward and furrowed his brow. "It's hard to explain. It was like I wanted to tell the truth. I mean, I wanted to. But as far as everyone knew, me being a murderer was the truth. So I didn't really know how to go about telling the truth without everyone saying, well, he's lying. So I tried to make it seem like I had still done it, but I was saying that I wasn't. I don't know if you can understand what I'm saying."

And the letter to prosecutor Wilson?

"That letter, basically, told the truth. I apologized for all the lies that I had told, as in saying that I killed Mr. Poage. [The letter] told that Diane had killed her grandfather and that I was in love with her, so I tried to help her get away. And I took the rap for her."

There was a recess in the proceedings, and then Mike Wilson arose to cross-examine. He was spitting out rapid-fire questions almost before he left his chair, a hard edge in his twangy mid-Missouri voice as he moved swiftly in a direct line toward the defendant. His strategy seemed as clear as it was brutal: Given that Zachary had already exposed himself as a liar, the prosecutor meant to tear down every last shred of his credibility and then trap him in moments of irrevocable truth.

He attacked the matter of Zachary's supposed attention deficit/hyperactivity disorder: "Isn't it true that the last doctor that examined you told you you didn't have ADHD?" ("Not that I recall, no.") He jabbed at little inconsistencies in the boy's direct testimony: If his mother and stepfather hadn't known of his return home from the treatment center, why would Zachary think it was Kirk driving that truck, with its flashing headlights, into the yard at two A.M.? "Well, there's only two hundred and nineteen people in Hunnewell. I figured he might have heard it from one of them." "Did you talk to all two hundred and nineteen people that night?" "No, but I'm sure they all saw me." "Pretty easy to see people in Hunnewell, isn't it?" "Yeah."

Here Wilson stopped the cat-and-mouse and turned abruptly to the boy's original confession. He bore in on Zachary's recitation of the gruesome details: the gurgling and snoring, the purple brains on the ceiling, "something about blowing the top of his head off. Is it possible you said that?" ("Yeah. I said a lot of things.") "Because you were trying to cover for Diane, right?" ("Exactly.") "Can you tell us exactly how it protects Diane by saying, 'I kicked the bed before I shot him'?" ("I believed that that would protect her because if I made it believable enough, you know, then they're going to believe it.") "So you thought it necessary to add just as many details as you could?" ("I was saying everything that came to mind, that she had told me. And anything else that came to mind from myself.") "Fiction?" ("Yes, sir.") "And that's why you said the color of his brains were purple?" ("No. That wasn't from my mind. That was the statement that Diane made to me.")

Now, and without seeming to do so, Mike Wilson abruptly shifted his line of questioning from the factual to the philosophical: "And that's why you said J. D. Poage deserved to die?"

Zachary, perhaps caught unawares, walked into it. "In all honesty, that's my belief."

"So you believe he deserved to die?"

"Yes."

"You just didn't do the killing."

"No, sir."

Having established this crucial mind-set, the prosecutor returned to the shaky line between Zachary's persona and his true nature: "But again, the reason you said things like, 'I want the injection, I'm guilty, and I'm not at all sorry, he deserved to die,' was a combination of what you believed was true, and also you wanted to look like the baddest dude you could so as to take the heat off Diane, right?"

"Yep. That's exactly—I wanted to look hard-core, per se."

Mike Wilson shifted again: "Well, you are fairly hard-core, though, aren't you, Zach?"

The defendant met his gaze. "No, sir."

"You've lived on the street before, haven't you?"

"Yes, sir."

"You've testified that you have an anger management problem, haven't you?"

"Yes, sir."

"You've engaged in assaults before?"

"Yes, sir."

"But you're not hard-core."

For the first time on the stand, Zachary seemed to struggle for his aplomb. "Not—not too—well, I suppose maybe to a certain extent. But not how I see hard-core."

Wilson now suspended his task of identifying and unmasking Zachary's pretentions and turned to the boy's letter retracting his confession. He bore home on the suspicious timing, just hours before Diane's sentencing for second-degree murder. "Was that an accident, was that a coincidence, or was that a plan, to change your story and retract your confession on the same day that she pled guilty?" ("That was not a plan.") "Just a stroke of luck, that same day that she pled guilty to second-degree murder for killing J. D. Poage, the same crime you're charged with, you withdraw your confession." Wilson took a step closer to the defendant. "Just a coincidence?"

Zachary had recovered his posture of the reasonable innocent: "I don't know how I knew that she was going to plead guilty, at two-thirty that morning. I don't know."

But now Wilson pounced again. "While Diane was in prison, did you ever write her?" ("Sure.") "Because you still loved her?" ("Yeah.") And then the prosecutor read portions of another letter into the record, a letter written to Diane by Zachary on September 1, 1998: " 'Your letter sounded like you didn't think I would write back. I felt that you would know better than that. I understand why you did what you did, but if you remember, I told you to do what you had to do. You can do something to change that, though. Come to my trial in November [the original trial date] and tell them a different story, or you were so out of it that you blocked it out of your memory, or anything for real. You've already been sentenced and they can't go back and change that.' "

It had the markings of a catastrophic moment for Zachary's acquittal hopes, and perhaps it was exactly that in the jurors' minds: a seemingly explicit plea to Diane to lie on the witness stand in order to save Zach from a murder conviction—complete with the knowing reminder that her sentencing protected her from further prosecution.

And yet the maddening sliver of ambiguity remained: "tell them a different story" did not *necessarily* equate with "tell them a lie." Moreover, in the drama of Mike Wilson's timing—introducing a letter that seemed to establish Zachary's cynical manipulations of Diane once and for all—the defense attorneys did not seize upon what Wilson had artfully glossed over: the lack of positive evidence that Zachary had corresponded with Diane, or with anyone in a position to know about her court schedule, *before* her June 4 sentencing.

In short, the highly improbable just might have been true: the timing of Zachary's retraction might have been a coincidence.

In his redirect, Frederick Tucker attempted to counter the effects of his client's troubling letter by producing the correspondence that triggered it: a letter written to Zachary on August 31 by Diane. Its contents, which added more layers to the central enigma—not to mention a few surfacings of standard adolescent lovesickness, which lent the whole of it a sad grotesqueness—read, in part:

> I started this letter a hundred times it seems like. But this is the one you will get, I hope. All this time, you've been on my mind. You're still my first and last thought every day. I had to write and tell you that I'm truly sorry about how things turned out. Like I said from the beginning, I was going to lose, no matter what I did. I just didn't know it would hurt so damn bad.
>
> I can't even imagine what you're going through, and knowing that I made it even worse tears me up inside. Not a day goes by when I don't think about how I've destroyed two lives, one by murder, one by what to me is selfishness. I would give my own life to be able to change things. Shit, it's mostly gone, anyways.
>
> In a way, I wish we never would have met. Not because I won't always cherish our short time together, but because then you and my family wouldn't have to go through this. I told you once I didn't have any regrets, but I was wrong. I regret hurting you and the other people I love. I regret that the wrong person died that night, and more than anything, I regret having to be away from you. It's just like, damn, I had a whole new life going on, one where I was happy, and I went and fucked things up.

Under Tucker's prodding, Zachary maintained that his invitation to Diane was a response to the sentence, "I would give my own life to be able to change things," followed by, ". . . because then you and my family wouldn't have to go through this." The implication Tucker hoped to establish, obviously, was that Diane was signaling a change of heart and her willingness to tell the true story.

Mike Wilson leapt like a leopard on fresh meat. "Can you show me where it says, 'I'm sorry I shotgunned my grandfather'?" he demanded of Zachary. ("Those exact words, no. No.") "Does it come even close to saying, 'I shotgunned' anybody?" ("Yes, in my opinion, it does.") "But is the word 'shotgun' mentioned?" ("No, sir. The word 'murder' is.") "Yes, and she's pled guilty to second-degree murder, hasn't she? So she's admitted her involvement, hasn't she?" ("Involvement, yes.") "It's just you that hasn't admitted any involvement so far, isn't it? At least today." ("I was involved after the fact, yes.")

And then the prosecutor introduced into evidence the letter he clearly regarded as the trump card. Written by Diane to Zachary, it was dated November 17, 1998.

Dear Zach, I'm not sure how to begin this. Guess I'll get right to the point. Not sure what happened, but you changed. Or maybe you were like this all along and I was just blinded by your "I love yous," and promises of forever. All I know is that I won't let you hurt me any more.

You should know what I'm talking about, but just in case you're playing dumb, I'll refresh your memory. What the fuck made you start telling people I did everything that night? Why are my two best friends telling me you're doing me wrong with the one bitch you admitted you fucked?

And most and worst of all, what gave you the right to bring my molestation up in all this shit? I fucking trusted you so much, and loved you so much, what you've done, are doing, is no better than what my brother did to me as a child. Both of you took away my ability to trust and love. How could you do all that and still say I love you to my face? . . .

There isn't really shit else for me to say, other than goodbye. I can't believe the person you've become, Zack. Just so you know, you can't play a player. Then again, I never thought you could hurt me either. Fuck promises.

Wilson put the letter on the table and turned toward Zachary, regarding him for a few moments. When he spoke again, his tone was acid.

"It appears she's pretty upset with you in this letter, doesn't it?"

"Yes, sir."

"It appears she knows at this point that you're blaming it all on her, doesn't it?"

"Yes, sir."

"No further questions."

Noontime on this second day was approaching. I had been aware of the dampness and the heaviness of the bodies around me. Big, solid Missouri farming people, nearly all of them Poages or friends of Poages, they had sat through this trial with a kind of ageless stoicism, ignoring strangers and, without making a show of it, holding themselves quietly apart from the few Wilsons and former Wilsons in the benches. Now, as proceedings paused while the attorneys drew around the judge's bench to discuss a recess, the accumulated intensity inside this small courtroom seemed to burst in on all of us, like the shock of silence after a steady noise had ceased. In the complete quiet—the absence even of whispers—I looked around at the fixed faces and rigid shoulders among the spectators and understood, for the first time, the weight of this death. J. D. Poage was and would remain an unknown entity to me, but I sensed his history a little under the skin of the bereaved people in my vicinity.

Noon recess.

The afternoon session.

Diane Myers took the stand.

She was called by the prosecution from her incarceration at Vandalia. As the storied but until now unseen "other" in this murder trial, she might have created a dramatic stir upon her entrance into the courtroom had she not been related to so many of the people there. I certainly found myself staring at her. If I had been unprepared for the actuality of Zachary Wilson, set against what I had imagined him to be, I was mildly stunned by Diane.

What drew the eye to her was her self-possession. It encompassed and went beyond the tired notion of poise and reached an eerie sort of coiled hauteur, a dignity that suggested she was beyond anything as trivial as self-consciousness. Her prison pallor, set against her blackened hair and black jersey, her habit of tucking her chin into her throat, and a set of her mouth that might have been a tentative smile and might have been something else, set her apart—not only from her straining kinfolk but somehow also from the region. If Zach Wilson was a boy of complex surfaces and depths, he had met his counterpart in Diane Marie Myers.

Elizabeth Kohler, Mike Wilson's assistant in the prosecution, conducted the questioning. Diane seemed coolly professional—a weathered criminal-justice system insider—as she answered the early, corroborating questions of identity and chronology in a small, terse voice. She referred to Zachary as "the defendant" and seemed intent on not offering one syllable beyond the minimal answer required.

She grew emphatic (but remained deeply guarded) only when Kohler led her into the events leading directly to J. D. Poage's murder, beginning with the first of the two evening walks she took with Zachary. "What did you discuss when you went on that first walk?"

"Different things. We, like, talked about I was upset and things."

"Why were you upset?"

"Part because I got into a fight with my stepdad, and part because I thought that I might have been pregnant and miscarried. I said that I wanted to leave, period. Leave, go somewhere else."

"Leave the state?"

"Leave. Anywhere. I didn't care where."

"Did you talk about how you would go about leaving?"

"Take a car."

"Steal a car?"

"Yeah."

"Whose idea was that?"

"I don't remember."

"Did you talk about whose car you were going to steal?"

"Yes."

"Whose car did you talk about?"

"Different people's."

"Like who?"

"Like whoever we knew. We talked about his mom, we talked about people we knew in this area. My grandfather."

"Your grandfather, the victim in this case?"

"Yes."

When Kohler prodded her about the specifics of the plan, she received monosyllabic vagueness from the motionless girl. Back to Mitch's house. "While we were at his house, the codefendant, he cut his hair." "The defendant?" "Yeah, the defendant." More hanging out: "We talked." "What did the defendant do?" "Nothing, really.

We just talked." The visit to wake her stepfather and to cook for her little brother. She dyed and cut her own hair. She walked back to her stepbrother's house. "And I got the defendant."

Back to Diane's house. The shotgun, stolen from the gun cabinet. The gathering of "bullets." Clothing. "Because we were running away." The attempt to hot-wire the LTD.

It was approximately at this stage that I began to hear, just at the edges of the icy girl's syntax and cadences, the traces of another voice: the faint voice of a lost child.

"Why did you take the gun?"

"To pawn, I guess."

"Do you know how to shoot a gun?"

"Kind of."

"Are you experienced in shooting guns?"

"No."

The walk to the victim's house. "Once you started walking, what did he say?"

"He said that he was going to kill him and, like, people, certain people deserved to die. Saying things like that."

They talked on about other things. "Where we would go, what we would do. A lot of it, we were just talking about stupid stuff, you know, nothing that was really important. He said something like he didn't have any feelings, or something, and—"

"He said he didn't have any feelings?"

"Yes."

And what, Kohler wanted to know, did Diane think was going to happen when the two reached her grandfather's house?

"I didn't really know. Nothing. I thought we were going to rob him, and that was it." Because they needed to run away.

The two approached within a town block of Poage's house. Diane stopped walking.

"Why did you stop?"

"I was getting nervous and scared."

"Why were you scared?"

"I just didn't want to do it anymore."

"Do what?"

"Anything. I just wanted to go back home."

"Did you tell the defendant that?"

"I just said, 'I don't want to go out there anymore.' "

"And what did he say to you?"

"He said, 'No, we walked all this way.' And then something like, well, maybe you should have stayed back there. I don't remember the rest, really."

Zachary walked on alone. Diane watched him. A hill separated the two of them from Poage's house. Zachary disappeared over it. After a minute or two, Diane started walking after him.

Kohler wanted to know why, given that Diane was now frightened of what was about to happen.

" 'Cause I didn't want to sit there in the dark, either."

Diane crested the hill in time to see Zachary reach the edge of the Poage house. By the time she got there he had disappeared inside. She remained outside, by the entrance to Poage's garage. Why? Kohler wanted to know.

"I don't know. I was just standing there."

"What happened then?"

"I heard the gun go off."

A single shot. Then Zachary walked out of the house, through the front door. He called to Diane to "come on," and she walked to where he was. She entered the house and stood beside the front door. Zachary went into a back room, "and I heard the gun go off again."

"What happened then?"

"He came out, and we left."

Zachary was carrying Poage's trousers, from which they later withdrew $100. On the way out Diane picked up a second shotgun that was leaning by the front door. Her grandfather's shotgun. The two teenagers put Diane's dogs—they had followed the pair to the house—in the bed of Poage's 4×4 truck and drove away. The far side of the Mark Twain Bridge. Quincy. Chicago. Rensselaer. Indianapolis. Ohio. It was in Indianapolis, after they'd bought the music tape, Diane recalled, that Zachary told her what he had done to her grandfather. "And then I was just like, I don't want to hear any more about it."

As to why she had eventually pled to second-degree murder: "Mostly because my mom said she was tired, and she didn't want to go through another trial. And I was just tired; you know, I was tired of the lies, I was tired of everything. I just wanted to get it over with."

In his cross-examination, Frederick Tucker bore in on Diane's antagonism toward her own family—establishing that her incarceration at St. Louis had been partly for stealing and forging her mother's checks—and in so doing, uncovered a new ambiguity not especially helpful to Zachary's defense: It was not her grandfather who had molested her, Diane casually testified, only her brother.

Actually it was her recollection of an earlier conversation, with the Ohio troopers, that brought this new twist to light.

"And you told the officers that you told Zach that you had been pregnant, but you lost the baby and couldn't have children because of abuse from your grandfather and brother?"

"No, I said my brother."

"Okay. You're sure that you did not say your grandfather?"

"If I did, I don't remember, but I know that it didn't have anything to do with him. It was my brother."

A bit later, Tucker tried a new way into Diane's chimerical memories and motives but was headed off by Elizabeth Kohler. He attempted to question her about a piece she had written for a creative writing class at Monroe City High School a few months before the murder. Kohler objected, and the two lawyers debated fiercely for a few moments at the judge's bench. The essay, according to Tucker, described Diane's love of getting high—"it was the biggest thing in the world," as Tucker paraphrased it. "And she also said that there would be no greater high than killing a person," he added, "and I do have a witness here to confirm all that if she denies it."

"Stephen King writes about killing people," Kohler countered. "He's not a murderer. This is not relevant to this trial." Tucker persisted that it was; it amounted to evidence that Diane had considered the aesthetics of killing. "She's thought it through. She's thought about the experience of it. To her, the experience is a good one." In the end, the judge sustained the objection, and the jury never heard about Diane's fantasies of murder.

With Diane's testimony, both prosecution and defense had exhausted their witnesses. Final arguments were set for the following morning, a Friday.

· · ·

DRIVING BACK TO Hannibal, I tried to analyze the impact of the two teenagers' testimonies on the jury, but my mind kept going back to a small moment involving Zachary. It had happened shortly after the judge banged his gavel for the noon recess and the spectators around me heaved to their feet. As usual, I sat for a few minutes watching the defendant. Routinely, in hiatuses such as this, Zachary liked to hobnob with anyone in his vicinity: bailiffs, family members. But this time he remained off to himself, his hands characteristically stuffed into his pockets. And then, when the room was nearly vacant, Zachary started to move. He began a casual saunter across the front of the courtroom, from my left to my right, toward the now-empty jury box and the expanse of windows that formed the wall on the right side of the room. I was seated not far from the windows, so his stroll brought him vaguely in my direction.

But Zachary was not looking at me. His gaze was set on the windows—the room's main source of light—which were covered by thinly slatted venetian blinds.

He withdrew one hand from a pocket and parted two of the slats, peering through the opening at the sunlit downtown of Moberly and the few trees that were starting to produce green buds. He muttered something to himself. I found as I drove that I couldn't get the phrase out of my mind.

What he'd said was, "It's a beautiful day in the neighborhood."

· 21 ·

VERDICT

Friday morning's closing arguments belonged to Mike Wilson. His summation was a devastating assault, honed, and deadly—a tour de force of old-fashioned courtroom oratory. In a trial dominated by shifting versions of a lone Gothic story, the prosecutor made himself the metastoryteller; he summoned all the conflicting elements of Zachary's and Diane's accounts and assembled them into the story *of* a story. As he spoke, in the brisk but distinctively whipsawed twang of the deep region, I could sense the elements of an older narrative tradition, at once indignant and slyly ironic, imposing themselves on the present.

"You have seen a very unusual murder case," he informed the jury, "for a number of reasons. But one is because we had a complete confession. The state obtained a complete confession before we even knew we had a body. That's pretty unusual.

"Something else that's unusual, if you've had any experience in trials at all, is that you haven't really heard very much disagreement about the basic facts.

"The only real issue is whether the defendant was lying back then, as his counsel says, or lying now, as the state proposes. If you've got a taste for irony, that's pretty unusual right there. We've got a state's counsel trying to prove that the defendant is a truthful person, and his own counsel trying to prove he's a liar. That's a little different."

Now Wilson began a remorseless, methodical paring away of possibilities.

"Was whoever did this aware that his conduct was practically certain to cause the death of J. D. Poage? When you go into a home, as this somebody did, and go into the bedroom, and look down at this sleeping, naked, deaf old man, put a shotgun to his head and pull the trigger, and see the kind of devastation that that first shot causes, the trench in the shoulder, and the hole in the head.

"And then you reload, and put that shotgun up to your shoulder again, and pull the trigger again. Do you think that whoever did it knew that his conduct was practically certain to cause the death of J. D. Poage? That's why he did it. There's no doubt. He'd be terribly disappointed if doing that didn't cause the death of J. D. Poage. That's what shotguns are supposed to do. And this one apparently performed exactly the way it was supposed to. Every rural five- or ten-year-old Missouri farmboy knows what shotguns do, and they know that they can cause a death, so that's pretty easy, too."

Wilson seized the elements of Zachary's "noble lie" in defense of Diane and wrenched them into a damning incantation.

"He was caught five hundred miles away from here, so he certainly wasn't hanging around. He knew the precise location of the murder weapon, in the middle of the Mississippi River. He knew the precise location of J. D. Poage's billfold, under a rock.

"And he had the precise details of every minute aspect of what went on in J. D. Poage's rural farmhouse on January twenty-eighth down pat. He knew what door was broken into. He knew that [Poage] was old and deaf. He knew that all the lights were on in the house. He knew that the phone was yanked off the wall. He knew that there was a semicircle cut in the shoulder before that first shot went in the side of the head. He knew that he was sleeping. He knew he was naked. He knew that after the first shot he was covered up. And he knew that the second shot made a hole in that sheet as it went through the top of his head, and on into the headboard, and on into the wall.

"And he offered a lot of details that he didn't have to, certainly not to protect Diane, his girlfriend, as he's told you on the witness stand. The details about the colors of brain, the gurgling in between, the kicking of the bed. He didn't have to tell you those things. He told them to you for one reason, and one reason only: They were true."

Now Wilson shifted his attack. He abandoned the incantatory recitation for a burst of pure outrage.

"Now, throughout the process, you haven't heard one drop of remorse or regret from the defendant on the witness stand. He said something the state regards as cold and amazing: 'I didn't do it, but he deserved to die.' He's clinging to the idea that he's done the world a favor by ridding it of J. D. Poage."

Having made this lacerating point, Wilson refocused his energies toward deconstructing Zachary's "noble lie."

"But the problem is, after he goes to jail for a while, the glory and the excitement kind of wears off, and he starts thinking, this isn't as much fun as I thought. And Diane, well, you know, she's in prison. Can't have sex with her anymore. Which was all he was using her for. She can't help him.

"Oh, yes she can! She can take the rap. And that's exactly what you've heard happen. Now, if you have doubt about that, if there can be any doubt about that, don't forget—please don't forget—this swell letter to Angela Hinds in which he lays out his plan. He gives you the blueprint for what he's going to do. He does a couple of just great things. He says, I'm guilty; although I think everyone knows who really did it, I just hope people don't look at me different. I mean, I had a really good reason.

"Yeah, he had a really good reason. *He wanted to steal his truck.*

"If you can come up with an explanation for how that letter can be anything but true, and lay out the plan, then you're better than Zachary Wilson was when he took the stand. You heard him stutter and stammer and try. He couldn't get it done. He couldn't make this letter go away. And in your deliberations, you shouldn't let this letter go away either."

As for Zachary's letter of retraction, Wilson made short work of it: "The problem was in the details, ladies and gentlemen, the little things. He retracted that confession on June fourth, but he made a point to date that letter to make it look like he wrote it in the middle of the night. That's about the only letter you've seen or read that was dated specifically with a time on it. It's dated two-thirty in the morning.

"Why did he do that? Because he wanted to make sure that letter was signed and sealed before Diane came to court and testified. The problem with that is, he didn't put it out to the outside world through that prison guard until that prison guard came on that afternoon. And that was intentional.

"Why is that important? Because the defendant lied and said there wasn't any correlation; it was just an accident that he came up with that confession the same day [Diane] pled guilty to second-degree murder. That was a lie. And you all know that, because the likelihood of that day being selected over all the other days between January and June fourth is absolutely impossible.

"It wasn't a great plan he had, ladies and gentlemen; it was just all he had."

And now the thunderous summation.

"Don't let him get away with it, ladies and gentlemen. Let him know that if you kill someone, you will get the rest of your life to regret it and repent. You won't get other opportunities to kill good citizens; you won't be out walking the streets. You'll be in the penitentiary for the rest of your life. Guilty, first-degree murder."

It was Twain, it was pure Twain. The mordant rhythms of a tensely building horror scene, as in the "what shotguns do" passage; the cadences of repetition ("He knew . . . He knew . . . He knew . . ."); the bluntly corrosive asides ("Yes, he had a reason—*he wanted to steal his truck!*"); the relentless naming and then excising of fraudulent possibilities, the sudden shaft of venom-tipped umbrage. It was all Mark Twain, and specifically, it was the Mark Twain of the later, "Great Dark" years, the angry father of American letters drawing on his dashed Missouri innocence and idealism to rail against an accursed, unjust universe.

But with this inversion, of course: Where Mark Twain had raged from the implied perspective of a boy disillusioned by corrupt society, prosecutor Wilson sought now to speak for a disillusioned society in its case against a corrupted boy.

The defense's closing argument was not memorable. It took the jury about an hour to convict.

The jury returned to the courtroom at eleven twenty-eight A.M. As the judge asked the foreman to stand and recite the verdict, I became aware of a terrific rumbling in the courtroom. It was a sound—a steady and insistent thunder, as of heavy things dislodging and gaining momentum—and also a sensation, a vibration that I could feel in the wooden bench beneath me.

I glanced around, to see whether the fixtures in the courtroom were shaking. My first thought was of an earthquake. The notion was far from fanciful. The New Madrid Fault, one of the deadliest quake zones in the world, lay less than three hundred miles to the southeast. In 1811, that faultline shifted with such force that the Mississippi River roiled and reversed its course for several days; walls cracked in Cincinnati, and church bells pealed in New York and Boston. The town of Hannibal could trace its origins in part to that convulsion. In consideration of the uprooted farmland in southern Missouri, the U.S. Congress authorized land certificates to refugees from the area, redeemable anywhere in the territory. Many of these certificates found their way into the hands of speculators; one of them, Thompson Bird, filed a claim on what is now the Hannibal riverfront.

Seismologists had been predicting recently that a recurrence of the great quake was imminent. Perhaps the fault was preparing to devour what it had created.

But not today. After a moment I realized that the tremor's source was nothing quite so vast. It was generated by three rows of Poage men and women, sitting close together on the spectator benches, their hands tightly interlinked, their knees bobbing up and down uncontrollably as they listened for the foreman's verdict.

The foreman spoke, and the collective bobbing ceased. Guilty, first-degree murder. Life in prison without possibility of parole.

· · ·

A HEAVY SPRING rain was falling as I left the courthouse and began my sixty-mile drive back to Hannibal. Each day on my way to and from the trial I had passed the turnoff to Hunnewell from the main highway—Route Z—and on this early afternoon, despite the bad weather, I decided to take it.

Rural Missouri had seldom looked sweeter. The rain had brought a glisten to the landscape. The fields gave off the promise of prosperity; the black soil had been freshly turned over in the pastures, ready for planting. I could see fine small herds of white-faced black cattle. The houses along the road, ranging from mobile homes to brick suburban-style houses, were clean and trim. I passed a couple of plaster-of-paris statues, twin hunting dogs on point, and an artfully half-buried wagon wheel, a signature of this part of the country. American flags hung wetly in front of houses and barns. Crocuses and dogwood blossoms were out; the rain was washing the land into the first blossoming of springtime. I drove past stands of oak trees, redbud, some willow. The underbrush had already been cleared from the winter and neatly stacked in piles.

It was all just a little too ripe looking. I could not help wonder, as I drove, whether the inhabitants of those neat little domiciles owned patches of the surrounding land, or were employees of it—wage earners in someone else's new agribusiness economy.

At the level of memory, it did not matter. I felt again the pull this kind of land had had on me as a boy. How it had drawn me into itself. How I could assign meaning to every feature of it, place invisible friends and enemies in its contours, make the rain personal and give it a function in the drama, watch for living things in the trees and against my shoes, things feathered and scaled. How the air had a fragrance and a taste. And how I could build all of that into a story of itself and me.

My father and I had hunted rabbits and squirrels on this land in my boyhood—me with my BB gun, him with his twelve-gauge shotgun. Sammy Clemens himself had roamed these acres a century before that. Hunnewell, and J. D. Poage's empty, violated farmhouse, just down the road now, lay about eleven miles north of Florida, where Sammy was born, lived till the age of four, and revisited in summers throughout his boyhood, his enchanted interludes at his uncle John Quarles's farm. That town itself was a played-out peninsula now— nearly surrounded by an artificial recreational lake called Mark Twain Lake—but I was driving in his essential realm. "A heavenly place for a boy," he wrote of the farm. He inventoried its pleasures as an aging writer in Vienna: the meals of fried chicken and roast pig and venison just killed and fresh corn boiled on the ear, apple dumplings and peach cobbler, all served on a table set in the middle of a shady and breezy floor inside the double-log cabin. He recalled the holy minutiae of that terrain: how the farmhouse "stood in the middle of a very large yard, and the yard was fenced on three sides with rails and on the rear side with high palings; against these stood the smoke-house; beyond the palings was the orchard . . .

"I can see the farm yet, with perfect clearness," he wrote. "I can see all the belongings, all the details; the family room of the house, with a 'trundle' bed in one corner and a spinning-wheel in another—a wheel whose rising and falling wail, heard from a distance, was the mournfulest of all sounds to me, and made me homesick and low-spirited, and filled my atmosphere with the wandering spirits of the dead . . ."

He recalled nights at the farmhouse with "my aunt in one chimney-corner knitting, my uncle in the other smoking his corn-cob pipe . . . half a dozen children romping in the background twilight . . . in the early mornings a snuggle of children, in shirts and chemises, occu-pying the hearthstone and procrastinating—they could not bear to leave that comfortable place and go out on the wind-swept floor-space between the house and kitchen where the general tin basin stood, and wash."

Ahead of me as I drove now, I saw a rusted water tower rising above a tree line. A metal sign, chipped black paint on a white field: "Hunnewell Pop: 219." (Zachary's recall had been right on target.) At the base of the tree line were the town's first visible houses, mostly run-down mobile homes.

I crossed an invisible line into Shelby County. The invisible line also marked a dramatic discontinuity between the robust fields and the exhausted hamlet. A freight train, ambling slowly westward, ob-structed my entrance into the town.

Freight trains were routine in Hunnewell, day and night. J. D. Poage must have heard them from his house, heard them swaying and bumping along that ancient line. All the Hunnewell Poages would have heard them. And Diane Myers. And Zachary Wilson. Hunnewell owed its existence to the trains. The railroad line created the town.

When the caboose cleared, I edged my car across the tracks and into the netherworld where Zachary and Diane had passed their brief time together, foraged for a vision of a life to come.

Not a human being was in sight. A kind of universal rusted brown lay across everything: buildings, lawns, street surfaces. A few early tulips poked out of some of the yards. Nearly all the residences were mobile homes, I realized, except for some older wood-frame shacks that looked abandoned. Fenced-in dog kennels were everywhere, but I saw few dogs. Trash bags, glistening from the rain, swelled on porches like black mushrooms. A sign on a white board, nailed against the shingles on the front of a low-slung brick building, announced: "US Post Office, Hunnewell, MO."

I found it hard to imagine children romping in the background twilights of these precincts. Zachary and Diane, it seemed likely, would always be able to see J. D. Poage's house with perfect clearness, and they too would find their atmosphere filled with the wandering spirits of the dead. But the land—the memories of it—would not likely restore them. Now it was the land itself that had gone invisible, had lost its capacity to heal the emptiness of a Missouri child.

Turning onto First Street from Maple, I spotted my first and only resident—a thin, solitary stroller wearing military camouflage pants and boots and brandishing a thick walking stick. I saw satellite dishes, propane gas tanks, cars with blue weatherproof tarps draped over them, a gas station/restaurant/store that looked to be closed and, on closer inspection, was up for sale. I saw the Christian church, a white clapboard building with two struggling cedar trees in its small front yard, and the Mt. Zion Baptist Church with its small white steeple. I saw some beetle-shaped bungalows that might have been built at the turn of the century.

But no other people. And no real trace of evidence as to why Hunnewell even existed.

As I let the car crawl aimlessly up and down the miniature streets and avenues of the town, I thought about the conversation I had had with Zachary's stepfather while the jury deliberated. After two days of nodding warily at Kirk Wilson, I had introduced myself to him on this morning before the court convened, and he had proved more open to an intrusive stranger than I'd expected. When court recessed so the jury could consider its verdict, Kirk and I left the courthouse in search of a quiet place to talk. We settled on the main room in the town's public library.

"You've never ever known anybody like Zach," Kirk told me when we had taken seats at a fiercely polished reading table. Taller and leaner than his brother Kyle, his face lined and sorrowful under his tinted aviator glasses and trimmed mustache, he had the air of a man who needed to get some things off his chest.

"He's totally into his inner self," he went on. "My daughter and I were talking about it on the phone last night. She has a degree in psychology. She said, 'Zach fits the profile of every serial killer you've ever read about. Down to a T.' Myself, I'm not sure that he fits any profile at all. But if I needed a baby-sitter for a six-month-old, I would take Zachary. Or if I had an old man who needed help walkin' across the street, an old woman, we'd stop. Zachary would say, 'Stop the car. We need to help them.' "

Kirk's voice, murmurous enough at the outset, dropped down lower, to something like tire wheels on gravel. "And yet he is cold to a fault. The only time I've ever seen Zachary cry, aside from the few times I've spanked his butt, was a few years ago when we thought I had cancer. He cried over that. And that's all."

Zachary was four when Kirk first met his mother, Lana. "She was sellin' hot dogs at the local IGA, near the field where I was playin' in a softball tournament. My kids and I had gone in there; it was real hot, so we walked in there to cool off for a few minutes, get some ice cream. We met her in there, we talked. I didn't think anything about it then. I met her a few weeks later, we went out, this that and the other, and it went from there. One of the *worst* decisions in my life. Without a doubt."

Lana and Kirk were married for eleven years. "Until the time she came home and said, 'Oh, my boyfriend's wife's going to call you, you need to talk to her.' That's what I was dealing with. And in a totally normal tone. Well, I'll tell you how twisted it was. I was sitting in my recliner watching TV in the family room. I said, 'No problem.' I said, 'You need to work on something, though, because you can't live here anymore.' I never raised my voice. She said, 'Okay.' Zach grew up in this environment."

The "super-sweet little kid," as Kirk remembered him, remained sweet until the second grade. He grew truculent with his teacher. And then everything fell apart. Then came the transfers: to public school, to Catholic school, back to public. The boy's behavior worsened. He became "the Babe Ruth of detention."

Then, at age ten, the medication began.

"He'd become uncontrollable," Kirk said. "The thing he said in court yesterday upset me: that we took him off the medication because of the cost. That was not an issue. The issue was that he was drugged and his behavior did not change."

Kirk fell silent. His chin tucked against his chest, he stared at the polished surface of the reading table. After a minute I asked him whether he could remember any happy times with Zachary.

"I'm a softball pitcher," he said, without altering his gaze. "Fastpitch. That's what I used to do with my summers; it was an all-consuming thing. My team would travel all over the country for about thirteen weeks out of the summer. We won a national championship in 1991. I played for a team out of Sikeston, Missouri. Superior Office Products. We won the national championship in 1991. I was the only pitcher. I wasn't good enough to win at that level, but somehow I *was* good enough over those four days. I don't know how to explain that. But that's not the point. The point was, it was a very big deal to Zach. A super-big deal. It was like him and I were buddies then.

"And there was one other time. He was in second or third grade. His class had to make a cake. It had to be nutritious, and the kids had to be involved in making it. Well, his mother was working till late in the afternoon, so I said, I'll help you make the cake. Yeah. Okay, Zach, let's make a cake."

Some animation came into Kirk's voice now, and he lifted his gaze from the table surface. For a minute he was not talking to me, but to a boy that only he could see. "You like chocolate, let's do a chocolate cake. Okay. You and me will make this together. Look you're gonna put it in the pan, you're gonna do all the stuff, I'll show you how. So we gotta make it nutritious, I mean it's gotta be good. I said, I'll get some apples, whole apples, and put 'em in. I said, I'll get some raisins and put chocolate icing on 'em and then drop 'em on top of it, like bird turds. He said okay!

"So we did it. We dropped six whole apples, leaves and all, stuffed 'em in it. Then we iced it and then we put raisins all over the top of it. Then we brought it in, and"—here Kirk laughed—"*God* it was awful! But then they had an auction and I had to buy it. We won for Most Nutritious. And it wound up costing me six bucks to buy it back. I had about ten bucks tied up in that cake." His face had taken on a mischievous expression. "And I gave it to my sister-in-law for her birthday."

Kirk looked at me. "He was in third grade," he murmured.

Another heavy silence, and I asked Kirk if there had been any good years in the life of the reconstructed family. He pursed his lips and considered this, and said no.

"The first year or two it was the alcohol and the drugs. I didn't know about the drugs; I was too dumb. And that's stupid. I thought I was more in tune." He eventually placed Lana in drug and alcohol rehab. "When she came back, she got pregnant by her boyfriend the day she got out of rehab. Had an abortion. My friend, a Baptist minister, said, She's a person, give it a shot. I said, Well, I'll do that. We had a cleaning company for a year where she went to work at four in the morning and worked a shift and then I went to work. I worked twelve hours a day then. She was excellent at this; she was great at it. She made it go. We had that for about a year, year and a half, then we bought us a house."

Then, Kirk said, it went away. The old destructive patterns re-emerged. "Zachary escalated. His life was a constant escalation."

What forms did that escalation take? I asked Kirk.

"He developed this . . . personality. He said to me once, 'You know all the times you said to me, don't hang around with these kids 'cause they're a bad influence on you?' He said, 'It wasn't them.' He said, 'It was always me.' "

I pressed Kirk for his exact meaning: So Zachary feels that he's a kind of Satan? I asked him.

Kirk whipped his head from side to side. "No, no, no no no no *no*. He's *Zachary*. He was in total control of that stuff." And then, as if to himself: "Yes, he was."

Kirk gave me a searching look. "Don't underestimate how intelligent Zachary is. Zachary is *brilliant* in his own way."

The notion of brilliance triggered something in Kirk's mind. Abruptly, almost violently, he shifted his thoughts to the murder trial and to the heart of the truth of the matter. The words came low and rapidly, and then in a torrent.

"Yesterday, while Zach was on the witness stand, I went outside. I had to; when I sit too long my back hurts. I went outside into the hall, and I framed his face through the window of the courtroom door. I didn't want to hear what he's sayin, or Diane; I know what they're gonna say. I know what he and Diane are going to say. If I couldn't hear the voices, I'd know, *Zachary, you were in charge.* And Diane: *You're lyin'.* Zachary's lyin' too, I'm sure. But Diane is lyin' and you can tell it. And I don't know what Diane said, I didn't hear her testimony. But I knew what it was. Diane was lyin', you could tell by her body language. Her hands, looking down, she didn't look anybody in the eye, she's lyin', you knew that."

Now emerged the notion at the epicenter of Kirk Wilson's pain. "*She was there, and she did it.* Or they did it together."

I gave him a questioning look.

"Because—it's some kind of bull-in-the-china-shop thing. He wouldn't try to hide that. It wouldn't be done. It wouldn't be necessary. He's not that foolish."

I thought to ask Kirk whether, by "try to hide that," he meant the covering of Poage's body after the first shot was fired. But Kirk's thoughts were tumbling on, accusatory and justifying at the same time, a last-ditch argument for the defense, three blocks outside the jury's hearing. Somehow, in this tortured construct, Zach's slovenliness was proof of his innocence.

"He's a pig to live with beyond anything you can imagine. He would spit on the floor and leave it. He would put cigarettes out on the wall. He was too lazy to get up. This is a routine thing. His toy box. I opened it up one time. There must have been a thousand cigarette butts. He didn't try to hide them, it would have been too much effort. So to do—to be as meticulous as he had to be—"

The focus of his thoughts lurched.

"One thing they didn't bring up in court was that Diane robbed a gas station one time. She was smart enough to wear socks over her shoes so they couldn't track her shoeprint. It was down in St. Louis. She was smart enough that she covered her feet with socks.

"Zachary and Diane are the same type of individuals. They are almost identical personalities. I met Diane at her mom and dad's house. This girl is stone. She looked right through me.

"Diane may be badder than Zach. Diane is colder than Zach. She could cut your heart out and never change expression.

"The day she visited him in rehab, I was there. I was with him, because we'd sat in an AA meeting a friend of mine ran. I was a member of AlAnon then. We sat down together, and Diane was there, and Zach was there.

"And I hear the next night, Monday night that this has all happened. Zach had left the center that afternoon.

"And I said"—he laughed sardonically—"You're kiddin' me! 'Cause, you know, we'd been talking about the Job Corps thing. That was the first smart move Zach's made! Let's go from here! We'll do whatever we gotta do to get you straight."

His voice lowered and slowed down again. "Well, we did that. And then this all takes place."

We talked on about a few other things. And then it was time to go back to the courthouse and hear the verdict.

. . .

MY CAR WAS motionless now, the motor dead, at the far edge of Hunnewell, near the all but physically visible border where the funky old town stopped and the efficient, superintended fields pressed in. My thoughts were now playing restlessly along that border.

Since I had first absorbed the news of the killings committed by Robie and then Zachary Wilson, more than a year ago, I had been preoccupied—consumed, maybe—with trying to fit those acts of befouled childhood into a context beyond the borders of my own sacred ground. I had wanted to "de-Hannibalize" those atrocities by showing that Hannibal itself had been denuded of particularity. That the town had been subsumed into the placelessness of a nation washed blank by its own conquests, by all the effortless intrusions of its economic markets and state bureaucracies into family and community, by the insouciant abolition of local, intimate cycles of work and ritual and reward, and their replacement by compulsive consumerism and empty, predatory wealth.

I had a powerful ally in this quest. Mark Twain had seen it all coming more than a century ago. He had seen the first contours of "a civilization which has destroyed the simplicity and repose of life; replaced its contentment, its poetry, its soft romantic-dreams and visions with money-fever, sordid ideals, vulgar ambitions, and the sleep which does not refresh; it has invented a thousand useless luxuries, and turned them into necessities, and satisfied none of them; it has dethroned God and set up a shekel in His place."

Or to put it into the compressed idiom of the age itself: an America grown besotted on comfort, technology, and existential rage.

I still believed that all this was true. I'd seen nothing, heard nothing, during these visits back to America's Home Town to mitigate my sense of the devastating toll this ever-accelerating social transformation had taken, or would keep on taking. Hannibal and its environs lay like a jackrolled body in the path of the onslaught, too many of its children emotional orphans.

But that view of things was inescapably grandiose and abstracted and a little too sterilized of human compost. It had "airs." And now, here, with everything settled that I'd come to see settled, and with the local rain drumming on the roof of my credit-card corporate-contracted car, and with Kirk Wilson's low voice reverberating beneath it in my head, and Kyle Wilson's voice beneath his brother's, I found myself facing up to the full possibilities of the older, meaner parallel story that had been unfolding itself at the edges of things. Pap's story. I was thinking about how fate and calamity and unexpected sorrow get worked out down through all the little histories of a place, through all the doomed, hopeful, daily gestures of families, through the small transmitted tragedies of fathers and sons.

The railroad that carried the freight trains through Hunnewell was known originally as the Hannibal & St. Joseph. It was chartered by the Missouri legislature in 1847 and completed in 1859, the first rail route to connect the Mississippi and the Missouri rivers. The railroad begot the town: Hunnewell was deeded July 28 as a supply center for the workers who eventually would stretch the road across the state and link it to the legendary Pony Express. Its very name was a company name: H. Hollis Hunnewell was an official of the Hannibal–St. Joseph Land Co., the land-acquisition arm of the railroad enterprise.

And who begot the railroad that begot the town? The answer to that question was embedded in the fates of J. D. Poage and Zachary Wilson and Diane Myers and all the Poages and Wilsons and Myerses and Powerses and all the other families that took up residence in Hannibal from the mid-nineteenth century onward. It was railroad wealth, not literature, that created Hannibal. It was the train, not statues to boyhood or souvenir shops, that swelled the little settlement outward from the Mississippi riverbanks through the gaudy labyrinth of Market Street.

Mark Twain abominated "the unholy train." He wrote bitterly about it on his great revisitation of the Mississippi River in 1882, that five thousand-mile tour that produced the second half of *Life on the Mississippi*. He returned, in part, to search out his own unviolated Eden, held in place by "the shining river, winding here and there and yonder," offering "glimpses of distant villages, asleep upon capes; and of stealthy rafts slipping along in the shade of the forest walls. . . . And it is all as tranquil and reposeful as a dreamland, and has nothing this-worldly about it—nothing to hang a fret or a worry upon."

Until the unholy train, which "comes tearing along . . . ripping the sacred solitude to rags and tatters with its devil's warwhoop and the roar and thunder of its rushing wheels."

It was Mark Twain's father who brought the unholy train to Hannibal. John Marshall Clemens—fierce, icy, ambitious, indebted, the doomed aspiring squire whose existence is all but lost to history, save in his son's fictionalizings—set it all in motion. The year was 1846. Sammy was ten and unaware. John Marshall, father of four surviving children, was the town justice of the peace and a failed store owner; he sold off the family's furniture that year to stave off destitution. But John Marshall was a visionary, a dreamer of public libraries and railroads and steamboat lines. In that year, he was at the center of a small group of civic boosters that conceived the Hannibal & St. Joseph. His law office at Hill and Main streets was the site of the meetings in which those boosters did the conceiving.

Their brainstorming brought quick results. The state of Missouri granted a charter to the Hannibal & St. Joseph the following year. A month later, John Marshall was dead at forty-nine, the victim of pneumonia caught during a ride by muleback in the rain, campaigning for circuit court clerk.

Sammy Clemens never knew about his father's connection to the railroad until someone wrote to him about it in 1886. But John Marshall's business legacy shaped the economic destiny of the river town more profoundly, in some ways, than his son's literary legacy.

The railroad arrived in the Mississippi Valley just in time to open up markets for lumber. By the 1850s, German-born speculators had already made modest fortunes by contracting with lumberjacks in Wisconsin to harvest white-pine forests and float the logs down the Mississippi to sawmills along the shore. The new railroad line at Hannibal gave these dealers a conduit to home builders far to the west. By 1870, twelve lumber companies were thriving in the town, with a combined capital investment of $3 million. The following year, a railroad bridge was built across the Mississippi. Suddenly Hannibal was no longer a white town drowsing in the sunshine of a summer's morning, as Sammy recalled it, but a booming center of manufacture and transportation. At the century's turn the town boasted 112 factories employing a fourth of its eighteen thousand residents. They included three shoe factories, two breweries, twelve cigar makers, and the largest portland cement plant in the world. Fifty-six passenger trains and thirty-four freights a day stopped alongside the turreted $100,000 depot that Mark Twain had observed during his 1882 stopover, scarcely imagining that his obscure, long-dead father had been its progenitor. ("In my time the town had no specialty, and no commercial grandeur," he mused; "the daily packet usually landed a passenger and bought a catfish . . . but now a huge commerce in lumber has grown up. A deal of money changes hands there now.")

The boom created a string of small railroad villages to the west, villages such as Hunnewell. It created Market Street in Hannibal, with its lunchrooms and saloons, a railroad man's playground. And it created jobs: tickets to the bright lights for generations of rural Missourians, uneducated, rough boys off the bean and egg and corn and cattle farms. They drifted into Hannibal to learn the engineer's trade, or the brakeman's, or the fireman's, shoveling coal from the coal car into the locomotive's furnace. They married, started families, and built small bungalows tightly grouped on the streets that combed the steep hills on Hannibal's south side, the hills above the great railroad roundhouse on the floodplain near Bear Creek. The railroad workers formed the core of the town-within-a-town that was the south side, with its school district and fire station and little family-owned grocery stores, and for several generations it flourished, if that is the right word; at least it held its own—a rough-and-tumble, lunch bucket part of town, insular but stable.

A few nonrailroad families lived up in those hills. One of them was Jasper Toalson's. A baker and the father of my mother, he kept his big family in a bungalow situated over a downsloping apple orchard and commanding a view of downtown Hannibal, the Mississippi River, and the Mark Twain Bridge. I sat on the suspended swing on the front porch of that house on summer nights in my 1940s boy-hood—the same front porch where my father, the Fuller Brush Man, had rung the doorbell and encountered my mother one day in 1937—and looked at the distant arcing lights on the Mark Twain Bridge and listened to the thunder of invisible boxcars being coupled on the roundhouse tracks to make up the long lines of a westward-heading freight train.

But by then it was already over. In the postwar years of my childhood, the two or three remaining lumberyards in town were artifacts of a vanished economy. The logs had all but stopped floating down the Mississippi; the white-pine forests of Wisconsin and Minnesota were effectively depleted by the early decades of the twentieth century. As for the railroads, they were steadily slipping into obsolescence, and the jobs they supported were shrinking apace. In 1953, the castlelike Union Depot, which Twain had admired seventy-one years earlier, was torn down and replaced with a featureless little flat-roofed hut that resembled the suburban branch of some savings and loan. The price was the same as the original: $100,000.

And thus the "unholy train" that had so offended John Marshall Clemens's son now took its place beside the steamboat as a symbol of a tranquil and reposeful dreamland banished by money fever, sordid ideals, and vulgar ambitions. The little railroad towns along the old Hannibal & St. Joseph line, the Hunnewells, withered. The tight-built bungalows on the hills of the south side went wanting for fresh coats of paint. Market Street sagged.

The father's vision of the town had finally run its course. Now in its economic desperation, the town began to market itself as the embodiment of the visions of the son. It became America's Home Town.

The postwar evaporation of the railroad economy in Hannibal had afflicted the stability of family life more acutely, over the long run, than the collapse of Missouri agriculture. This was especially true on the south side. The tough farm boys drawn there by the fulfillment of John Marshall Clemens's vision, and their sons and grandsons, found themselves faced with rapidly diminishing options. One option was the one always available at the edges of the hardscrabble river town. I sat in my rented car, looking at Hunnewell through the rain, and the efficient fields pressing in, and replayed the last few things that Kirk Wilson and I had talked about before leaving the public library and returning to the courthouse to hear Zachary's verdict. Those things involved the little histories of a place as worked out through the small transmitted tragedies of fathers and sons.

Kirk had spoken to me, as Kyle had, of their father, John Wilson, the railroad man—the grandfather of Robie and the step-grandfather of Zach. They had spoken about his memories of his father, growing up on Hannibal's south side.

"When we were kids we had nothin' " he had observed. "We were raised on welfare.

"My daddy was—God, I wish I could explain my father to you. He was a woman chaser. Matter of fact, I had a call from a woman last year at one o'clock in the morning, who said, 'I thought I'd call you and let you know that your father had a child by me in 1958.' I said, 'Ma'am? There is no such thing as a forty-year-old orphan. I can't help you.' She said, 'And there's another lady that's a friend of mine had a child by him too.' I said, 'I am not responsible for my father's conduct.' 'Oh, I just thought I'd let you know that you have a brother and a sister.' "

He smiled a private smile and went on in his low rumble, "I've got a strong sense of irony. It keeps me in line. If you had my father for a father, you'd better have one or you'd be dead.

"He was a control freak. He controlled by fear. I watched him beat my mother, pull her hair out, break her nose. I watched him take the steering wheel of the car one time and break it in half because the car died, and then push it back up again." He shot me a sidewise glance. "Do you realize what that takes, what kind of anger and strength that would take?"

He paused and thought a moment. "I watched a man make a hole in his head from here to here. I lived with that."

I had to ask it: How did he get the hole?

"Car ran over his head. The night he was leaving my mother." A pause. "You want some irony. The night he was leaving my mother, he had his bags packed, sitting in the doorway. He was going to come back and get them later. First he had to go out and chase some women. The motorcycle he was riding on bumped into the car with the women in it. And a wheel ran over his head.

"He died three times on the way to St. Louis that night. He went from two hundred and thirty-three pounds in the hospital to one hundred and twenty in six weeks. They removed his skull"—Kirk made a swiping motion around the front of his head—"from here to here. He basically had a lobotomy.

"And from then on—" Kirk blew through his cheeks. "He always had a bad temper before that. But *afterward*. My mother decided to stay with him. She did, until he beat her so bad that we finally left. That took another couple of years or so.

"Kyle and the rest of us spent the rest of our childhoods growing up with my mom. She did whatever she could. She couldn't really be a mother; she did what she could do. She got pregnant by a guy she wound up marrying years later. She told us the day that her water broke that she was pregnant. We said, 'Mother, we're in high school; you think we didn't notice?' "

The stories went on for a while, until it was time to leave. Replaying them now, I comprehended how oddly familiar they were to me. Kirk and Kyle Wilson were not strangers from some distant place I had inhabited once, in another lifetime. They were my people. They could have been relatives. Friends of the family. I recognized their voices perfectly. They were the voices of uncles of mine, or cousins, from places that were still more real to me than the places I had lived since then: the bar and grill at Fifth and Broadway my uncles Abe and Roy had run; somebody's backyard on a barbecue Sunday afternoon, the bright-lit lanes where I watched my dad bowl with his buddies, and heard their low rumbling voices, until the cigarette smoke and stale beer smell made me sleepy.

The stories were dark—Gothic—harrowing—but they were not alien. They weren't the kinds of stories I tended to remember, as an adult, looking back on the people of my Hannibal childhood. But they were familiar. In a sense, these stories, and stories like them, comprised the metastory of Hannibal: the great, inevitable narrative between the meeting in John Marshall Clemens's law office in 1846 and the uses of Ronald Poage's twelve-gauge shotgun in 1998.

And, hell, I knew a few things about shotguns. They were part of my family too. And not just from hunting these fields with my father. My brother Jim took up a shotgun himself back in 1977 and used it for lethal purposes. The difference was that he turned it on himself.

· 22 ·

JIM

WIDE MISSOURI
By Jim Paul Powers (1945–1977)

In the small town everything seems lazy. Even the radio announcer sounds relaxed and more sincere than the announcers on big city stations. Traffic seems just to drift along, as do the people browsing in the old stores. At the park, old men and mothers watch the boys play ball with teams from nearby towns. No one is in a great hurry; anyone is glad to help a stranger find a street or a good cafe.

In towns along the Mississippi, boys hike or ride bikes to their secret forts on the bluffs, where they explore faint trails. Sometimes a barge comes laboring by, so near that a far-thrown rock would hit it.

In the city, action is all around. Overhead, a low-flying jet struggles skyward, beginning a trip to New York or, perhaps, Los Angeles. Sports cars pull onto the highway, anxious to be unleashed and given full throttle. Great buildings are everywhere, dwarfing the trees along the walk. Tires squeal, bells clang, newsboys yell, and a siren wails. The faultless sky gives simple beauty to the great midwestern city.

On the farm, the teen-age boy feels that he is a king. In a sense he is, for he can do as he wishes with his calf; he can challenge nature with his dad's tractor; he can enjoy life as no one else quite can, swimming in the river or napping in the warm, friendly sun with his dog. When supper is over and evening chores are done, God treats the family to a red and purple panorama as the orange sun steadily sinks below the towering mass of angry clouds that have grown from the meek bits of fleece in the noon sky. Now from their peaks and canyons lightning flares, and a cool wind brings the tingling smell of a Missouri thunderstorm.

—Written at age 16 and printed in
Missouri's Youth Writes,
the Missouri Association of Teachers of English, spring 1962

He had a feeling for Hannibal too. I never knew that.

By the mid-1970s I could barely remember Hannibal. The Patrol Boy corner, the Rialto, the cars, the parents, my goofy flattop, the river, the night, first kiss, my brother. Childhood. All that was over. Beyond over. It hadn't existed. By the mid-1970s I had long since scraped Hannibal off my shoes, strained Hannibal out of my speaking voice, learned to control my tongue in the men's room, learned how to pronounce "chablis" and "hors d'oeuvres," and landed a job on a big Chicago newspaper as a columnist. My beat was radio and television. I got the big article published in *Playboy* magazine. I had a big apartment on Lake Shore Drive. I wore big clothes with big collars and big ties. I grew some big media hair and a big new media beard to go with my big media mustache. In my more candid moments I had to allow to myself that I was big.

If I had stopped to think about it, I might have told myself that I'd finally made it up out of the seats and onto the movie screen. But I didn't stop to think about it.

I pursued a big itinerary: I thought nothing of jetting off to the Coast, skying to Stockholm, working Paris into the schedule for a couple of days. "Just time for a quick note between London and Hollywood . . ." I was actually capable of writing to my parents one June. I wrote a lot of letters and postcards like that. My mother, as uncritical of the rube-in-paradise jabber as I was, glued or taped each one of these into her scrapbook. They stare out at me from those yellowing pages now, unabashedly lurid as a collection of cocktail napkins from around the world.

"London is as beautiful as ever," I find myself gassing from June of 1973, on Berners Hotel letterhead. "A couple of nights ago I saw Carroll O'Connor (Archie Bunker) at a play starring Alec Guinness. We exchanged pleasantries." I was this TV critic, see. This big, big TV critic. For God's sake, I *exchanged pleasantries*.

Well, let me prove how big. This, from the back of a shingle-sized postcard showing a "Spectacular Night View From Mulholland Drive of Scintillating Hollywood, California": "Sorry it took me so long to get this off—*packed* week of work. I visited the set of Laugh-In & met Dan Rowan. Interviewed many other, lesser TV personalities and saw Sinatra perform at the Hollywood Bowl—free!" Note that last-name-only reference to Sinatra. Ol' Blue Eyes. Chairman of the Board. And the price was right—right?

And I see now when I review Mom's old scrapbook that while I was sending postcards of Mulholland Drive and the Parthenon and the Hotel Excelsior at Dubrovnik, Jim was sending them postcards of the hellfire blast furnaces at Bethlehem.

Nineteen seventy-seven was shaping up to be my biggest year ever. I'd quit the newspaper, written my first book—about the awfulness of TV news—then joined the TV news department of a Chicago station. While traveling to research my TV news book, I'd met a beautiful woman on an airplane whom I would marry. My TV station had sent me to Stockholm to cover the Nobel Prize ceremonies in December of 1976, because two Chicagoans, Saul Bellow and the economist Milton Friedman, were among the Nobel laureates that year.

The following spring—it was a Friday night in early June 1977—the Chicago TV stations had their annual Emmys banquet. I persuaded my mother and father to fly to Chicago for the event. Honoree, my wife-to-be, flew in from New York. She wore a light-blue chiffon gown that still hangs in her closet. Her hair was braided down her back. A TV legend from our 1950s Hannibal living room viewing, Steve Allen, was the master of ceremonies. They had their first taste of Côte de Boeuf Rôti au Jus that night, and some Carottes Veronique as well. I managed to win an Emmy, as did nearly every other employee of every station in town. We all drank champagne. Near midnight, I looked at my mother and saw that she was red-faced and about as happy as I had ever known her to be. It was a big night.

Just a few weeks after the banquet, in June, my big-deal media career got another exotic boost. With my awfulness-of-TV-news book on the verge of publication, I found myself packing my suitcase for a flight to Cuba. My TV news department in Chicago was sending me.

It seemed more than just fifteen years ago that my generation of college students had watched and listened, in 1962, for the destruction of the world to originate from Cuba. Now I had my chance to visit there. Fidel Castro had made overtures to reestablish trade relations with the United States. A group of midwestern businessmen had been invited to Havana to discuss this. TV crews from two Chicago stations were allowed to come along. I was to be included in one of those crews.

I remember all of us on the airplane taking off from Chicago—all us snappily dressed TV people, giddy as little kids on a bus trip to a theme park. Wisecracking and hooting. Somebody floated the rumor that a Polish hijacker had forced his way on board and demanded that the pilot take this plane to Cuba. It was like we were playing hooky from America—going somewhere we didn't exactly belong, someplace a little dangerous, to lay eyes on one of the legendary rogues on the world stage. I remember wondering if my life was just going to keep on getting more and more fantastical.

The island itself proved beautiful, almost eerily so. White-sand beaches, among the purest in the world, lapped by warm Caribbean waters. Havana a great old seaside capital in the Spanish style; wide boulevards lined with palm trees, cathedrals, plazas; the fifties-style lobbies of its hollowed-out hotels preserved, waiting. But almost no people. Castro had relocated the urban population to the countryside.

We saw Cuba's hospitals and its schools and its happy garment workers. We saw the successful side of the Revolution. We didn't see the graveyards or the jails. One morning, as the entire contingent— anchormen, reporters, producers, sound crew—were herded into a jitney and driven off to our next stage-managed tour of a happy orphanage, a walrus-mustached cameraman opened his mouth wide, let a handful of peanuts slide into it and down the sides of his face, and offered the elegiac caption for the entire trip. "Twenty years ago, they had girls fuckin' donkeys here," he mumbled between munches. "Today, it's a dyin' nation."

On the final night of our visit, Castro held a reception for the

American businessmen in the great hall of his governmental palace. We television people were discreetly shooed outside, onto a balcony with its own table of food and liquor. From there, we could look through the windows into the brilliant room and see, under crystal chandeliers, the American capitalists and their gowned wives lined up to shake the hand of the glamorous Communist who'd nearly destroyed the world.

Along about midnight, the balcony doors shuddered open and Fidel Castro glided out into the cool night air, among us. He was wearing his famous military fatigues and campaign cap, and he puffed a monstrous cigar: The man was in costume. Mark Twain's voice whispered: *"For he was showing off too."* He made a courtly, fraudulent shrug of embarrassed hospitality—*How could we possibly have forgotten our friends from the press?*—and then he swept briskly from person to person, shaking hands. This liberator and killer and shaper of the destiny of the world. The light of his cigar glowed brightly under its rising cloud.

We departed Havana on a Friday. By early Friday evening I was back in my Chicago apartment. I disconnected the telephone, dropped into bed, and slept for maybe fourteen hours.

When I awoke, at midmorning on Saturday, I reconnected the telephone and called my parents in Missouri, something I did on returning from every trip I took.

Instead of my mother's voice, I heard the voice of my sister's mother-in-law on the line. Her voice sounded flat and mangled, and she quickly put the receiver down to go and find my mother.

It took a little while for my mother to reach the phone. When she finally did, she told me this: "Ronnie, Jim's dead."

I can't remember what we said after that. She was not in much condition to talk, and neither was I. But I do remember what I was thinking as I put the receiver back on its hook: I was thinking that every time I had ever called my parents after being away, I had expected that news. Including this time.

I packed a black suit. On my flight from Chicago to Missouri I probed the words endlessly, as you might probe a soft tooth with your tongue, trying to summon feeling. "Jim's dead," I informed myself again and again. "Jim's dead." Nothing. Numbness. I felt as though there were some powerful, even dreadful emotion down there among the nerves, but it wouldn't dislodge. I started to observe myself from somewhere outside my body. I formed a ridiculous image of myself flying not on a jet plane but on a giant bird, a celestial bird. "Jim's dead," I kept saying to myself, trying it out. "Jim's dead. Jim's dead."

The pain I was begging for never broke the surface.

I tried to imagine how he had died. My mother had not been specific; it was strange, on reflection, that I had not asked her to be. Jim had taken up gliding as a sport: piloting an engineless, wide-winged craft after being towed into the air by a propellor plane, gliding aloft on the wind's currents like a giant bird. I decided it was likely that he had crashed. My parents had worried about this hobby of Jim's. It seemed terrifyingly reckless to them.

It was deep twilight when I touched down in wide Missouri, a firefly and bullfrog time of evening. The little brick compound of an air terminal glowed with orange light, and the runway lights were on; a searchlight swept the sky; there were lights everywhere. My sister Joyce and her husband, a good man named Stanley, were waiting for me just inside the glass door, and when I came through it carrying my clothes bag, Stanley said to me, in a voice of infinite sadness and understanding, "Ronnie, it's worse. He killed himself."

For a while there was some misinformation about the means. It was only a day or two later that we learned about the shotgun, the sanitation dump where he'd gone, the note he left that I never to this day have read.

At the family house my father sat at the kitchen table, his face in his hands, motionless for long spells, then erupting into desperate sobs. It was the first time I'd ever seen my father cry. My mother, whom I'd thought of as the emotional one in their marriage, had gone somewhere deep and silent; she moved through the house with an eerie private calm.

Neighbors brought covered dishes.

I went into the living room, where the telephone was, and sat down and called every relative and close friend I could think of. I went right down the list. I amazed myself with my chilly efficiency. "I have some bad news," I said to each person I reached. I listened to my calm voice saying, "I have some bad news." I listened to the way they took it.

After that, I lay down on the sofa for a while, on my back, with the back of my wrist resting on my forehead. I lay there trying to figure out how I felt, how I was supposed to feel.

At around ten o'clock, I did the one thing I really hadn't wanted to do. I called out to Pennsylvania, to Jim's house. It was essential for someone to make arrangements for the visit out there, for the funeral.

I spoke briefly to Jim's widow, and then she put her mother on the line. Her mother was in a combative mood; she seemed under the impression that we wanted Jim's remains shipped to Missouri. "If you think we're going to fly the body out there—" she began.

I cursed her gently, politely, and hung up. After that, there was no talk of the Powers family traveling to Pennsylvania for Jim's funeral. We just didn't go.

We had a memorial service at the First Christian Church, conducted by a minister I'd never met before. He jotted down some details of Jim's life for his eulogy. I read Jim's essay, "Wide Missouri." I'd been afraid that I would be overcome by tears as I read it, but I was not.

And that is all. Except that from that day onward, I have tried to forgive myself for having pulled that shotgun trigger.

Guilty, first-degree murder. Life without possibility of parole.

· 23 ·

PLANS

I had wanted to speak to Robie Wilson almost from the day I heard about the calamity on Pleasant Street, but for one reason or another I was never quite able to. Things got in the way, including my own reluctance to force the issue. His estranged mother and her relatives bristled at the idea of my meeting with him, along with any probing of mine whatsoever into the case, and I found that I could not really blame them for this and in fact respected them for it. Whatever my motives, and however intimate my connections with Hannibal, I was a trespasser in the Wilsons' misery and I knew it. I knew how James Agee felt, rummaging in the lives of the Gudgers and the Woodses and the Rickettses back in 1936, while castigating himself as a "cold-laboring spy." I knew all of this, but I couldn't help it. I was drawn to these killings and their implications as powerfully as if they had opened up a buried chapter in my own history, which in a way they had. Still.

Still, there were limits as to how far I was willing to push, and the threshold of Robie Wilson's psyche was one of those limits. The reasons why I hesitated were the same ones that made him so compelling to me. Of all the personalities in this sad and grisly web, all the perpetrators and all the victims and all the victims' bereaved, Robie seemed to me the most conditional, the most transitory, the least formed. He was the kid who had gotten into a car one winter afternoon to kill a little time and ended up with a man's blood on his hands. A few murky moments of chance, whim, testosterone, and clueless bravado had turned this high school hanger-on into a criminal, a killer. In the ensuing months, as everyone else caught up in his and Zachary's lethal mischief had gained definition by their predicament, Robie seemed to lose it, to grow transparent, shapeless: less a person than an integer, a bargaining chip, an example, a statistic. He was seen but not heard—a blurred figure in a newspaper photograph, a mute kid with a nosebleed at the lawyer's table, a disembodied demon to the surviving Walkers, a set of imperfectly formed passions and regrets in his own father's mind.

An American adolescent, in sum.

I had been within speaking distance of him a couple of times. Once, early on, while he was out on bail, in his father's custody awaiting trial, I walked past him on the sidewalk as I left Kyle's house, a watchful smooth-faced boy in a fresh haircut and a plaid shirt. We nodded, but Robie was clutching the collar of a straining Akita, and it didn't seem the right time to open up a soul-searching conversation. I saw him again at his trial. And then he vanished back into the Missouri criminal-justice maw.

It was there—in the correctional facility at Boonville, Missouri—where I finally reached Robie Wilson, months after his trial, by telephone.

Kyle had talked him into the interview, an act of faith, as he made clear, in my intentions. I had promised Kyle that I would not grill his son about his part in the death of James Walker, or about his degree of remorse for what he had done. I was more interested, I'd told Kyle, in getting a sense of what sort of person Robie had become and what the effects of incarceration had been on him.

Kyle had some thoughts on that. "He's not takin' any lip," the elder Wilson told me on the phone. "They leave him alone now, because they know he doesn't take shit. That's different from before. Before, Robie might back off a little bit. Not anymore. He's getting hard." It sounded like a compliment.

Robie himself had not been keen to cooperate with my request, his father told me, but he'd agreed. And as our conversation began, I had the sense that Robie was resigned, at this point, to do just about whatever anyone required of him.

His voice on the phone was deep-pitched in the way that adolescent boys can make their voices deep-pitched, toneless, distant in a way that could not be described in terms of miles. His journeyings since the verdict in his case had taken him to places that few people visit in their lifetimes.

We began by reviewing his prison itinerary in the many months since the events on Pleasant Street. The tour had been extensive. "First I did eighteen months in the Boone County Juvenile Justice Center," he told me. "That's where I went back and forth to and from court. Then, when the bunks filled up there, I got sent to the St. Charles Juvenile Justice Center near St. Louis. Then the St. Charles County jail where I waited for my certification hearing—I got certified to be tried as an adult.

"Then after that I got sent back to the Marion County jail [Marion is Hannibal's county] where I finally got bonded out and waited for the trial.

"After the trial, they put me in the Pike County jail near Bowling Green on a change of venue. Then I went to the Fulton Correctional Center, a diagnostic center for psychological testing. IQ, mental health, emotional stuff." Here Robie paused a beat and then said the only thing that brought a little life to his voice: "They said I had the knowledge of a sophomore in college."

After Fulton Correctional—located in the town where in 1946, during a speech at Westminster College, Winston Churchill first alluded to an "iron curtain" descending across the European continent—Robie was transferred to a substance-abuse treatment center at Farmington, where he underwent 120 days of therapy. "It opened my eyes to life and drugs," he said, although the phrasing sounded a little rote. "All of it. We had groups, classes. We were reading over stuff."

When his drug therapy was completed, Robie was returned to the Fulton facility, "at the custody level," he said. Then, after a year, he arrived at his current site at Boonville.

I asked him if he would tell me his impressions of the various jails and prisons and centers he had been shipped to.

"They all had their advantages," he said after a minute. "When I first got locked up, I didn't get to finish my schooling and I was separated from my family. So I was pretty down for a long time. But over all it helped me to grow up, I think."

Then came an appraisal—concise, detached, almost professional, it struck me—of several of his ports of call.

The "JJC" (juvenile justice center) in St. Charles had been clean, really clean. The county jail, though, was rough, nasty. Filthy, in fact. Fulton had been all right because of the way they ran the cells; you were expected to keep your cells clean. The "Hole" at Farmington was infested with rats and mice. Robie had gone straight to the Hole, a punishment for fighting, where he'd spent seven days. "It was rough in there at first," he said. "Just a space with a couple of lights and a toilet. I had no one to talk to."

And his present quarters?

"Boonville is an old boys' camp, for orphans," he said. "Before that it was a boarding school. It's all brick, all the houses. It runs on the college system. You get credits for taking certain classes. I had to drop this program because I wasn't passing. I missed too many days. I had a job, I was sick. My job was in the education department, doing filing."

Besides his work routine, Robie told me, life at Boonville wasn't too bad. "Every day you get to go outdoors for a few hours," he said. "Play catch with a softball, run track, play handball. We're inside for chow from eleven until one, then we go back outside from one-fifteen to four o'clock. In the evenings we watch TV."

I asked him about the subject that Kyle had cited as the standard for Robie's adaptation to prison life. I asked him about the fighting.

Robie seemed reluctant to take it up, but dutifully, he did. "There are not really a lot of fights here," he said. "They crack down. You always have to fight in prison at first, to prove yourself. After that it depends on how you carry yourself. I didn't know how to carry myself at first. Now I do. You have to watch behind you a lot. Have a few partners around. Don't get caught in a place where you ought not to be.

"It's kinda hard, going through certain houses here. People have a chip on their shoulder, maybe because of what somebody said." After a pause, he went on. "It's racial. Everywhere you go, it's racial."

Racial? I asked him.

"All over Missouri," he said. "All the camps. They're full of white supremacists, and Bloods and Crips. Most of 'em are aged about seventeen to thirty-five. They're in here for armed robbery, man-slaughters, assaults, theft, parole violations. And drugs. A lot of drugs."

He offered a cryptic remark that, by implication, indicated another arbiter of how much fighting went on. "A lot of times the officers have power," he said, "and they like to use it." I asked him what he meant by that, but his answer was vague. "It all depends on how you carry yourself," he repeated. "Being respectful, having respect for yourself. Don't let anybody take advantage of you."

I asked Robie if he could estimate the number of fights he'd had since entering the prison system. He thought it over for a moment and then said, "About fifteen. Fifteen fights."

There was a silence for a few beats, on both ends of the telephone, and then I asked Robie about his plans after his release from prison.

"I've had plans for a long time," he said. "I want to sit back and stay out of trouble. I want to spend time with my mom, get a job with one of my brothers. Move out, be on my own. Run my parole down. Settle down with somebody."

Are you a different person now? I asked him.

He thought about that. "I'm more patient on certain things," he said. "I deal better with stress. I look out for myself, mentally and physically.

"I guess you'd say it has made me tougher all around. I'm not a bad guy. But I don't feel like a little kid anymore. I'm nineteen, and I feel like I'm about thirty-five."

I hung up the telephone with the feeling that somehow, with a break or two, Robie Wilson might come out of all this all right. At least he didn't seem likely to suffer too much more abuse from his enemies inside the prison walls. I remembered something that Kyle had told me: Robie had thirteen fellow inmates from Hannibal now to back him up.

. . .

I DECIDED THAT there was one last thing I had to do, having established contact with Robie Wilson. I needed to go see Zachary.

· 24 ·

THE DREAM PALACE

The Federal Corrections Center at Potosi, at the edge of the Mark Twain National Forest, eighty miles below St. Louis in southeast Missouri, is set in some of the densest and most pristine woodlands left in the lower midwestern part of America. Driving there in the early spring, on rising and dipping two-lane blacktop, you pass thick stands of ash and hickory and oak trees, blossoming dogwood and redbud. There are bright stretches of stream and creek for a few miles, small, flat, cultivated patches of farmland. You pick up the quaint staccato hammer of a woodpecker when you stop on high ground to savor a view of the hazy St. Francois Mountains to the south. It is easy to forget exactly where it is you are headed, and why.

The center itself has nothing to do with its surrounding landscape, or with the shriveled and Wal-Marted little lead-mining town a couple of miles below it, or with anything except itself. It rebuffs expectations and is the more horrifying for it. Far from being a dark, weathered, brooding dungeon of the type beloved by moviemakers, the center is blisteringly white and featureless, as antiseptic as a eugenics lab. Blinding coils of concertina wire looped near the top of an electrified chain-link fence separate the approaching visitor from the deserted exercise yard and the featureless walls that seem to erase themselves from memory even at first glance.

Inside, in the visitors' reception area, only a few of the prison's many armed, watchful, controlling presences are visible; these project a massive disinterest bordering on contempt as they herd each new-comer through the surveillance process. I watched the visitor ahead of me, a portly black man in a carefully pressed but worn business suit—the father of an inmate, as his signature on the sign-in sheet stipulated—return through the electronic scanner several demeaning times, until finally he was obliged to strip off one, and then the other, of his polished loafers.

The corridors and elevator banks leading to the room where visitors talk with inmates on telephones, separated by reinforced glass panes, are almost triumphantly featureless: no color, no objects, no striations in the floors and walls to interrupt the aura of being nowhere at all. One has the constant sense of being watched through thick panes of tinted glass; of violence incipient; of time obliterated, hope abolished, volition surrendered; of narrative leached from the possibilities of imagination. Of not much to do.

In these respects the Federal Corrections Center at Potosi bears a striking resemblance—far more of a resemblance than the forested countryside around it—to the United States of America from the point of view of many of its young.

· · ·

I WATCHED HIM enter his side of the small interview booth, his hands behind his back, and immediately kneel down. I glimpsed the blue-shirted guard behind him before the door closed, and then I glimpsed the open rectangle cut into the door at a kneeling man's handcuff level. This was not something I felt completely entitled to watch.

When his hands had been set free, Zachary Wilson rose to his feet, and before he sat down in his plastic chair I impulsively reached out my hand and placed the palm flat against the Plexiglas. Zachary placed a palm on the glass opposite mine. I wasn't sure why I did this; it seemed awkward, and perhaps a shade too comradely, given the offense for which he was serving his life sentence. But there is something about watching a person freed from handcuffs on his knees that makes you want to acknowledge his humanity. At any rate, the gesture was over in a second.

We were communicating through glass via telephone, instead of at a table, as I had hoped, because Zachary was serving a period of "administrative detention"—solitary confinement. He had told me of the situation by telephone, over frequent interruptions by a recorded voice from the prison advising me that if I did not wish to take this call I could push certain buttons and then hang up: "A nigger came on to me for sex, and I had to open his head up," was the way he had offhandedly explained it.

He had taken on a prison pallor, but he looked beefier through the shoulders than he had in court. His face was unmarked except for a small tattoo, a twist of barbed wire, and still conveyed the quizzical, focused attitude I'd noticed from him on the witness stand. A boy's face, but not for much longer.

The questions I had for him probably sounded more purposeful than they actually were. I had no idea, really, what I wanted to know from Zachary Wilson. There were no missing pieces to his puzzle, as far as I could tell, and I hardly expected a soul-baring confession. His letter to me, accepting my interview request, carefully hand-lettered on lined paper with little circles for dots over his *i*'s, had abruptly abandoned its elaborately courteous tone ("Greetings and salutations! First of all, I would like to appologize for my delayed response to your original message as well as my horrible handwriting . . .") to demand a little brass-tacks accounting from me: "I have one condition for doing this interview and I believe you will find it extremely simple. I want to know what you think. Plain and simple." I'd written him back that while the case against him seemed pretty convincing, I had formed no final opinion, and could not, simply because I had not been present on the night of the murder. That was the truth, and apparently it satisfied him.

I suppose that I'd come there just to hear him talk a little bit and see whether I could hear any Hannibal in his voice or thoughts, or any remnants of my people, living or shotgunned, or of me.

We opened up on childhood recollections, and I was struck by the strong visual imprint of his memories: a decorative cluster of iron grapes that hung on the front porch of his parents' little house in the floodplain near Bear Creek, the house's false black shutters with diamonds painted onto them, the dog pen for Porky the beagle, who "bit my dad one day when he tried to spank my brother." A Frisbee he'd learned to throw into the wind, so that it would come back to him, during the many long days he spent alone in the house as a small boy, both parents gone: "I don't remember a lot of good. I have bad memories and nonmemories, and then it goes blank. I can see myself standing there, something's about to happen, and then it goes blank."

A sort of nonmemory intruded: "We never had a welcome mat at our door. But at some point in time we got a mat with a Tasmanian devil on it that said, Go Away."

An early memory of family strife: "Mom and Dad [his natural father] were sittin' on the couch talking and watching TV. I came in, watched with 'em a while. It got to be about eight o'clock, my bedtime, and I said, 'Well, I better go to bed, good night.' For some reason my mom said, 'Oh, it's not your bedtime, don't worry.' I said, 'It's eight o'clock . . .'

The fury! 'GET YOUR FUCKING ASS IN THERE THEN AND GO TO BED, AND FOR THE REST OF THE FUCKING WEEK YOU'LL GO TO BED AT FUCKING SEVEN O'CLOCK!'

"I was trying to be good. I didn't get a lot of recognition for being good."

His mother was doing a lot of drugs then. "She liked speed a lot. Had a complex about her weight. My grandpa and grandma were getting divorced. That put her under pressure.

"My mom wears sunglasses a lot. She's got twenty–two hundred vision in one eye and is blind in her other eye. My dad used to bust her eyes open. He broke her ribs. Mom got so she could fight pretty good. She'll start a fight. She can throw her hands up like a man. She'll get on a tirade, and she won't stop till you're cowering in a corner in submission." Zachary said that one of the first beatings administered by his mother happened because he left his new box of seventy-two Crayolas on the windowsill, and the heat from the sun melted them together.

I asked Zachary about his dreams. Literal dreams, dreams about the future; I hadn't narrowed the question. But as it turned out, that didn't matter.

"I never remembered my dreams till I came here," he said. "That's why I call this place the Dream Palace. It's because your old dreams come back to you here. And your new ones die out."

He described a dream from his early childhood, its imagery taken from television, that he'd never recollected until he was incarcerated at Potosi: "My Little Pony is drowning in quicksand. The Witch is makin' fun of it drowning. Rainbow Brite is standing in the quicksand with a rope, tryin' to pull My Little Pony in.

"I'm readin' Freud's *Interpretation of Dreams*, tryin' to figure out what that one meant."

Zachary's natural father left for Arizona, Kirk Wilson came into the picture, and the family moved to a somewhat better subdivision when Zachary was about nine. The contrast was not lost on Zachary. "I got a sense then that I was different from the other kids," he said. "One day I was at my friend Trevor's house. We were playin' in the front room. He knocked over a glass of Kool-Aid. It was red. He went, 'Mom, I spilled some Kool-Aid.' She came in and cleaned it up and said, 'Boys, be careful when you go outside.' And I remember thinkin', *'What's wrong with this lady? He's got a beatin' comin'!'*

"A lot of things like that. Billy's mom would call him to come in after supper, and he'd call back, 'Hold on!' And I'd see him the next day, and he wouldn't have a black eye."

It wasn't long after that, Zachary said, that he himself introduced the concept of fighting to his new neighborhood.

What is it about picking a fight that you liked? I asked him and drew the first cold, appraising stare of our conversation.

"I guess you meant to ask me what was it about fighting that I liked," he said after a long minute and paused to let the subtle distinction sink in. "I don't know, it was like—I really don't know. I mean I can't remember having any feeling. I just really don't know."

He recalled that in about 1991 his mother and stepfather shipped him out to Arizona to live with his natural father, "because they couldn't handle me." He and his natural father were buddies for a while. Then, "out of nowhere," his natural father started getting short-tempered. Maybe it was because his wife had taken a job in Washington—State or D.C., Zachary wasn't exactly sure which. "Well, we're getting the house ready to have a garage sale, and I'm weed eating the yard, and I snapped the line on the weed eater. That happens, happens to everybody. And he went off on me. Hit me with the weed eater," Zachary claimed.

Not long after that, Zachary's natural father returned him to Hannibal. That was when the serious attention deficit kicked in: the record-setting detentions, the in-building suspensions, the out-of-building suspensions, the different schools, the treatment centers, the medication.

Not all of his teachers despaired of him, though. "There was Mrs. Ferrell. Seventh-grade social studies. She thought I had potential. I got A's from her. She used to let me teach her class. Matter of fact, when I was in eighth grade, I used to get in so much trouble that they just made me a hall monitor. And I'd sneak off from that and go down to her class and she'd let me teach it. I snuck into it through her window one time. She was cool."

It seemed like a good moment to work my way toward what might have passed, if anything did, for a purpose to this interview: to test the theory I'd worked out on the first day of his trial, in which Zachary works out a Huck-like sacrifice on behalf of his beloved fellow fugitive. I made the first question general: do you still, I asked him, have a bent toward classroom learning?

His answer was unhesitating: "I want to learn everything. I want to know why we do what we do and why we are who we are, and at the same time I want to know what magic spells can best be cast against a dragon. You know—I want to know *everything*. I want to know about warfare, I want to know tactics, why these people do things like this; I want to know why Phil Jackson's triangle offenses work so much better than anybody else's that has coached the Lakers.

"I want to know why everything in prison is a money game, why the rules seem to be more about a power trip, more to show you just who is in control than to have any purposeful function. You know, I want to know everything." He looked at me expectantly. I took it a little closer in.

You ever read Mark Twain?

"I love Mark Twain. I read of course Tom Sawyer and Huckleberry Finn, you know."

I couldn't help it: Do you ever see yourself as Huck Finn?

I was expecting a shrug or a smirk, but I got neither. He was completely deadpan. "I think every young boy growing up in Hannibal does." His brow furrowed. "But at the same time, I think that had Huckleberry Finn grew up in the twentieth century he may possibly be here in Potosi, Missouri. You know. Because Huckleberry Finn was good. He was a kind man. He was a kind man and for real if you put Huckleberry Finn in front of, say, a Dr. Daniel, he's quite likely to tell him that he is a sociopath because he would do things, I mean repeatedly do things, wouldn't care, he would just keep on doing them and take his punishment and go on, you know."

Agitated, Zachary was talking fast, now, conflating Twain's myth with his own. Dr. A. E. Daniel was the psychiatrist in Columbia, Missouri, who had evaluated him after his arrest and incarceration early in 1998. This was when Zachary still insisted on his guilt in the Poage murder. As I would later learn from talking to Dr. Daniel, Zachary had refused to allow the psychiatrist to recommend an insanity plea, which might have significantly reduced his sentence. Now, it seemed, Zachary was indeed imagining himself as the noble renegade of the raft, struggling to maintain his purity in a world polluted by adults. The "he" of the scenario just described was Zachary himself, repeatedly doing things, good but misunderstood things by inference, and taking his punishment: *I felt good and all washed clean of sin for the first time I had ever felt so in my life . . .*

But it was impossible to pause and develop this inference, because Zachary was talking on in a rush. What he told me next surpassed any boundaries of astral convergence that I could have imagined. Zachary, it seemed, had actually spent some time performing Mark Twain's characters for tourists to America's Home Town.

"One summer I went to the Mark Twain Outdoor Theatre [an open-air tourist attraction] out on Highway Sixty-one toward New London, and I got a job there. I was in that theater. The director told me I was too big to play Tom Sawyer. Oh, I was mad. I was mad for real. But I ended up playing Injun Joe for a while. I played the judge, I played the sheriff, I played all kinds of stuff.

"I played Mark Twain," he went on. "They wanted me to play Mark Twain because I could do the voice. There are two quotes that I love from Mark Twain, one of them is"—here he switched to a gravelly approximation of the famous Hal Holbrook cadences—" 'To quit smoking is the easiest thing in the world to do! I must have done it a thousand times.' And the other one, and I do a little voice on this one, too, he says: 'When it's his time to go,' he says, 'I'm going to ask the Great Creator what all this human life is about. I have got a feeling I know what he will do. Plop me down on a raft in the middle of the Mississippi on a starry summer night, and I can fairly match what rapture is.' "

A pastiche, that last, but deftly rendered—as had been Zachary's recitation of his Miranda rights to the arresting patrolmen in Ohio.

"I have laid down at the John Hay Recreation Area," he went on. "I have laid down on the grass there and stared at the stars above the Mississippi River, because it seems like they're not clear anywhere but there." The John Hay Area was where Zachary hurled the shotgun into the river the night J. D. Poage was killed. "But I don't know, it's kind of special, it's kind of magic if you let it be, and that is where I think my character differs from a lot of people that grew up at the same time I did. That I can allow myself a more romantic side to kind of dwell on the more beautiful things and the things that I can see and consider to be more meaningful in a spiritual type way, I guess."

No sense holding back now: Do you, I asked him, identify with Huck Finn?

"Well, that would be me. I mean, that would be me. I'm corresponding with this kid from England, and I told her a little bit about the case. I told her that I was trying to help a friend, you know, and I told the police a lot of things and I got myself in a situation that is not good at all because I felt that it was my duty and I thought that I was being noble. And I put something in the letter like, Well, I guess chivalry is dead. You know?"

· · ·

WHEN I RETURNED to the center the following day, the noble Huck had receded and had been replaced by a somewhat more brooding presence.

The talk quickly moved to Diane. What drew you to her? I asked him.

"She's cold," Zachary said. "She's a cold person, and I think that's what attracted me to her. She puts up defensive walls around herself. And that was a challenge for me. To break down those defensive walls.

"I'd just come off a bad relationship with my son's mother." This was the mother of the boy Zachary had fathered in 1997, the boy whom he had never seen. "And Diane needed somebody. And I needed somebody to need me."

I asked Zachary about the amazing coincidence of timing that involved his letter recanting his confession, written and dated on the same day as Diane's plea. "She told me to do that. She wrote me and told me to do it. It's amazing. She was thinking of me. And she was thinking of my son. And she was thinking of my dad. I would have handled it different if I'd been thinking."

But the timing? An incoherent burst of responses from Zachary.

Because Diane had told me to. Because if the fucking town marshal had done his job. Wanda Jo was the guard there, and I says, Jo, and she says, Yeah? I says, What time is it? She says, Two-thirty. I said, Are you sure? She said, Yeah. I said, What is the date? She said, June fourth. I said, June fourth, two-thirty. She said, Yeah. I said, Because this is important. I said, I need the exact time because it's important, this is a legal matter, and she says, Okay, it's two-thirty right now.

But why two-thirty?

Because Diane had asked me to do this, had told me this is what you should do, because I'm taking this between and I can't turn around and change my time. Okay. And I had told her no, I had wrote her back a letter and told her no. She wrote me back a letter and told me yes, I wrote her back a letter—see, this is why it took so long to get up to the date she pled, letters back and forth, and I'm telling her, Are you sure? And she's telling me Yes, do it now. Hurry.

I changed the subject: Why didn't your lawyers plead you to an insanity defense?

"That wouldn't have worked because the doctor in Columbia said that I was too smart, that I purposely placed myself, due to circumstances of my situation, in a negative light to gain a certain response, and that my test should be considered invalid. But in all reality, I didn't mind. And to tell the truth, you know, I was always under the impression that you don't have to be stupid to be crazy."

Do you really believe Diane was pregnant? I asked him

"Now? No. But at the time I wanted her to be so badly."

Why?

"Because I thought I could start a new life with her."

A new life. Within a family. As a father. That was Zachary Wilson's ultimate notion of escaping from his familiar pattern: the legacy of violence, the blankness, the addiction. To live in a family environment, as the father of a child.

There suddenly did not seem to be very much else to talk about.

Before I put the telephone on its hook for the last time, I asked Zachary whether he felt he could handle a lifetime in prison. He gave me a blankly quizzical look, as though he couldn't quite figure out why I had asked.

"Prison is not hard for real," he said. "I mean for real it's not. You get in a pattern and you live the pattern."

·   ·   ·

A FEW DAYS later, in Columbia, Missouri, I looked up the psychiatrist A. E. Daniel, who had administered Zachary's pretrial evaluation. Daniel, a native of India who was small and fastidiously dressed in a goldish sport jacket and necktie and who maintained a thick thatch of white hair, had agreed to speak to me on condition that I obtain written consent from Zachary, which I had done.

"I found him to be a severely disturbed youngster," Dr. Daniel told me. "I diagnosed him as hyperactive, with an attention deficit disorder. He is very impulsive, an extreme impulsiveness. A boy with an exalted sense of his self-worth, a boy who prides himself on being in control. And he's a boy who is unable to trust. In the early months of life, it's the mother who becomes the focus of emotional attachment with the infant, but it is the father who is the facilitator of trust. And Zachary's father did not help him establish trust, or a sense of empathy with people. And so Zachary lacks the necessary mooring, the necessary base, for dealing rationally with the world.

"*But Zachary is not a vicious killer.*" Dr. Daniel stared at me a moment as if to be certain the words had sunk in. "I don't believe that he would be a particular threat to kill again if he were released from prison. It is my belief that this killing was not random. In his mind, the killing was justified. Mr. Poage had caused the death of his child.

"He told me during our interview that people who are like that should be killed." Dr. Daniel paused and cleared his throat delicately. "What he actually said was that they should be fucked."

I recalled a detail of Zachary's confession to the Ohio patrolmen. He said he had kicked Poage's bed to make sure his victim was awake and aware of his executioner. In a story filled with incomprehensible details, that one had always struck me as particularly depraved. I recalled his words about Diane's pregnancy near the end of our conversation at Potosi: *I wanted her to be so badly.*

Dr. Daniel went to his filing system and withdrew a folder. He pulled a sheet from it and carefully put on a pair of reading glasses.

"This is from the transcript of one of my last conversations with him," he said. He read: " 'I did it for my son or daughter who is up in heaven. . . . Being a father is the best thing in the world. . . . That was taken away from me. . . . If I did not have a son I would not have felt this way. . . . This adult penetrated this young girl. The adult male sex organ is too large. I believe in my heart that this is why it [the miscarriage] happened.' (Under his breath, to himself) 'It is an act of personal justice.' "

Dr. Daniel put away the file with careful and precise gestures. "I would have said, if called as a witness, that because of his attention deficit disorder, Zachary could not have formed an intent to commit first-degree murder. He probably would have been convicted in the second degree and received a sentence of fifteen to thirty years.

"He refused to let me use the diminished-capacity defense. I believe that he refused out of pride."

At the door to his office, Dr. Daniel seemed at pains to sort out his own feelings about Zachary Wilson. "I was raised in a small state in India, called Kerala," he said. "In the town where I grew up, everyone knew everyone. There was a string of small towns, in fact, from the north to the south in our region, where that was true. One interesting statistic that I remember about the region is that the literacy rate was ninety-eight percent, as opposed to fifty-five percent nationally.

"But the pressures against that kind of community are mounting," he went on. "As India modernizes and becomes more urban, people grow more selfish and turn more deeply into themselves. That is what happens when any traditional community is threatened by that kind of change. I have practiced in America for a long time. What I see here, in the last ten to fifteen years especially, is that family members have distanced themselves more from one another. And families have distanced themselves more and more from community. And that—" He sighed as he opened the door for me.

"And that empathy is not there among the children," he said.

· · ·

I HAVE MY own Dream Palace. It is inside my head. My past, or versions of my past, live there. In one dream, or perhaps a dream mixed with memory, my father and I are together and he is doing something splendid. What he is doing is driving his Nash, with me in the passenger street, at breakneck speed along the streets and boulevards of St. Louis toward Busch Stadium, where Ken Boyer and the St. Louis Cardinals are about to play a baseball game against the New York Giants. In the dream, or memory, our family has driven from Hannibal to a St. Louis suburb to attend a barbecue thrown by some of my father's Fuller Brush colleagues, but my father has—perhaps miraculously—obtained these last-minute tickets to the game, and he has said, "How about it, Ronnie?" and we have escaped that boring barbecue party, the envy of everyone there, and now we are surging along in this moment of tremendous spontaneity, this freedom, this release, the likes of which I'd never experienced with him before. Jim is alive, in the dream, or the memory, but he has decided to stay at the party with my mother and my sister, and it is just my dad and me in the Nash, racing toward the stadium to see Willie Mays bat in the top of the first. My father is driving brilliantly: fast but safe, only one hand on the wheel, the other arm resting nonchalantly on the window jamb. We're passing cars and rumbling over railroad tracks, and I am looking out at the brightest lights and the biggest billboards I have ever seen, and we're not even stopping for red lights, and that is okay, because I am the Patrol Boy, and I'm alongside my father who is suave and fearless, and I am going to grow up and marry and have sons regardless of what may have passed between my father and me up until now, or my father and Jim, because this is what men do: We have sons and risk going to hell, despite Pap, despite all, under the salving illusion that nothing can possibly happen to us. The river is always there, waiting for us. We're going to make it.

INDEX

abuse reported in families, 14, 66, 108–
13, 131
line between punishment and abuse,
78–79, 213
perpetuation of, 275, 279
reactions against state protective
measures, 116–17, 126, 212, 213
Wilson stories, 154–55, 279–80, 295–
96
See also father-son relationships;
sexual abuse
adolescents
alienation of, 4, 13–17, 28, 69, 92–
95, 109, 112, 186, 227, 228
anger among, 109
changed behavior models for, 140, 141
concepts of good and evil among, 98–
101
corporate exploitation of, 16, 228–29
criminal-justice system and, 191–94
disruptive and violent, 16–17, 50–59,
107–13, 170–71, 186
drug use by, 50, 69, 109, 111, 148
emotional shifts of, 130
gangs, 50–51, 145, 155–56
high school experience, 160–66
lack of activities for, 153
lack of adult contact with, 227
1950s-era, 158–66

people's fear of, 111
psychological distress of, 69
subculture of, 50–59, 155–56
Adventures of Huckleberry Finn
(Twain), 22, 78, 141
"racist" charges against, 40
"raft chapter," 148–49
See also Huck Finn
Adventures of Tom Sawyer, The
(Twain), 33, 39, 40, 84
advertising, 227, 228–29
African Americans. See race relations
agribusiness, 66
alcohol abuse, 14, 15, 25, 69
alienation
adolescent, 4, 13–17, 28, 92–95,
109, 112, 186, 227, 228
material wealth and, 229
social-service agencies and, 115
Twain and, 131
Alternative School. See Hannibal
Alternative School
American Cyanamid, 90
anger, 109, 126
Ashcroft, John, 111
Assemby of God, 115
Atlantic Monthly (magazine), 39
attachment disorder, 69
Aunt Polly (Twain character), 34, 39